An Englishwoman in the Philippines

(Illustrated Edition)

by

Mrs. Campbell Dauncey

The Echo Library 2019

Published by

The Echo Library

Echo Library
Unit 22
Horcott Industrial Estate
Horcott Road
Fairford
Glos. GL7 4BX

www.echo-library.com

Please report serious faults in the text to complaints@echo-library.com

ISBN 978-1-40689-129-4

AN ENGLISHWOMAN
IN THE
PHILIPPINES

BY

MRS CAMPBELL DAUNCEY

WITH ILLUSTRATIONS AND A MAP

NEW YORK
E. P. DUTTON AND COMPANY
1906

FIRST EDITION *July 1906*
Reprinted October 1906

INTRODUCTION

In the following letters, written during a stay of nine months in the Philippine Islands, I tried to convey to those at home a faithful impression of the country I was in and the people I met. Since I came home I have been advised to collect and prepare certain of my letters for publication, and this I have done to the best of my ability, though with considerable misgivings as to the fate of such a humble little volume.

It is impossible to mention the Philippine Islands, either in daily life in the country itself, or in describing such life, without reference to the political situations which form the topic of most conversations in that uneasy land. On this subject also I wrote to the best of my power, faithfully and impartially; for I hold no brief for the Americans or the Filipinos. I merely aimed at a plain account of those scenes and conversations, generally written within a few hours of my observing them, which, it seemed to me, would best convey a true and unbiassed impression of what I saw of the Philippines as they are.

CONTENTS

LETTER I.

MANILA 17

Journey from Hong Kong. First sight of the Philippine coast. Manila Bay. The Pasig River. A drive through the streets. Old Manila. Spanish influences. Manila hotels. The Virgin of Antipolo. Inter-island steamers.

LETTER II.

FROM MANILA TO ILOILO 21

Beautiful islands. Coin divers. A glimpse of Cebú. The hemp industry. The Island of Mactan. Magellan. A curious record in orthography. Fellow-passengers. Soldiers and school-teachers. American theories. Social and racial equality. The Filipino race.

LETTER III.

FIRST IMPRESSIONS OF ILOILO 26

Arrival at Iloilo. Situation of Guimaras and Negros. The Island of Panay. Climate. House-hunting. Native methods. Conant coinage. Philippine houses.

LETTER IV.

A PHILIPPINE HOUSE—AMERICAN PRICES—NATIVE SERVANTS —FURNITURE 31

We find a house. Domestic architecture. The Azotea. Results of American extravagance. Iloilo shops. Filipino servants. Settling down. Chinese shops. Furniture. "Philippines for the Filipinos." Rumours of the Custom House.

LETTER V.

HOUSEKEEPING IN ILOILO 38

Housekeeping. Strange insects. Chinese bread. The washerwoman. Domestic etiquette. A hawker of orchids.

LETTER VI.

A WASTED LAND 43

The road to Molo. Picturesque scenes. Custom House methods. An unpleasant surprise. Philippine trading firms. An over-zealous law. The Philippine bed. Christmas Eve. The tropic dawn. Christmas Day. The water-supply. Food and drink. Scarcity and high prices. Book-learning versus agriculture.

LETTER VII.

CUSTOMS AND DRESS OF THE NATIVES 48

A Filipino *Fiesta*. The national hero. Doctor Rizal and his work. A languid festival. A musical people. Dress of the native women. *Piña* muslin. Dress of native men. Scrupulous cleanliness. A walk on the beach. Gorgeous colouring.

LETTER VIII.

SOCIAL AMUSEMENTS 52

A ball at the Spanish Club. The *Rigodon*. Curious costumes. Bringing in the New Year. A painful interlude. Position of Eurasians. New Year's Day. The suburbs of Iloilo. Filipino children.

LETTER IX.

TARIFFS—INSECTS 57

More Custom House surprises. Official blunders. House-lizards. Roof-menageries. *Anting-anting*. Snakes. *Cicadas*. Ants. Cockroaches. Mosquitoes.

LETTER X.

A FILIPINO THEATRE—*CARABAOS* 61

Dramatic clubs. The Iloilo theatre. An amusing experience. An operetta. The Jaro road. *Carabaos*. An evening scene by the river. The fashionable *paseo*.

LETTER XI.

SOME RESULTS OF THE AMERICAN OCCUPATION 66

Heat and drought. Bathrooms. A handsome cow-boy. Cost of living. Military manners. Camp Josman. The Government of the Philippines. A "pull." An arbitrary tax. The Plaza Libertad. Effects of fire and bombardment. Story of the American occupation. Unwelcome saviours. A pretty garden. The "unemployed." Scale of wages. A Philippine cabstand. Filipino dignity. A charming scene.

LETTER XII. 74

CHINESE NEW YEAR—LABOUR CONDITIONS—
A CINÉMATOGRAPH SHOW 74

The Chinese New Year. Question of Chinese labour. A cinématograph entertainment. Unpleasant habits. An interesting audience. Diplomatic warfare. A half "'cute" native. A Filipino philosopher. Tropical rain.

LETTER XIII.

SOME INFLUENCES OF CLIMATE, SCENERY, AND RELIGION 79

The *Rainbow*. Sugar industry. A beautiful view. Unchanging charms. "Always afternoon." The fascination of the East. Missionaries. A keen advocate. La Iglesia Filipina Independiente.

LETTER XIV.

VOYAGE TO MANILA 83

A journey to Manila. The mail steamer. Food for Esquimaux. A comfortable night. Dream Islands. Dress for Europeans. Manila. The harbour. Curious reasoning. American hustling. A charming house. The Luneta.

LETTER XV.

AN OFFICIAL ENTERTAINMENT **89**

Evening on the Pasig River. Malacañan Palace. An evening *fête*. The Arms of the Philippines. "The Gubernatorial party." "Manila at a glance." The Gibson Girl. An amusing episode. A drive in Manila. The fashions. Manila shops. A market for the best diamonds. A "mixed" wedding.

LETTER XVI.

MANILA AND ITS INHABITANTS **94**

The suburbs of Manila. Hawks. A nursery-garden. Orchids. By the bandstand in the evening. Manila society. A city of cards. Intramuros. Americanised Filipinos. The American Ideal. Blind pride. Bilibid prison. Arts and crafts. The "Exposition" and the inquiring voter. The Philippine sky. A steamer on fire. A procession of death and degradation. "Sport." A visit to Malacañan. A beautiful woman. Some lovely embroideries. Manila prices. Mr Taft and his Chinese servants.

LETTER XVII.

DEMOCRACY AND SOCIETY IN MANILA **104**

A *Mestizo* party. Seeking for democracy. And finding aristocracy. A shopping expedition. Chinese enterprise. Bridge again. A devotee and enthusiast.

LETTER XVIII.

THE RETURN VOYAGE AND MY COMPANIONS **109**

Home letters. The Simla of Manila. The return journey to Iloilo. A crowded ship. My cabin-mate. Filipino schoolboys. The first-fruits of the American Ideal. Filipino manners. Some Filipino views. Philippine Spanish. Dawn at the mouth of the Iloilo River. Expensive religion. Wonderful costumes. Lax port authorities. A hearty welcome home.

LETTER XIX.

A *BAILE*—A NEW COOK AND AMERICAN METHODS 115

Carnival festivities. Lenten relaxations. A Palais Royale farce at the Filipino Club. "Hiawatha." At a *baile*. A walk through the town. A Chinese graveyard. A troublesome cook. Wily native ways. A change of staff. Municipal marvels. *Noblesse oblige.*

LETTER XX.

FILIPINO INDOLENCE—A DROUGHT 120

The rising thermometer. A Filipino watering-cart. A harrowing story. The Filipino employé. *Mañana.* A demonstration in racial equality. More drought. A new acquisition.

LETTER XXI.

THE WHARVES—AN OLD SPANIARD 123

Roofs of Philippine houses. A walk along the quay. Chinese sailors. A mistaken policy. Native shops. Curious cigars. Desolate mud-flats. One of the results of high wages. A Spanish courtier. *Los Indianos.* A cause for panic.

LETTER XXII.

A TRIP TO GUIMARAS—AN ASTONISHING PROPOSAL —HOUSEBUILDING 128

A little trip on the sea. Marvellous scenery. The ship of the Ancient Mariner. Coast villages. A band in the Plaza. Oriental tastes. The difference of Eastern and Western minds. Little comedies. How we drive in Iloilo. An importunate visitor. Strange American customs. A peaceful scene in the sunset. Building a house.

LETTER XXIII.

A TROPICAL SHOWER—OUR SERVANTS—FILIPINO CUSTOMS ... 133

The mails. A good butler. "The inevitable *muchacho*." Palm Sunday. Negritos. Curly hair. Beggars. A Filipino funeral.

LETTER XXIV.

EASTER FESTIVITIES 135

Easter holidays. Superfluous precautions. A gruesome procession. The Funeral of Christ. Rival religionists. A midnight pageant. A pretty procession. Happy children. A dull *baile*.

LETTER XXV.

A DAY AT NAGABA 139

A trip to Nagaba. A native house. The "Philippine cuckoo." *Nipa* thatch. Ylang-Ylang. A swimming-bath. A stroll along the rocks. A fisherman's hut. Country-folk. The village. Pig-scavengers. The fire-tree. The *tuba* man. Mistaken temperance enthusiasts. Cocoanut-growing.

LETTER XXVI.

THE MONSOON—AN ITALIAN OPERA COMPANY 144

Love-birds. Traces of the Filipino mind. The S.-W. Monsoon. Typhoons. A horrible custom. A wandering Opera Company. Increasing heat.

LETTER XXVII.

A WEEK-END AT NAGABA 147

The departure for Nagaba. An amusing landing. Morning on the beach. A fish *corral*. Trading vessels. A native kitchen. Betel-nut. A row up the river. Up in the woods. A magnificent prospect. Wild fruits. A primitive hut. The simple life. The American theory of education before food. Wanted a Colonial Office. Harlequins of crab-land. The tropic night. Fishing by torchlight. A *parao*. Skilful sailorising. Home again.

LETTER XXVIII.

A LITTLE EARTHQUAKE, AND AN OPERA COMPANY UNDER DIFFICULTIES 154

A slight earthquake. Grand opera under difficulties. Barbaric laughter. The exodus to Hong Kong. Vagaries of the Monsoon.

LETTER XXIX.

AN EVENING ON THE RIVER—RIVAL BISHOPS 157

Evening on the Iloilo River. Pleasant natives. A cocoanut-grove. The *bolo*. Green cocoanut. Salt pits. More trouble with the Customs. The verdict of Solomon. A hopeless grievance. Curiosities of taxation. Religious enthusiasm. Rival bishops. The Cardinal Delegate and the Aglipayano Monsignore. The Plaza at Jaro. A handsome old belfry. The Angelus. Peace and goodwill.

LETTER XXX.

PHILIPPINE SANITATION—DECORATION DAY 163

The coolness of 90°. A letter from Benguet. Expense of travelling. Baby mongeese. Native neighbours. The sanitary control. An appeal to *verguenza*. An ill-kept town. An inhuman custom. The new hospital. Decoration Day. Digging up American soldiers. Unwholesome sentimentality.

LETTER XXXI.

MR TAFT—TROPICAL SUNSETS—UNPLEASANT NEIGHBOURS —FILIPINO LAW 168

News of the coming of Mr Taft and his party. Miss Alice Roosevelt. A simple-minded damsel. Relaxing wind. By the Molo road. A lovely scene. An Eurasian household. A melodrama. And a farce. A flitting. Filipino justice.

LETTER XXXII.

OUR MONGEESE—A FIRE—THE NATIVE EDUCATION QUESTION 172

A distressing malady. Habits of my mongeese. An alarm of fire. A strange state of affairs. "Arbitrary race-distinctions." Undemonstrable theories.

LETTER XXXIII.

A PAPER-CHASE—LACK OF SPORTS—PREPARATIONS FOR MR TAFT 175

A paper-chase. Lack of sports. Ladies astride. A problem for Mr Taft. Amusing headlines. Sad little pets.

LETTER XXXIV.

TRYING HEAT—AN AMERICAN PROSPECTOR—NEW LODGERS —BARGAINING FOR *PIÑA*.. 178

Damp heat. An enterprising millionaire. New neighbours. A happy household. Buying *piña* muslin.

LETTER XXXV.

DECLARATION DAY—THE CULT OF THE FLAG— A PROCESSION, FESTIVITIES, AND A BALL 181

Declaration Day. The cult of the Stars and Stripes. An angry critic. The procession. American officers. Methods of horsemanship. A cruel vanity. American soldiers. The Veteran Army of the Philippines. "Little brown brothers." Representative parades. Celebrations in the Plaza. Strange developments of athletics. A melancholy contrast. Official ball at the *Gobierno*. An ardent anti-Taftite. An amusing assembly. Unconventional bandsmen. A keen pro-Filipino. An ill-bred *Mestiza*. Balancing a *quilez*. Some of the drawbacks of civilisation.

LETTER XXXVI.

COCK-FIGHTING—PULAJANES 190

A sad loss. The Filipino and his fighting-cock. Tricks of the ring. Off to the front. Peace and prosperity. A horrible story. A plague of flies. A slovenly guest. The poll-tax and some of its workings.

LETTER XXXVII.

A PEARL OF GREAT PRICE 194

Philippine flowers. A town of swamps. Monotonous scenery. Hawking a pearl. Pearl fisheries. Plentiful fish-supply.

LETTER XXXVIII.

AGRICULTURAL POSSIBILITIES 197

A Gymkhana on the beach. An *alfresco* domestic servant agency. Road-mending. The foreign cemetery. Justice for the white man. Treatment of servants. The Filipino tiller of the soil. Wasted opportunities. A terrible disease. Some native fruits, and some more wasted opportunities. A welcome invitation.

LETTER XXXIX.

A LAST DAY AT NAGABA—THE "SECWAR" 200

Farewell to Nagaba. The three-card trick. The Secret Police. A pleasant sail. Through the village. A native shop. Corn pone. An Anglipayano church. An idyll. Filipino coffee. Lack of American enterprise. A strange word. The coming of the *Secwar*. Human mosquitoes. A familiar type of character.

LETTER XL.

PREPARATIONS 205

Preparations for the Patron Saint. Arcadian animals. Mr Taft's intentions. Determined patriots. A famous phrase. The blessings of a free press. American altruism. Political Pecksniffs. The spell of indolence.

LETTER XLI.

THE FESTIVITIES **208**

The *Comitiva Taft*. A reception that failed. Unappreciative guests. The decorations. A culinary treat. A call in the dark before the dawn. Gay streets. The visitors. "Miss Alice." Mr Taft. The "Taft smile." Looking for equality. A well-instructed journalist. Floats. Some strange banners. Mr Taft's opinions. An amusing *contre-temps*. A very informal reception. A little mistake in tact. The banquet. Disappointed admirers. A haphazard feast. The mermaid. Speeches. A fiery patriot. Instructive applause. A splendid orator. Mr Taft's mission. Two critics.

LETTER XLII.

WEIGHING ANCHOR **220**

An Iloilo hotel. A faithful servant. Complaisant Americans. Echoes of the visitation. Skilful reporting. A disappointed well-wisher.

LETTER XLIII.

HOMEWARD BOUND **223**

A pleasant prospect. Comfortable quarters. Chop-sticks. A happy little slave. The Chinese pigtail. An unspoilt Filipino. The dignity of the white man. The dregs of East and West. A last whiff of the sugar-*camarins*.

LIST OF ILLUSTRATIONS

DISCHARGING HEMP FROM PARAOS (NATIVE BOATS)......... 22
A FILIPINO GIRL, AGED 10............ 25
A CASCO (BARGE).......... 25
OLD SPANISH HOUSES AT MOLO.......... 29
THE BACK OF OUR HOUSE. Showing Azotea and Outbuildings........ 32
FILIPINO SERVANTS........... 35
RIDING A CARABAO.......... 64
SPANISH ARCHITECTURE IN THE PHILIPPINES. An old church at Daraga.......... 69
MANILA. Malacañan Palace........... 90
MANILA. The Escolta.......... 92
A STREET IN MANILA. Showing Electric Tram.......... 94
MANILA. The Luneta........... 96
BIRD'S-EYE VIEW OF INLAND SUBURBS OF MANILA........... 100
A PHILIPPINE PONY.......... 123
NATIVE HOUSES........... 140
THE TRACK OF A TYPHOON........... 144
A FILIPINO MARKET-PLACE........... 149
A THREE-MAN BREEZE OFF GUIMARAS........... 152
A PARAO........... 152
A PALM GROVE........... 158
CATHEDRAL AND BELFRY AT JARO........... 160
A SUBURB OF ILOILO........... 165
AWAITING SHIPMENT. Coffins containing Bones of American Soldiers stacked in Malate Cemetery, Manila........... 166
A VILLAGE COCK-FIGHT........... 190

WATERING CARABAOS. 195
A FILIPINO FISH-MARKET. 196
THE PHILIPPINE ISLANDS (Map) 226

AN ENGLISHWOMAN IN THE PHILIPPINES

LETTER I.

MANILA

MANILA, *27th November 1904.*

We arrived here early yesterday morning from Hong Kong, after three days of rather a horrible sea voyage, as the steamer was more than crowded, the weather rough, and we carried a deck cargo of cattle. These conditions are not unusual, however, in fact I believe they are unvarying, as the 362 miles of sea between here and Hong Kong are always choppy, and the two mail steamers that ply to and fro, the *Rubi* and the *Zafiro*, are always crammed full, and invariably carry cattle.

The poor beasts stood in rows of pens on the main deck, each fitting tightly into his pen like a bean in a pod; many of them were ill, and one died. We watched the simple funeral with great interest, for the crew hoisted the dead animal by means of a crane, with a rope lashed round its horns, standing on the living beasts on each side to do it; but they had a good deal of difficulty in extracting the body from its pen, in which it was wedged sideways by two live neighbours, who stubbornly resented the whole affair. Finally, with a great deal of advice and swearing, the carcase was slung over the side, and it looked very weird sailing down the ship's wake in the sunset.

That was the only event of the voyage, till we sighted Luzon, the biggest and most northern of the Philippines, some time on Saturday afternoon—this is Monday, by-the-bye.

The *Zafiro* kept all along the coast, which loomed up dim and mountainous, but we could not see anything very clearly, for the atmosphere was thick and hazy. Here and there on the darkening mountain sides a column of smoke rose up very straight into the evening air, and I was told they came from forest clearings, but we saw no signs of human habitation. A man who had been many years in the Philippines, and was returning to what had become his home, told me that such fires on the mountain sides had been used a great deal as signals between the insurgents during the Spanish and the American wars, and had been made to indicate all manner of gruesome messages.

About two in the morning, the *Zafiro* arrived at Manila and anchored in the bay, and when it was light, about five o'clock, we came up on deck and looked round, but the land lies in a section of so vast a circle that one does not realise it is a bay at all. The morning was very dull and grey; hot, of course, but overcast, and the sea calm and grey like the sky. The city of Manila lay so nearly level with the water that it was almost out of sight, just a long low mass, rather darker than the sea. Far, far away inland a faint outline of mountains was perceptible, but Manila is built, for the most part, on a mud-flat at the mouth of a broad river called the Pasig. This is a curious river, only 14 miles long, coming from a big lake called the Laguna de Bayo, but yet it is wide and deep enough at the mouth for 5000-ton steamers to anchor at the wharves and turn in the stream.

About seven o'clock, or earlier, our friends' launch came out for us, and in this little craft we steamed up the mouth of the Pasig, past rows and rows of steamers anchored at the quays, and hundreds of huge native barges covered over with round roofs of brown matting. I noticed numbers of brilliantly green cabbages floating down the stream, sitting on the water like lilies, with long brown roots trailing behind, and thought a cargo of vegetables had been wrecked, but was told these are water plants drifting down from inland bays up the river. They are the most extraordinary plants, of intensely crude and violent emerald, and make a marvellous dash of colour amongst the grey and brown shipping on the yellow, muddy water.

We landed at a big wharf, right in the town, and close to streets with shops, all looking strangely European after China and the Straits, the whole place reminding me more of the suburbs of Malaga or the port of Las Palmas than any other places I can think of. Here a carriage was waiting for us, and we drove all through the outskirts of the town, till we came out upon the bay again, and saw the open sea, where our friends' house is situated in a quarter called Ermita. All Manila is divided into quarters, or wards, with curious Spanish or Filipino names—Malate, Pasay, Intramuros, Binondo, etc., and many names of Saints.

The days get very hot here after eight o'clock, whether the sun happens to be shining or not, so I did not go out until the cool of the evening, and spent the day in the house, unpacking and resting, and trying to forget the smell of those cattle. Never again, I am sure, shall I linger with pleasure near the door of a byre!

Everyone here goes about in diminutive victorias, very like the Italian *carrozza*, and all the horses are tiny ponies, the result of a cross between the little Chinese horse and a small Spanish breed. They are sturdy little beasts, and remarkably quick trotters, with thick necks, and look pretty if they are well kept; but some of those in the hired carriages are very poor little creatures, though they tear about with incredible loads of brown-faced natives.

We drove about the town, which all looks as if it had been put up in a hurry. There are no indications of antiquity outside Intramuros, the old Spanish Manila, founded in 1571, which stands, as its name signifies, within walls—crumbling grass-grown old walls, very high, and with a deep moat.

This Walled City, as the Americans called it, is the town the British took under General Draper in 1762, and these are the walls our ships bombarded at the same time, under Admiral Cornish, papa's great-uncle. When we were at home, it seemed strange that just before I came to the Philippines, I should inherit the lovely old emerald ring which the priestly Governor of Manila gave to the Admiral, when the former was a prisoner of war in the British Fleet, during the few days we held the Philippines, before we gave them back to Spain. But when I was actually under the walls they fought for, I looked at the old ring, and the coincidence seemed stranger still. I wished it were a magic emerald that I could rub it lightly, and summon some mysterious spirit which would tell me all the old ring had seen and heard. But now, Old Manila is only a backwash leading to nowhere, for the modern town has spread itself all up the banks of the Pasig River.

Our way did not lie through the Walled City, but along outside it, down a broad avenue, bordered by handsome trees, over a bridge across the Pasig, and into the town of shops and streets. The whole place looked dull, grey, ugly, and depressing, and after Hong Kong it seemed positively squalid. Big houses like the magnificent stone palaces of Hong Kong, would be impossible here on account of the frequent earthquakes, but such buildings as there are look mean and dilapidated, and the streets are badly paved or not at all, weeds grow everywhere; in fact, there is a sort of hopeless untidiness about the place that is positively disheartening, like going into a dirty and untidy house. I think a great deal of the hopelessness, too, consists in the air of the natives, who appear small and indolent after one's eye has become accustomed to the tall, fine figures of the busy Chinamen.

I was particularly struck with the fact that I saw no traces of anything one is accustomed to think of as Spanish—no bright mule-trappings, or women with *mantillas*, or anything gay and coloured, and the houses are not built round *patios*. I was told that the reason of this is that the Spaniards who settled in the Philippines all came from the north of Spain, from Biscaya, and of course the Spain one knows and thinks of *as* Spanish is Andalusia and the South, with the wonderful glamour and poetry of the Moorish influence.

In the course of our drive we went to a certain bridge to see a religious procession, and as we got near the place where it was to pass, the streets were crowded with people, and there were triumphal arches scattered about, all looking quite pretty in the rosy-pink glow of the sun, which was just beginning to set. We pulled up in a mass of carriages and traps on one side of the bridge, and waited an hour or more for the procession, which was then about three hours overdue.

While we waited there, we met and talked with a Mr —— whom I mentioned to you before as having come out from England in the same series of steamers as ourselves. He told us that he was putting up at the best hotel in Manila, which, he said, was haphazard and dirty beyond belief. We said we had had the same account from other people, and considered ourselves more than lucky to be staying with friends.

"Yes," he said, "you are in luck, for you can't imagine what a Manila hotel is like. And yet it is full of decent people. I wonder why they can't run a better one."

It does seem odd when one comes to think of it, because, though Manila is off the tourist track of the world, and there is no reason for any mere traveller to come here, still, people do come sometimes, and anyhow there are the Americans themselves, who want a shelter of some sort, and that nation has the reputation of being accomplished connoisseurs in the matter of hotels. One would imagine that a good hotel would be the first thing they would demand or establish, but they have been here six years now, and the Manila hotels are still a byword for unutterable filth and discomfort.

Well, about this procession, the occasion of which was the bringing down to Manila of a very sacred image, called the Virgin of Antipolo, from the town of Antipolo, which is inland, to deposit her in some church in Manila. She had been four hundred years in Antipolo, and was a very precious and much-battered relic, so her journey was a great event, and the procession had been travelling, by road and river, ever since before the dawn.

At last the long lines of people began to appear, crawling over the bridge in the last grey shadows. It proved to be a very dull affair, simply consisting of endless files of the faithful, carrying unlighted candles, with every now and then a band of music, and every now and then a group of paper lanterns carried on poles, or some gaudy banner, and all moving along to the accompaniment of a weird, unearthly chant. This kind of thing went on and on, and after an hour we got tired of it, and drove away without having seen the actual image, which was, we were told, a little, armless, wooden figure, dressed in a stiff tinsel robe, perched up on an immense high platform, decorated with lamps and flowers, and surrounded by priests chanting, and acolytes swinging censers.

We are to sail for Iloilo to-day, after lunch, having got a permit to go in the *Kai-Fong*, of the China Steam Navigation Company. We were to have come in this same steamer from Hong Kong, as I told you at the time, in which case we should have gone in her right through to Iloilo, touching here and at Cebú, but we received the telegram too late, an hour or so after she had left, and as we were told to start at once, we followed by that pleasing craft the *Zafiro*.

By this manœuvre we have clashed with a vexatious local law that forbids foreign (*i.e.*, not American or Filipino) steamers to convey passengers from Island to Island of the Philippines, so we had to apply for this special permit, as they say the regular mail steamers, which ply between Manila and Iloilo, are exceedingly dirty and uncomfortable. They are owned by a Spanish Company, trading under the American flag. However, it is all settled now, in favour of the English boat, and we sail this afternoon.

I have only caught a passing glimpse of Manila, but I hope to be able to tell you more about it later on, as I have been invited to come back and pay a visit to our friends here in a month or two's time.

LETTER II.

FROM MANILA TO ILOILO

S.S. "KAI-FONG," CHINA SEA, *December 1, 1904.*

I hear there will be a mail going out from Iloilo to-morrow, the day we arrive, so I will write you a letter to go by it, that you may not be disappointed—six weeks hence!

We left Manila at three o'clock on Monday, in lovely sunshine, and had a delightful voyage through scenery which was simply a miracle of beauty. The sky was intensely blue, with little white clouds; the sea calm and still more intensely blue, dotted with dreams of islands, some mauve and dim and far away, some nearer and more solid-looking, and a few quite close, so that we could see the great forests of bright green trees and the grassy lawns, which cover the hills and clothe the whole islands down to long, white, sandy beaches, with fringes of palm trees.

The islands are volcanic, mountainous, and of all shapes and sizes, from Luzon, which is nearly the size of England,[1] and Mindanao, which is larger still, down to tiny fantastic islets, but all rich, green, fertile—even a rock poking its head out of the brilliant sea, has its crown of green vegetation. I don't know at what size an island ceases to be an island and becomes a mere rock, but anyhow, there are two thousand Philippines considered worth enumerating.

I noticed very few signs of cultivation, or even of human habitation, but was told that even if there were villages in sight, they would be difficult to distinguish, unless we passed close to them, as they are built of brown thatch, and placed amongst the trees. Here and there was a little group of white buildings, generally, in fact always, clustering round a huge church. We passed quite close to some of the islands, so that we saw the trees and beaches clearly, but even those at a distance were very distinct, and I was particularly struck with the absence of colour-perspective, for the islands some way off, if they were not so far away as to look mauve, were just as brilliantly green as those close at hand. One after another, like a ceaseless kaleidoscope, these fairy islands slipped past all day—in fact, as I write, I can hardly keep my attention on my letter, the scenery is so wonderful and so constantly varying.

We got to Cebú, which is the chief town of the island of that name, at six o'clock on Wednesday morning, and anchored just off the town, which appeared as a flat jumble of grey corrugated iron roofs and green trees, rather shut in by high mountains close behind. On account of these hills, they say Cebú is much hotter than Iloilo, as the latter town lies open to the Monsoons.

These are the chief towns of the Philippines: Manila, the capital, in Luzon; Iloilo, in Panay; and Cebú, in Cebú; and that is the order they come in as to size, though

---

[1] England is 50,823 square miles in extent, and Luzon is 40,885.

between the two provincial towns there is endless rivalry on the subject of importance. In fact they are a sort of local Liverpool and Manchester—bitterly jealous, and yet pretending to despise each other. There was a P. and O. cargo steamer anchored not far from us, the first ever seen at Cebú, and everyone seemed very proud of the event.

When we went on deck, we saw a couple of canoes, hollowed out of big tree trunks, circling round, and containing natives dressed in loin-cloths, offering to dive for coins, in the approved fashion, west of Port Saïd. They were fine young men, yellowy brown in colour, and they made a great deal of noise, but did not dive very well. After breakfast some of C——'s friends came off in a launch and took us ashore, when we drove in the usual little victoria, drawn by two small ponies, to the British Vice-Consulate, a large house on the borders of the town, where the Vice-Consul, Mr Fulcher, entertained us royally.

DISCHARGING HEMP FROM PARAOS (NATIVE BOATS).

Here I followed the same programme as I did at Manila, resting in the cool house all the long, hot day, and driving out in the evening at about five o'clock, when the sun had begun to go down. We drove all through dim streets, with a gorgeous sunset fading in the sky, and I could not make things out very distinctly, but could see that we were passing along ramshackle, half-country roads with overshadowing trees, and every now and then we passed a row of little open shops with bright lights in them, and natives squatting about. There are no bazaars in this country, by-the-bye, only little mat-shed shops where food is sold.

That was all I saw of Cebú, as I did not go out this morning, and we sailed in the afternoon. When we came down to the wharf to get on board, the tide, or the Port Doctor, had allowed of the *Kai-Fong*, drawing up to the wharf, so we came on board up a plank, when one had to look at the ship instead of the water on each side! The ship was very busy getting a cargo of hemp into one of the holds, hemp being the peculiar produce of the Island of Cebú and the opposite ones of Samar and Leyte, all long-shaped islands lying almost parallel in the middle of the Archipelago.

The hemp comes on board in great oblong bales, looking like oakum, and a man told me it was the fibre of a plant like a banana tree, which the natives split and shred very skilfully, and then it is dried and done up in bales, and "that is all there is *to* it," as the Americans say.

Opposite the town of Cebú is a long, low island called Mactan, where the great Portuguese Navigator Magellan was killed in the year 1521. The story is that the natives of the islands, finding Magellan invincible, and believing him to be enchanted, lured the great explorer away by treachery to the little island of Mactan, where they had prepared a pit covered with branches, such as they use to trap wild pigs. Magellan fell into this trap, whereupon the savages rushed out of their hiding-places and shot him in the joints of his harness with poisoned arrows, and one bold man finally finished him off with a spear. They poison their arrows to this day as they did then, by dipping the tip into a decomposed human body.

There is a monument to Magellan on the spot where he died, but we did not have time to go and see it, so I had to be content with looking at a photograph, which gave me a very good idea of the quaint old three-decker edifice of grey stone, tapering to a column at the top. The real and original spelling of Mactan is as I have written it, but it is now altered to Maktan, and for this change there is a very curious reason, dating from the days, some ten years ago, when the Filipinos, headed by a patriot of the name of Emilio Aguinaldo, revolted against the authority of Spain. The chief element in the uprising was a secret society, called the Katipunan, the device of which, on flags and so forth, was K K K, and to make this fact memorable, or to prove his power, Aguinaldo ordered the hard letter C to be replaced by K in all names in the Philippines, making Mactan, Maktan; Capiz, Kapiz; Catbologan, Katbologan, and so on. This alteration the Americans, some think unwisely, have not taken the trouble to abandon, so the revolutionary spelling remains a monument of the success of disloyalty, to say nothing of the names having thus lost all philological significance.

We are now passing round the north end of the Island of Cebú, for Panay lies to the westward, in a rough parallel. Sometimes the north passage is taken, and sometimes the south, according to the wind and current. The currents are very strong between these islands—all the Philippine Islands, I mean, and in many places the sea is always rough, in fact it is very seldom really calm anywhere, I believe.

Our fellow-passengers are all Americans, half of them military, officers and privates, who address each other in most unceremonious fashion, and the rest school-teachers. A most appropriate and characteristic company, as the American scheme out here is to educate the Filipino for all he is worth, so that he may, in the course of time, be fit to govern himself according to American methods; but at the same time they have ready plenty of soldiers to knock him on the head, if he shows signs of wanting his liberty before Americans think he is fit for it. A quaint scheme, and one full of the go-ahead originality of America.

I can understand the conduct of the free and easy soldiers, for such equality is not inconsistent with American social theories; but what puzzles me is the use of these astounding pedagogues, who are honest, earnest, well-meaning folk, but their manners are those of ordinary European peasants. And as to the language they speak and profess, it is so unlike English that literally I find it difficult to catch their meaning when one of them speaks to me direct, and quite impossible when they talk to each other. Yet I could forgive them their dreadful lingo, if only they would not use the same knife indiscriminately to lap up yolk of egg, or help themselves to butter or salt. Of course these good people are fresh from America, and utterly ignorant of all things and people outside their native State (such ludicrous questions they ask!), but quite apart from that, and the hopeless blunders they must make on that account, it seems a pity that such rough diamonds should represent to these natives the manners and intellect of a great and ruling white nation.

But here comes the most curious phenomenon of all, for I am told that the United States does not pose as either "white" or "ruling" in these islands, preferring, instead, to proclaim Equality, which seems a very strange way to treat Malays, and I find myself quite curious to see how the theory works out. I only hope it won't mean that we shall have unmanageable servants and impudence to put up with. Our friends in Manila told me ominously that housekeeping was "difficult," and I begin to wonder if Equality has anything to do with it!

They are a funny little people, these Filipinos, the women averaging well under 5 feet, with pretty, slender figures and small hands and feet. The original race was a little, fuzzy-headed, black people, remnants of which are still to be found in the mountains and in the smaller islands, but the Filipino, as one sees him, is the result of Malay invasions. Up in the north, in Luzon, the Malays are a race or tribe called Tagalo, but all this part of the Archipelago is called Visaya, and the people Visayans. Of these broad outlines there are many subdivisions of type of course, in the way that physique is different even in different counties in so small a space as England; but the average Filipino is the same everywhere. The Filipinos (by which are meant the Tagalos and Visayans) are, as nearly as one can say, a short, thick-set people, with yellowy-brown skins, round, flat faces, very thick lips, which frequently jut out beyond the tip of the nose, and more bridge to the same said nose in proportion to the amount of foreign blood in the owner's veins. It is not easy to lay down any very definite rule about their appearance though, as the race is so hopelessly mixed with Spanish, Chinese, European—every nation under the sun, that it is difficult to say what is a Filipino face. One feature they have in common, and that is magnificent, straight, jet-black hair, which the women turn back from the forehead, where it makes a roll so thick that it looks as if it must be done over a pad, while they twist the back high up, in shiny coils. The men look as if their thick mops were cut round a basin, and they have no beards and moustaches—I mean they can't grow any, not that they don't want them! As far as I have seen, they appear to be very lazy, and to talk a great deal. They are not a bit like the Chinese or Japanese in any way, unless they happen to have a strain of that blood in them, and even then the resemblance is only physical, for though the type may be varied, the universal character remains unalterable.

I forgot to tell you that at Cebú we "collected" C——'s dog, a dear old brown person, with one of the sweetest faces I ever saw, who answers to the name of Tuyay, which is the Visayan for Victoria. I really must leave off writing now, as it is long past time to "turn in," though I feel as if I could write on for hours, there is so much to tell you.

A FILIPINO GIRL, AGED 10.

A CASCO (BARGE).

LETTER III.

FIRST IMPRESSIONS OF ILOILO

ILOILO, *December 4, 1904.*

We arrived here on Friday last (the 2nd), and I at once sent off a letter to you, written on board the *Kai-Fong*, which letter ought to reach you some time in the middle of January.

We are so glad to be at the end of this long journey—exactly seven weeks from London—seven weeks to the very day, for we left London on a Friday and got here on a Friday; and all that time we have been travelling steadily, and have seen so much that it seems years already since we left home. I hope you got all the letters I wrote on the way? One each from Gibraltar, Marseilles, Port Saïd, Aden, Colombo, Singapore, Penang, Hong Kong, Manila, and lastly, Cebú. I give you this list because I always have a fixed conviction that letters posted on a sea voyage seldom turn up, as the last one sees of them is going over the side in a strange land, in the clutches of some oily, dark person, who swears he will spend the money one has given him in stamps. I try to believe him, but he, like Victor Hugo's beggar, thinks he has to live somehow, I suppose.

Well, so here we are at last on our "Desert Island," as you call it—which is really a vast and fertile country, with several big towns, of which this is the chief and largest.

We got in at dawn as usual, the run from Cebú (which I notice the Americans call *See*-boo) being about twelve hours, so our first view of the Island of Panay and the town of Iloilo was in the early morning light, from the deck of the steamer, which lay, waiting for *pratique*, in the "roads," at the mouth of a river. We saw a long, flat, dark-green coast line, with a high range of purple mountains far inland, and the town of Iloilo, like Manila, almost imperceptible, as it lies so low on the mud-flats of a big estuary. It did not look at all inviting, just a line of very green trees, with some grey iron roofs amongst them, and it seemed as if it must be baking hot, but, as a matter of fact, the very flatness and the direction of the mountains keep the place cool, for, as I told you before, it lies exposed to the N.-E. and S.-W. Monsoons, the great arbiters of fate in the China seas.

On the map you may find marked a small island called Guimaras, which is about 4 or 5 miles off, but in this air it looks so close that trees and houses can be seen over there with the naked eye, and yesterday evening, in driving down a street of Iloilo and seeing Guimaras at the end, I thought it was part of *this* island at the end of the road!

Guimaras is very small, with low, pointed hills, covered with forests, as are all these islands; and behind it, 7 miles further away, lies the big island of Negros, the mountains of which loom up, a dim, pale purple outline behind bright green Guimaras, making one more of these marvellous colour effects. One of the high peaks we see is a volcano called Malaspina or Canloon, which is 4592 feet high, and only half quiescent. At any rate, if we cannot actually see it, there is such a volcano in Negros. There are plenty of volcanoes in the Philippines, twenty-three of them all told, and that fact and the frequent earthquakes give an uncomfortable impression, as of a thin crust of rocks and trees over vast subterranean fires.

Here, in Panay, the mountains are 20 miles inland, away to the west—a long range of peaks and serrated ridges, behind which the sun sets with magnificent effects. From the foot of the mountains the land stretches away quite flat, watered by big rivers, and where one of these streams forms a wide estuary, this town is built, as I told you, on the mud, in the same way that Manila stands on the mud-flats of the Pasig.

The first settlement of white men in Panay was only a Spanish garrison, inside a fort built in the days when a few Spaniards in armour lurked under shelter from the poisoned arrows of the savage natives, while now and then a priest ventured out to see what a little talk and baptism would do towards making life more pleasant for everyone concerned.

When the island became more civilised, or settled, or subdued, or all three, a town called Jaro (pronounced Hahro) was founded about 3 miles up the river, and became the capital of Panay, but now the tide of commerce has swept down-river, and the chief town is Iloilo, all crammed down at the edge of the sea, with many of its suburbs nothing more nor less than sandy beach. It is a big town, with long, straggling streets, and the houses, all two stories high, with grey corrugated iron roofs, stand apart, separated by little bits of garden with palms and flowering trees, which makes it quite pretty, in spite of all the buildings being totally devoid of any architectural beauty whatsoever.

At present the N.-E. Monsoon is blowing, and everyone is anxious to point out to me how deliciously cool the weather is, and it is certainly not so overpowering as I had expected, but all the same I find it quite hot enough to be pleasant and a little over. Though there is no dew, the nights are refreshing—almost cold by contrast with the day, and the evenings charming, while the early mornings are simply delicious. Dawn begins at half-past five, and by six the sun is up, but the air is exquisite till about half-past eight, when it begins to get too hot for anything but shade and fans, if one has any choice. I think the average Fahrenheit now is 83°, but as life here is adapted to such temperature, you must not think that means anything like what 83° would be in England. Still, when all is said and done, it is very hot, and if this is what they call "winter," I am only thankful that I have not plunged at once into "summer." This "winter" goes on till March, and then the weather begins to get hotter and hotter till June, when the Monsoon shifts to the S.-W., and the rainy season begins.

Four months dry and cool; four months dry and hot; four months wet and hot— that is the climate over most of the Philippine Islands, but it varies in sequence in different places—areas is a better word—and on the Pacific seaboard the seasons are quite reversed, so that it is rainy there when it is dry here. By rain and dry, however, I gather that a great deal of drought or a long, steady rain is not meant, for all during the dry season there are heavy showers, and everything remains green, while in the wet season there are spells of fine weather. Now I think I have described to you all I can of Iloilo till I see more of the place, but I know how anxious you will be to have some idea of what it is like.

We are busy house-hunting, which is a tedious and toilsome business, as there is not such an institution as a house agency—you allow a rumour to get about that you want a house, and then people tell other people to tell you where an empty building, such as you say you want, is to be found. Then you go off and "find" the house—a matter, usually, of infinite difficulties and sometimes quite impossible, as the Filipino cab-drivers don't know the names of the streets, or the numbers, or the names of the people. The best plan is, get into a rickety old trap and let the man drive about, while you lean out and ask for the house you started out to find, and end by seeing another one with *se aquila* (to let) written up, and stopping as near to it as the driver can pull up his pony, and getting out there instead.

Having thus "found" a house, you set to work to "find" the owner of it, who is probably at the club, or a cock-fight, or playing cards; and when he, or she, appears, you ask—and this is quite necessary—if the house is to let; for the board does not signify much, as they seldom take the trouble to remove one when once it has been put up. Most of the boards are obligingly going through the process of removing themselves, one nail at a time.

When the house really is to let, you ask the rent, and whatever the answer is you throw up your hands in horror, and declare it is *muy caro* (very dear), and that you will give half, calling assorted Saints to testify to all the drawbacks which make the house unfit for human habitation at any price.

Then a long argument ensues, for the people never really want to lose a tenant, as they know there is no lack of choice, for trade is very bad, and so many houses stand empty. All the same, the rates and taxes are appallingly high, and the rents are preposterous for this sort of town, and for the accommodation offered. Moreover you have a strangely lazy, supercilious, half-bred sort of people to deal with, who would rather keep a house empty and say they must have 100 dollars a month and starve, than take 50 for it and live on the fat of their land.

The money here is a dollar currency called Conant, which is worth 2s. 1d.—half the American dollar. This is the Philippine currency, and is named after its inventor, an American called Conant, and I wish he had invented a cheaper unit, for 10 Conant dollars, or *pesos*, as they are called, are nothing to spend, whereas the equivalent, an English guinea, is an important sum, and represents four times the spending value of 10 *pesos*. It is a silver currency, dollars and notes, and the coins have rather a pretty design of a man sitting looking at the sea, surrounded by most amusing inscriptions. For instance, the 5-cent, piece is: "Five Centavos," and underneath is "Filipinas." Why not "Five cents." and "Philippines," or else "Cinco centavos, Filipinas?" Why such mongrel? One can only suppose it is the notion of Equality coming out in some mysterious way by meeting the natives half-way in Spanish, which, by-the-bye, is not their native language, and only a few of them speak it at all.

The houses here, as I said before, are all two-storied, the upper part of wood, and the lower of stone or concrete. The floors are of long planks of hard, dark, native woods, which the servants polish with petroleum pads on their feet, sliding about till the surface is like brown glass. The walls are merely wooden partitions, painted white or green, and in the corners of the rooms appear the big tree trunks to which the house is lashed, sometimes just painted white like the walls, or encased in a wooden cover. The word "lashed," I must tell you, is not a figure of speech, as the houses really are tied together with *bejuco*, rattan (a strong, fibrous vine), so as to allow sufficient play for earthquakes, which, it appears, are so frequent in these islands as to be in no way remarkable.

OLD SPANISH HOUSES AT MOLO

The "windows" are really the greater part of each side of the house left open and fitted with shutters, sliding in grooves. Even with these "windows" closed against rain or sun the rooms remain cool, as the shutters are composed of wooden slats a little apart. Inside these is another set for very rainy weather, made of small square panes, each filled with a very thin, white, pearl oyster shell.

Taken all round, the Philippine houses are very pretty, and capable of a great deal of decoration, though, of course, one does not want any draperies or many ornaments about in such a climate, where such superfluities would simply become the homes and nurseries of clouds of mosquitoes and other small fry, besides being unendurably hot even to look at.

At first it appears very odd to see houses without chimneys and rooms without fireplaces, though I can't think why they have none, as it must be very difficult to keep the houses dry in the wet Monsoon.

LETTER IV.

A PHILIPPINE HOUSE—AMERICAN PRICES—NATIVE SERVANTS—FURNITURE

ILOILO, *December 10, 1904.*

I am sure you will be pleased to hear that we have already found a house to suit us, in fact we are quite charmed with it, and can't be too thankful that we did not hastily take any of the others we saw. C—— went to look at some on Tuesday, but on the way he saw this one, and liked it so much that he at once came back for me to look at it, and I went off to inspect, even in the middle of the day! I agreed with him in thinking the house charming, so we took it at once—or as soon as we had finished the preliminary pantomime with the Filipino landlady, a pleasant woman, married to a Spaniard.

The house is in one of the two nicest streets, a little out off the town, on the spit of land formed by the estuary and the open sea. These two streets run parallel, but as the spit gets narrower they leave off, and end in the Government Hospital, the Cavalry *Corral* (stables), some Government buildings, and diminish gradually to a long road, a house, some barren land, a few palms, a pilot's hut, a little bit of beach, some pebbles, and one small crab.

Our house faces S.-W. on a garden, and the back is all open to the river and the N.-E. Monsoon—the most important consideration here, for houses that do not get the wind are stifling and unhealthy. We saw two or three that would have suited us very well, but for the fact that they stood the wrong way, or because the through draught was impeded by some tree or building outside.

The house we have taken is in the usual style, such as I described to you in my last letter, and in one-half of the lower part lives our Spanish landlord, while in the other half, rather vault-like, *se aquila*. The lower parts of the houses are unhealthy, because of the malarial gases arising from the soil, and the damp, so no one lives in the basements if they can afford anything else.

The upper part of this house we are going to live in is quite a separate dwelling, as it is approached by an outside staircase, coming up upon an open balcony running round three sides of the upper story. The balcony is a great charm, and very few of the houses have this addition. I thought that the Spaniards would have made open balconies the fashion out here, but was very much surprised to see none, and can only attribute the lack of them to the fact that the settlers came from the North, in the same way that the houses have no *patios*, and so forth. A roofed balcony like this is not only a delightful lounge, but it keeps the house very cool, besides catching a lot of the heavy rains, and it seems incomprehensible that any sane person could build a house in this climate without one. Verandahs are, of course, quite unknown, but I daresay there is a reason for all this in the terrible Typhoons which sweep over these islands, and would make short shrift of any fancy out-works.

We come into a big hall at the back of the house, with the outer side almost all (with shutters) open to the estuary, and the front portion of the house is the *sala*. Off these two, open five rooms, all large and airy, and freshly painted white. In many of the houses the top of each room has a deep frieze in the shape of a pretty wooden grill, a Chinese fashion, which allows the air to circulate freely through the house—to say nothing of the remarks of the dwellers! We have not got this extra luxury, which I suppose has not been considered necessary in so airy a house.

THE BACK OF OUR HOUSE.
Showing Azotea and Outbuildings.

At the back is what is called the *Azotea*, which in this case happens to be built over the house below. It is a big, sloping, concrete floor, on which are built the kitchen, bathroom, store-room, etc.—all very compact, and quite away from the house, and not coming between us and the wind. In this, again, some of the houses we saw were impossible, for the outbuildings on the Azotea were placed so that they stopped the draught through the house. You may think I am a little foolish on the subject of a current of air, but I assure you I am not, for in a position with no draught the pores of the skin open like so many sluices, and one's head begins to throb.

So that is our house, which, after genuine Spanish haggling, we got for 50 *pesos* a month, a sum working out at about £60 a year, a very low rent indeed out here. In fact, when we set out and said we meant to give no more than 50 dollars a month for a house, we were simply laughed at, and at first were almost inclined to think it could not be done, but when we saw the numbers of houses standing empty in all the nice streets, we stuck to our sum, and are very glad now that we did so. A Spaniard or *Mestizo* (Eurasian) would not dream of giving more than thirty for a house like the one we have taken, but an American would give a hundred. That is where the trouble comes in—in making the people understand that we don't mean to grind them down, nor, on the other hand, to pay foolish sums, but to give the right value for what we get.

You know the way Americans go about in Europe spending the unit, which is lower than their own, like water, with no sense of value? And how they raise prices wherever they go! Well, they have done the same thing here, and an American woman, who was talking to me the other day, told me it was now beginning to be apparent to them what a mistake they had made, and they bitterly regretted having made the Philippines as expensive as America, but that it was very difficult for them to go back now to the more reasonable scale, for as soon as a Filipino found out you were an American, nothing would move him from American prices. Poor thing, she was very bitter about it, and I felt very sorry for her (as well as rather alarmed for myself), for the sums she was paying in rent and wages to live at all in Iloilo, would have kept her in comfort in London or Paris.

Well, when we had settled on the house, we drove straight to the shop-streets of the town—or rather, street, for there is only one with shops, the principal thoroughfare, called the Calle Real. Some of the shops have quite big, handsome windows of plate glass, with wonderful things displayed in them, but when you get inside you find they are, like the shop window in Browning's poem, only "astonishing the street," and beyond the window there is nothing but a large half-empty hall, where a few languid, sallow Eurasians stand trimming their nails behind long, untidy counters. These are the Spanish, Filipino, and German shops; but the Chinese are just the reverse, with no show in the little low window, and the inside a small, poky room, crammed with everything any human being ever invented, and kept by energetic, slant-eyed men who simply won't let you go without buying something.

The principal shop, however, is the great Store, which is kept by an English firm called Hoskyn & Co., and is said to be the best in the islands, and there we bought elemental necessaries, in the way of a few pieces of furniture, some groceries, china, glass, and so forth, at prices, when translated into shillings, to turn one faint with dismay. It was maddening to think of the lovely things we could have got for the same money at home, nevertheless these were very cheap for the Philippines, for this is a notoriously cheap "store," which can afford to sell at low prices, as they have such an immense business, even being able to compete with the shops in Manila, where they send all manner of life's necessaries. Though I am once more reminded of papa's remark that he never realises what a curse human life has become till he reads through a store list.

When we had done our shopping, we came back to the house and unpacked our new household goods as they came in, hung lamps, and so on, and all that day worked hard at the house. At intervals prospective servants kept dropping in, for servants are secured here in much the same way as houses—people tell other people about the opportunity, and the news flies about in servant-land.

All shapes and sizes of Filipinos loomed on the balcony at intervals, and drifted into the hall and stood watching us till we had time to attend to them. In this country all the doors stand always open for coolness, and there are no bells, and when you go to a house you walk in at the door and sing out for a servant. Some people go so far as to have a hand bell at the top of the stairs, but the whole system seems to me ridiculous, so I have persuaded C—— to invest in a door bell, which he is going to fix to the main door into the hall.

We were unpacking and going about the house, and every now and then we would come upon a silent figure waiting, just waiting, anywhere, leaning up against something, and perfectly indifferent to time or place. This stamped him as a candidate. To each one C—— put first of all the question:

"Can you speak English?"

And when the man said "Yeees, sair," he was refused without any further parley, for nothing will induce us to take servants who can understand what we are saying, which would make life impossible in these open houses. Besides that, when they speak English it means they have been with Americans, who spoil the Filipino servants dreadfully with their well-meant notions of equality, and give ridiculous wages as well. In the Spanish days a Filipino head-servant got 5 or 6 *pesos* a month, and the *peso* then was the Mexican dollar, which is only about two-thirds of the Conant unit. It was, and is, riches to them, but so changed are these things now, that we are considered wonderful because we have found a *mayordomo* or head boy willing to come to us for 10 *pesos* a month and a second boy for 6. An American would give them twice as much, if not more, which would simply turn them into drunkards, or gamblers, or both, or worse.

All the Philippine servants are men, as all over the East, though some women do have a native maid; but as all the women I have met do nothing but complain of the laziness and uselessness of these handmaidens, I have no idea of saddling myself with such a burden.

The two men we have engaged are about twenty years of age, but it is always very difficult to tell how old Filipinos are, as they look old when they are young and young when they are old. They can give no particular account of themselves, these two, and have unaccountably mislaid their little books of references; but we are taking them on the recommendation of their faces, which are nice, and that is just as good a standard to go by in a Filipino as in anyone else! One is a native of Guimaras; the other a Tagalo, from Luzon; and both are short, thick-set, sturdy-looking fellows who ought not to give us much trouble with falling ill. Half the time here the servants are ill with fever, or colds, or heaven knows what, for it is a race without much stamina.

One of the most aggravating characteristics of the Filipinos is the way they murmur, for they have naturally very soft voices, which become positively a whisper with shyness and awe. The English people here adopt the custom, which prevails throughout the East, of calling their servants "boys," but the Americans use the Spanish word *muchacho*, and that is unfortunate, as they give all vowels the narrow, English value, making it this word *muchaycho*. It sounds so odd, this lack of ear, and quite alters some of the Spanish names—such as saying Cavyt for Cavite (the naval port of Manila), Caypiz for Capiz (a town in Panay), and so on, and though they pronounce Jaro exactly the same as the English town of Harrow, thank goodness they don't go so far as to call this place Eye-low-Eye-low!

FILIPINO SERVANTS.

But I am wandering away from the servants, and I have not yet introduced the cook to you. We had less trouble to get this treasure than the others, as all the natives cook well by instinct—at least, they know how to make the best of what food there is to be had, which is all one wants. This particular *chef* is a shrivelled, pock-marked person, about 4 feet 6 in height, with an array of immense teeth, and an air of intense importance; this last characteristic being funny or annoying according to the mood one happens to be in oneself. His wages are 15 *pesos* a month, and as he is a married man, or says so, he is to live with his family in the town.

And that was the end of the first day, and a very long and fatiguing one in this climate.

When we came back next morning we found that the *boys*, who had been left in charge of the house and what furniture we had fixed up, had already swept and polished the floors, which made an immense difference to the appearance of the place, and the lamps were filled and trimmed. There is electric light in the town, but it is so very bad, and is the cause of so much complaint, that all have to supplement their expensive electricity with oil lamps before they can read. We are, therefore, not going to have it put on, though it would be quite easy, as the wire passes over us from next door. The efficiency and intelligence of the new servants pleased us very much, but all the same we observed cautiously to each other: "New brooms sweep clean."

We left the new brooms still sweeping, and went off to the shops again, and once more spent important and heart-breaking sums on the bare necessities of life. This time it was furniture, at the shop of a Chinese Eurasian, where we got a lot of things that look very nice, though they are not anything wonderful in the way of wood; but in these light, open houses with no fires and no carpets, it is not necessary to have such rich-looking furniture as at home. If one likes to spend still more money, there are beautiful things to be had made from magnificent hard Philippine woods, but the high price of labour, the poverty everywhere, and lack of capital and enterprise, have made these hard-wood things so dear that they are luxuries. The ordinary furniture is, in spite of the cent.-per-cent. import duties, either made out of Oregon pine, or else imported ready made from Vienna; but an insect called *buc-buc*, with which the country abounds, eats these soft pine woods, though it will not touch the native mahogany, teak, ebony, etc. It is not as if this Philippine timber were swept off for export, for no trade is done with it as no cheap labour is to be had, and splendid trees just decay in the crowded forests on the hills.

For our *sala* we invested in basket furniture, a necessity in this heat, for padded chairs or cushions would be unendurable. The bamboo and rattan, of which Chinamen would make all sorts of pretty chairs and couches for a few *pesos* a piece, grow plentifully here, but in the Philippines such articles are only to be had at three times the price, as they are imported from China, for the Filipinos are too lazy and stupid to make anything of the materials given them by "*el buen Dios*," and if they did, the scale of wages, set by the American Government, would make the things even more expensive than those imported. So the reeds rot, and the woods rot; and we, for our part, cannot cease to regret that we did not, while we were in Hong Kong, invest in some of the cheap and beautiful furniture we saw there, but we took local advice and forbore to import anything into this land of prohibitive tariffs; though now we discover that, tariffs and all, we should have found it cheaper to have brought the things with us.

All this expense of life springs from the accepted interpretation of the maxim, "Philippines for the Filipinos," which saying was invented by the late (and first) Governor-General of the Philippines, a man of the name of Taft, who is now Secretary of War in the United States. I suppose the idea caught on in America, and the good people there, whose opinion controls affairs in this country, which they have never seen, think that prohibitive tariffs and the exclusion of cheap Chinese or Japanese labour, must be a good thing for these depopulated islands if it is a benefit to the overcrowded U.S.A.

As a matter of fact, when applied to an indolent, indifferent race, the result is stagnation and starvation prices, which is a terrible state of affairs in a hot country like this, where food and labour ought to be plentiful and cheap, or nothing will pay. I can't think that the Americans really believe the Filipinos to be as high a development of the human race as they are themselves; but since they wish, with the best intentions, to allow the Filipinos to benefit by American systems of government, these Malays must first learn the A B C of such a system. Whether they are capable of profiting by such lessons, or whether they are so foreign to the essence of this race as to ruin it, remains to be demonstrated.

Well, I must get back to the house again, and the end of the story is that we moved into our house on Thursday, the 8th, and slept here that night. We were able to do this so soon, as people have been very kind in lending us things—sheets and towels from one, table-linen from another, and so on—but all the same I wish our cases would come, as there is such a responsibility about other people's gear.

À propos of these same cases, we are rather uneasy in our minds about them, as we are beginning to hear alarming rumours of Customs duties to be paid. Wedding presents used to be exempt, but quite lately duties were levied on them, and I am afraid we shall have to pay for our own things, which is a bore, not to say rather a blow.

We got through all our trunks, etc., that we had with us with a perfunctory opening of one box, a few questions, and the signing of papers, the only trouble being C——'s gun, which they took away, and he will not be able to get a licence, or allowed to have it out of the Customs House before he finds two "bonds" of 100 dollars each. That is, in clear English, he must find two people who are prepared to bet the American Government 100 dollars each that he is not going to sell the gun to an Insurgent.

So, barring the gun anxiety, we got our boxes in all right, and are told it would have gone equally well with the cases had we had them with us, but as they are coming out by freight, they will be subject to the duties. However, the authorities tell us it will not be very severe—C—— went and inquired about it, as he said he would rather not take our spoons and forks and things out of bond, but would prefer to send them back to Hong Kong rather than pay a large sum. So, all things considered, C—— is not reassured, so he has arranged to have the cases sent here unopened and in bond; and is going to open them, in bond, at the Custom House, and have the contents appraised before he decides what to do with them. The only reasonable hope is that many of the contents, such as plate, may be exempt, or very lightly taxed, as they are articles that could not possibly be produced in the Philippines; but when I mentioned this to a Customs official, he replied that such an idea had nothing to do with the system of taxation.

This is a fearfully long letter, but even now I feel I have not told you half I wanted to.

LETTER V.

HOUSEKEEPING IN ILOILO

ILOILO, *December 17, 1904.*

We are settling down very comfortably into our charming house, which we like more and more, and are continually congratulating ourselves on our luck in having found such a nice home.

There is nothing special to tell you about since I last wrote, so I will try to give you some idea of my housekeeping, of which I think I have not yet told you anything beyond just mentioning how many servants we have.

I find that the cook—he with the important manner and the big teeth—has been an under-cook in an American hotel, or what he is pleased to call an American hotel, by which I take it he means one of the saloons or eating-houses in the town. So far, however, he has proved himself a very good cook indeed, which is even more necessary here than anywhere else, for food in the Philippines has but little variety, and is not nourishing at its best. Every morning I give this person a *peso* and a half, with which he goes off to the market and buys whatever takes his fancy, or, more probably, what is to be had, which generally takes the form of an incredibly small and thin fowl—alive; one or two little fish; some green peppers or egg-plants, and always a few very small, half-ripe tomatoes. With these and with help from the store-room, he concocts a very good lunch and dinner, and, doubtless, makes a good thing out of it, but most cooks charge 2 dollars for the same *menu*, and he really provides for us very well. I supply tea, salt, butter, lard, tinned fruits, potatoes, macaroni—in fact all the dry provisions usually kept in a store-room, I don't know what is the technical name for them.

The store-room (*dispensa*, they call it), where these treasures are hoarded up, is a very nice little dark cabin, with shelves all round, which I made the boys clean out and wipe everywhere with petroleum, an excellent precaution against the numberless and extraordinary animals with which one has to share the house. I got tall glass jars for protection against cockroaches, and tins to keep mice off, and wire-netting for rats, and naphthaline to astonish the scorpions and spiders; and last, but by no means least, a good strong padlock for human beings! When the tins and bottles were all arranged, they looked very home-like.

We get up at half-past five or six, and I give one of the *boys* 20[2] cents, with which he goes out and buys bread for the day at the shop of some Chinaman down the street. It is necessary to get small daily supplies of everything, for food will not keep.

---

[2] Fivepence. The amount of bread this sum will buy in the Philippines is equal to half the English 2d. loaf.

Some people have told me fearful anecdotes about the horrors perpetrated by the Chinamen in the making of their bread, and these faddists have theirs made at home, but the Chinese bread tastes quite good, and is much more light and digestible than that made by the house-cooks. As our cook has cooked for Americans, he knows how to make the hot cakes which are the great feature of American breakfasts, but we won't have them, for they are deadly anywhere, especially in the tropics.

After our seven o'clock breakfast, which consists very largely of eggs, and after C—— has gone to the office, I open the door of the *dispensa* and serve out the day's supplies; but this routine was not brought about without a struggle, for at first the cook persisted in coming to me intermittently all day long to ask for things. At least, he invented wants, but I had an idea his only object was the key of the *dispensa*, as these Filipinos have a full measure of the cunning of the brown-faced person all the world over. However, I disappointed him about that, always leaving whatever I was doing to go and open the door and get out what he wanted, at the same time remarking, as best I could, that if he did not ask for things at the proper time he must do without them. Then once or twice I carried the threat into effect, and when he heard what C—— had to say about the dinner, that cured him. Everyone tells me doleful tales about the way the *muchacho* or *boy* robs them, so I thought it would be better to start from the first by giving as few opportunities as possible for trouble of this sort.

In the morning the servants' food is also given out, each one getting an allowance of rice (for which purpose we lay in a large sackful), and this they boil and eat with some tiny fish which they buy for themselves with a few extra cents I give them. I believe it is unheard-of extravagance to give the extra money; and I never measure out the rice, but let them take it, for, after all, it is all the poor souls live on. All over the Philippines the natives of all classes live almost entirely on rice, which formerly used to be grown in all the islands, but rinderpest destroyed many of the *carabaos* (buffaloes), which worked the soil, and high wages and heavy taxes have wrought even greater havoc, so that now the supply nearly all comes from China. You see, high wages are offered in the towns, and what with that and the unsuitable education they receive, the country-people all flock into the towns, and the country places are empty. It is on the coast, in the towns, that rice is so much eaten, for inland the staple food is *camote* (sweet potato); so the country-people think rice a luxury, and the town's-people eat *camote* as a treat.

When I wrote last, I don't think the staff was completed by the washerwoman, was it? A person with a huge, almost black, pan face came and stood in the picture of blue sky and green palm-branches framed in the doorway, dressed in a skirt formed of a tight fold of red cloth and a muslin bodice with huge sleeves (the native costume), holding a big black umbrella in one hand, and muttering in an undertone, while she kept one dull, rolling eye on Tuyay, who was disposed to growl and sniff.

We were at breakfast at the time, and as we ate we conversed patiently with her till we found that this person wanted to be taken on as a *lavandera* at 20 *pesos* a month, which is about twenty-six guineas a year. This offer we refused with imprecations, and we added that we would not give more than 10.

She melted away, murmuring, from the front door, and presently reappeared at the back door (both opening upon the hall, but at different ends), and murmured afresh. I must tell you, by-the-bye, that, following a very general custom here, we use one end of the hall as dining-room, though there is a room which has been used for that purpose, but it looks on the alley between this house and the next, and is not so cool as the hall.

After more conversation, we decided to engage this pan-faced individual at 12 *pesos* a month as a stop-gap, till we should be able to find some more intelligent woman, and there and then I gave her a bagful of soiled linen, and off she went.

Next day at lunch she suddenly reappeared, perfectly cow-like and stolid, leaning up against the door-post and murmuring so that C—— simply got *wild* with her, and would have thrown everything on the table at her head, I believe, if I had not been there.

As the cook is the only one of the servants who speaks above a whisper, he was sent for, and he told us that pan-face wanted soap, starch, and charcoal. All the washing is done in cold water at some well, it appears, and they only want a little charcoal to put in the iron. So C—— wrote an order, a *vale* they call it, upon Hoskyn's for soap, a box-iron, starch, and charcoal, and away went the new *lavandera*.

But we had not seen the last of her, for the next day she came again, at breakfast this time, and murmured again, clutching the bulgy gamp and leaning against the door-post. This time the cook told us she wanted tin tubs, and C—— gave a sort of roar as he asked her when the devil she was going to begin the washing, but she only looked more hopelessly stupid, and her face became more like a gorilla's. At last she got her *vale* for tubs, and off she went—but about mid-day she reappeared, on the balcony, outside the front door, with the tubs, huge tin baths, sitting beside her.

C—— managed to control himself sufficiently to ask her if there was anything the matter with the tubs, and she was understood to say no, but she only wanted to show us she had got tubs; and she melted away.

Next afternoon I was told the *lavandera* had arrived, so I went out to tell her the *señor* would soon be in and ready to listen to her, though I really had some doubt about the latter statement, but I found her undoing a huge bundle of washing—all finished and ready! And such beautiful work, C——'s white linen suits done to perfection, my frocks and blouses like new—I never saw clothes look more fresh and lovely. It was a pleasant surprise.

So pan-face remains, but all the same we are quite prepared to find this standard not kept up for long, and if any remonstrance has to be made, we know we shall have that blank look and that murmuring to face again.

The *boys* are shaping very well, and if they go on as they are doing, no one could wish for better servants. I did not bewilder them more than I could help at first, but sprang a routine on them by degrees in a mixture of pantomime, Italian and a word or

two of Spanish, that seems to answer the purpose very well. Two things C——
insisted on from the first: one, that the servants should wear native costume and bare
feet in the house; and the other, that they must address us as *señor* and *señora*, none
of which little marks of etiquette are insisted on in American households, but we
think, and I believe rightly, that they are of the greatest importance in dealing with
Orientals. C—— said if they didn't like these rules they could go, but apparently they
did like them, and they have stayed.

We asked some friends to dinner a few nights ago, and just before they arrived
C—— went into the hall and found an unknown young man, in a very smart, white,
buttoned-up, linen European suit with starched collar, and white canvas shoes,
standing on a chair in the middle of the hall, doing something to one of the lamps.
When the man turned round, we saw, to our amazement, that he was Domingo—our
second *boy*!

When he saw C——'s expression, the servant was quite frightened, not having
any idea what crime he could be committing or have committed, but he very soon
understood that if he did not take off those shoes and that coat he would be fired out
of the house. I don't think the poor creature meant any harm, in fact he was supposed
to be got up in his best to do honour to our guests, but he fled at once to the Azotea,
and has never been seen again except in the Filipino dress, which is a loose shirt rather
like a Chinaman's coat, only fastening up the middle, and with bare feet.

Yesterday the cook appeared, carrying four huge, tall orchid plants, with very
green leaves and pale mauve flowers, such lovely things, which he suggested would
look well in the *sala*, and I quite agreed, so we began to negotiate for them. The
countryman who had brought the flowers was ushered to the back door, and there was
understood to murmur that he wanted 2 *pesos* (four shillings) for the four plants, but
the cook, who said this was *muy caro*, got him down to a *peso* and 20 cents; only, the
people here use many terms applicable to the old coinage, such as *real*, *peseta*, and so
on, which make it so extremely puzzling to discover what the price of things really is,
that I found it difficult to make out what to give; but the cook fished out a *peso* and
20 cents out of a pile of money I put on the table, and the man picked the two coins
up and went off quite content. In my ignorance, I thought it rather a shame to insist
on so low a price for such lovely plants—and orchids, too! However, I have since
found out that these plants grow wild in great profusion in the woods over in the
Island of Guimaras, and that what I had paid was like giving a man at home two
shillings for a bunch of primroses. In spite of this, I decline to consider myself
swindled, or to be dissatisfied with my bargain.

When the orchids had been bought, I asked the cook where he proposed to find
pots to put them in, and he smiled in a very superior fashion, and said they only
wanted some earth and a piece of sacking to live in, and they could be kept alive by
certain airings and drinks of water; and when I said, "Who is going to do all this?"

"Domingo, *señora*," he said in a great hurry. "Domingo is the only one who really
understands plants"—and he grinned and nodded his head with marvellous rapidity.

I rather fancied the placid Domingo would be told he knew about plants and have to attend to them, after the fashion of one or two other "jobs" I had noticed, but I thought it best not to interfere, as Domingo is twice the size of the cook, and ought to be able to look after himself. Later on I saw the two of them fixing the tall plants, with roots neatly tied up in sacking bags, to the walls of the *sala*, or rather, Domingo very adroitly tying and nailing up, while the cook stood by to talk twenty to the dozen, and came afterwards to me for approval.

We had a very amusing scene of this description at the very beginning, when we fixed up the mosquito nets, on which occasion all hands, myself included (with needle and cotton) did something tangible, while the cook devoted the time to talking and jabbering and hopping about, uncannily like a monkey.

The orchids are really lovely, and make the *sala* look charming with their masses of little blooms of mauve and yellow against the white walls, and in time I must try to get some small trees in tall Chinese stands of blue and green earthenware, which adorn the houses here in profusion, and suit the white paint and brown floors admirably.

LETTER VI.

A WASTED LAND

ILOILO, *Christmas Eve, 1904.*

We have just come back from a delightful drive, to a town called Molo, which lies inland, in the direction of the river, but on the opposite bank to Jaro, the latter, as I think I told you, having been the capital of the Island of Panay in the olden days. There is a good road out to both of these towns, which crosses the river at Molo, and makes a circle, passing through a village called Mindoriao, and this is the great drive of the place, in fact the only one. The whole round is about 8 or 9 miles, however, which is too long for a *paseo* (promenade), so the carriages roll out at sunset to one of the two towns, turn round the quaint, ramshackle, old *plazas*, and return whence they came, spinning along in the fresh night air, with lamps lighted, and all the little ponies gallantly determined to pass each other.

Along the sides of the road, for a long way out of the town, stretches a vast suburb of picturesque native huts of palm thatch, built on high poles in the jungle, or standing in the edge of the river, surrounded by palms and all sorts of tropical trees of different brilliant greens, through which may be caught glimpses of intensely blue river or sea and exquisite mauve mountain ranges.

We enjoyed our drive immensely, and kept wishing that Papa could see the endless pictures of brown and yellow huts, women in bright red dresses, the groups of children and animals, the grey old Spanish churches and belfries—I think if you ever came out here he would spend his whole time on a camp stool, sketching for dear life!

Our cases have come from home at last, though I don't know why I should say that, as they have not been so very long after us, but we were rather grubbing along till they came, which made the time seem longer. When C—— was informed they had arrived, he went down to the Custom House and spent a long day with the official appraiser, a most polite and patient young man, weighing and examining everything. The methods of doing this are wonderful and alarming, for they weigh the silver and plate with their leather or wooden cases, and the duty is charged by so much on the kilo! Imagine what the proportion is on a dozen silver spoons or knives in a handsome oak case! All the italics and exclamations in the biggest printing house in the world could not convey my sentiments upon this subject. The textiles are examined with a magnifying glass, appraised as materials, and taxed as such, at the rate of 50 per cent., upon what the Customs people choose to say was their original value. If the material is made up, there is extra duty of 100 per cent., which makes me glad that I put so few of my frocks in the cases. The only way to console oneself is to think that even with the duty added, they cost about half what they would if one bought the materials and had them made up here.

Well, the end of it was that C—— came home late in the afternoon and told me that the duty came to 300 *pesos*—a little over £30!—and did I think the things were worth it, or should we send them back to Hong Kong in bond?

After we had discussed the matter, going into it all carefully, we came to the conclusion that we could not find substitutes for our things here for that sum. So we decided to take them, and the cases were brought up here by coolies, two or four carrying each one slung with *bejuco* ropes on to a hard-wood pole.

It is very nice to have all our own things about, but all the same it is a fearful hardship to have to pay their value for things that belong to us, and particularly annoying in the case of the wedding presents.

This, the arrival of the cases, has been the great excitement of the week, and from the look of the box-room, bids fair to continue to excite all hands for some time to come.

When we get the sketches hung up, the house will look very pretty, I think, and we are going to have some of them put in some frames that came in an old case full of C——'s things from Cebú. They will look very nice done up with enamel, and we can get some glass at a Chinaman's shop, but all "crystal" comes from outside, of course, and is subject to a very heavy duty. You may be surprised, perhaps, to hear me mention Chinese shops so much, but nearly all the "stores" in the Philippines are kept by Chinamen, one (as I told you) by an English company here, and I don't know if there are others, but I fancy not, and the rest by Spaniards and Germans. The chief businesses, big trading firms, are English all through the islands, and have been so for fifty years or more; and there are some Spanish companies, dealing in tobacco chiefly, and besides these, one or two Germans and Swiss, who import their native productions. Nearly all the Americans are official, military, educational, or missionaries. I am told that a few of the American soldiers, when the war was, or was said to be over, settled down on small plantations in the southern islands, and there are some saloon-keepers in the towns, a boot shop in Manila, and a struggling mechanic here and there; but so far, that is the extent of the American business interest in the place. Planters bringing in capital, such as our colonies profit by, do not, and never can, come into this country, for a new American law exists which prohibits all persons who are not natives from acquiring more than 40 acres of Philippine soil, and 40 acres in the tropics is not worth having, I believe.

I rigged up my bed with my own pillow-cases and sheets yesterday. They were delicious to sleep in, and the idea of linen pillow-cases for coolness and cotton sheets for health is excellent, for a cotton pillow-covering would be very hot and uncomfortable, and linen sheets would be dangerous in such heat. I have got myself an iron bed with a wire mattress, for I cannot sleep on the Filipino bed, which is a little platform of woven cane, and quite hard and unyielding. They are wooden four-posters, these native beds, with a cotton roof, usually red, set off by a frill of lace all round the top, above the mosquito curtains. Some of the bedsteads I have seen, made of native woods, are very prettily carved round the pillars, and a really handsome piece of carving fills the space at each end to the height of two feet or so. All right so far as looks go, but the bed itself is an appalling instrument of torture to lie on, for in pattern and material it is the same as the seats of cane chairs, and as hard as iron—all for coolness. On the cane is spread a native grass mat called a *petate*; the luxurious and faddy add a sheet, but humbler folk sleep on the mat, which is aired in the sun every day, or ought to be, and frequently washed. In the bed there always lies a small, round bolster, called in Spanish an *embrasador*, but the Europeans name it Dutch Wife, and this is used to fling a leg and an arm over, for, in this climate, to lie with the limbs touching would be intolerable discomfort. It is also a well-known fact that the *embrasador* is a great protection for the stomach against chills and fevers, which are a danger towards the small hours of the morning. Bedclothes, in the way of covering, are out of the question, but in every bed a small, thin blanket lies folded up, ready for the sudden chill of a rainy night. Once or twice people have said to me: "It was so cold last night. I was shivering even with my blanket." This is the winter to them, you see. I only wish it struck me in the same way, for though the nights are by no means stifling or anything like that, it would be delightful to feel cold now and then.

It is so difficult to realise that this is Christmas Eve—so odd to hear people talking of children's parties; and Christmas trees seem absurdly out of place! The churches began to get excited some time ago, and for the last week some deadly bells have begun to clang before the dawn.

The dawn, by-the-bye, is not what I expected, for I have often read descriptions of the coming of the tropic day—that is, night one minute and broad daylight the next. I find, however, that there is a considerable interval of twilight, both morning and evening. The other day I read a book by a very well-known writer, in which a description was given of the dayspring in Egypt coming like "the opening of an oven door," which I knew to be nonsense as applied to Egypt, and now I find the same sort of hyperbole about the tropics equally false; for I have watched the grey dawn come gradually nearly every morning here, and I sit reading on the balcony in the twilight, in the evening. It is certainly not a long twilight, but all one reads about the sun shooting up from the night into the tropic day, and so forth, must be what they call "word pictures," because it is certainly not truth, or even decent exaggeration.

Christmas Day.—I always write my letters to you all at one sitting, but I had to break off yesterday before I considered that I had covered enough paper to satisfy you, and I feel I can't begin again to-day without this fresh heading; though it is not like Christmas a bit, and I think the bright green palms, blue sea and sky, and scorching sun are a very poor substitute for the lovely brown and purples of the winter landscape at home, the invigorating cold, and the exquisite skeletons of oaks and elms.

I should not complain, though, for the weather here is really delicious just at present, with frequent heavy showers, which keep the vegetation fresh, and fill the water-tanks. There are lots of wells, in which the water is very hard, and people say it is sea-water filtered through the soil; and it must be so, for at high tide the wells are at their fullest, and quite brackish. So the water-supply one chiefly depends upon is that out of the rain-water tanks, which are fed from the corrugated roofs of the houses. However, it is not safe to drink even that unfiltered, and some people are very fanciful and boil it first, but that is rather absurd if one gets a good filter.

Out of the filter, Sotero, the head boy, fills up soda-water bottles, which he takes to the English Club, where they are laid on the ice for a charge of 2 cents apiece, and these, after an hour or two on the ice, give us very refreshing drinks. Good and light beer is to be had, brewed in Manila; it works out at about a shilling a bottle, and the Americans drink it, but the English people consider beer an unwholesome beverage in this climate, and stick to whisky and soda very faithfully. Some adopt the Spanish custom of drinking light red wine, *vino tinto*, which is supposed to be strengthening and blood-making in a country where the prevailing trouble is anæmia. This wine comes from Spain in barrels, and I expect it really is the most wholesome of all. For my part, I keep pretty generally to lime juice and soda, or lemon squash. Lemons, which come from China, are about 2d. apiece. At this season, in the way of fruit, small tangerines are to be had also, hailing from China, and oranges, another luxury, 6d. each. It is rather a bore that such necessary and wholesome fruit should cost such ridiculous prices. Bananas, everlasting bananas, are the chief fruit, and even they are not astonishingly cheap, as they are sold here at exactly the same price as in London. Vegetables there are none, except miserable tomatoes and egg-plants. The lack of fresh fruit and vegetables is very trying, especially the vegetables. Whatever is sold is imported, except the bananas, tomatoes, and egg-plants. Fresh meat, too, would be a boon, and butter, and milk, for all these can only be obtained tinned—"canned" as they call it here. Once a week we get some provisions from the Cold Storage in Manila, Australian meat and butter, and sometimes vegetables, but this is only a private enterprise of a few of the English community, who club together and get down an ice-chest by the *Butuan*, the weekly Manila mail. It would be unwise to venture to lay in more than one day's supply, which has to be cooked and eaten at once before it goes bad, even with an ice-chest to stand it in.

It might be possible to put up with these discomforts with more or less philosophic calm, and not mind the deprivations if they were inevitable, but they are not so by any means, as the soil of the Philippines is one of the richest in the world, volcanic and full of natural chemical manures, the islands having also every sort of advantage and variety of climate from the plains to the mountain-tops, and being plentifully watered. I am for ever being told that anything and everything will grow and flourish here, which is so aggravating when all the fresh food to be procured is miserable poultry, fish, and egg-plants, tomatoes you would not look at in England, and costly bananas. Rice and potatoes from China, live cattle from China, or frozen meat from Australia, and *everything* else under the sun in tins from London or America! This, after six years of what we are told is the most enlightened system of Colonial or Tropical Government yet invented. It is useless to point out that no roads exist inland, except one in Luzon for the Governor and his family to go to the hills; or to remark that labour is too dear for any enterprise to pay, and that all healthy foreign competition in the way of labour is excluded—the reply is an invitation to contemplate the splendid work that is being done in education. For these schools and swarming schoolmasters this pastoral country is taxed and tariffed to breaking point—schools to which the natives are being taken from the fields, and in which they are taught a crude wash of bad English and mathematics. The chief result is to bring all the "scholars" into the towns to loaf along in clerkships, if they can get them.

You will laugh at my vehemence! But it does seem such a pity to see a splendid country wasted, as it were, thrown away, for the sake of a windy theory propounded by some well-meaning though ignorant sentimentalists at the other side of the globe.

LETTER VII.

CUSTOMS AND DRESS OF THE NATIVES

ILOILO, *December 31, 1904.*

I think you may be amused to hear about a Filipino *Fiesta*, which took place yesterday, called Rizal Day—the anniversary of the death of the national hero, a Filipino of the name of Doctor Rizal. He was the William Tell of the Philippines, except that his existence was a reality, not a myth, for he died only eight years ago.

This patriot obtained the degree of Doctor (of Philosophy and Medicine) in Spain, where he went to be educated and enlightened. When he returned from that land, Doctor Rizal set to work, endeavouring to free his countrymen from the frightful Spanish friars, who were the real rulers of the Spanish Philippines, and whose cruelty and wickedness were almost incredible. Any friars who were not good enough for Spain, were sent out to the Philippines, where each man became a little god and tyrant in a tiny *pueblo* (village or district), in which his authority was unbounded and unquestioned. I suppose some of these friar-priests must have been good men, but no one can tell me they ever heard of such a being, for the enervating climate, lazy life, complete irresponsibility, and the irresistible power of the priest over the superstitious, childish Malays were too much for these men of God; and the stories of their cruelties, rapacities, and immoralities are all terrible and often simply sickening. I have heard them from people who lived in the *pueblos*, and the things that went on were like the Decameron and the Inquisition rolled into one.

Well, this Doctor Rizal started a revolt against the power of these dreadful *men*, if one could call the friars by such a name, about 1872; and from that time the rest of his life was a series of plots, captures, escapes to Europe, imprisonment by the friars, banishment, return, recapture, till at last, by the simple device of the friars having Rizal cabled for to Spain and getting him back to the Philippines, the avenging Church had him executed, by order of the Spaniards, on the Luneta, the Promenade at Manila, on December 30, 1896. I have met people who were present at the execution of Rizal, and they tell me that the crowds were vast, and relate how Rizal faced a line of soldiers bravely and was shot. Rizal had a nice, clever face of a refined Filipino type, if one can trust the portraits on the Conant bank-notes, and the Filipinos simply adore his memory.

It was in consequence of Rizal's revolt that Aguinaldo and the Katipunan arose, who lived to revenge their hero's memory, completing his work by turning the Spaniards and their dreadful priests out of the Islands. To do this, as you know, they had to get America to help them; which the Americans did, and stayed on. The idea is that they are going to teach the Filipinos how to govern themselves, which, it appears, ought only to be done by all peoples and races after the American method. The Filipinos are said to be delighted about this, but the puzzling anomaly is that they fought, and are still fighting the Americans tooth and nail to get their own liberty, their own way, but they are not asked what they think at all, and if they show any signs of wanting to get rid of this American burden and govern themselves in their own fashion, they are called Insurgents and knocked on the head, or dubbed common robbers and strung up to a tree.

On account of this state of affairs, the natives seize on this anniversary to give relief to some of their patriotic emotions. The day is a public holiday, they hang out flags and lanterns, and every Filipino knocks off what little work he ever does, and crawls about the streets and spits, and every one of them who is not carrying some musical instrument, is to be seen taking a cock to or from a cock-fight; while the women slouch along in gangs with myriads of children, or else jolt up and down in hired carriages—and that is the *Fiesta*.

They abandon these delirious joys during the hot hours of the day, from two to four, but swarm out again in redoubled numbers in the evening, walking about the streets till midnight in long processions, carrying paper lanterns of every shape and colour, and led by a guitar and mandoline band; while nearly every house is lighted up, and the big room full of people dancing.

The Filipinos have a natural gift for music of a very light sort, and I am told by people, who I do not think are very competent judges, that the natives perform classic music pretty well too, when well directed. Everyone plays an instrument of some sort, the men forming themselves into little and large societies, bands, in fact, which, on an occasion like yesterday, go about the streets and play "Hiawatha" on the slightest provocation. The trail of Sousa and "rag-time" is over them all, and their own plaintive, minor melodies, some of them very beautiful, are never heard now. At least I say "their own" melodies, but these tunes have a great flavour of Spain about them, and, of course, after four centuries of Spanish influence, it is difficult to say what is original Malay and what is imported.

The dress of the women is a mixture of the two races—Malay and Spanish—for the tight skirt (which is not worn in Manila, by-the-bye) is the *sarong* of the Straits; and the muslin blouse or jacket, with its huge starched sleeves and *panuelo* (a sort of folded *fichu* collar which sticks up behind) is an interesting survival of the fashions in vogue in Europe, in the days when Spain took these Islands on one side of the globe, and fought the mariners of Elizabeth on the other. Beyond these two garments the outfit is simplicity itself, for it consists of one long cotton chemise. I don't think you've ever seen a *sarong*, by-the-bye, which, when it is off, is like a bottomless sack; and when it is on, is drawn tightly across the back and tucked in over itself at the top, when it makes an outline exactly like the petticoats in Egyptian monuments, quite close at the back, with a fold like a kilt in front. Then over the upper part comes the muslin bodice, which is made in one piece, with a hole to slip over the head, after the fashion of a jibbah. It looks very cool, but the cut is clumsy, and the fashion is dwarfing to the tiny Filipino figures; while the big sticking-up collar gives a round-shouldered effect, and spoils what is one of their best points, a graceful set and carriage of the head and neck. They walk very straight, with all the motion from the hips, and their feet very much turned out, and generally wear no jewellery of any sort, except perhaps a pair of gold earrings, or a ring or two, or a rosary of European patterns. There is nothing characteristic in the way of native work or beads. The well-to-do Filipino women wear more trinkets, and the *Mestizas* (Eurasians) cover themselves with cheap and tawdry ornaments.

The favourite material for the *camisa* (bodice) is a native muslin woven from the fibres of pine-apple leaves, called *piña*, an exclusive manufacture of the Islands of Panay and Negros, where the pine-apples grow wild in the jungles. This the Filipino women weave with or without silk stripes and checks, and dye all sorts of colours; but the lower classes and peasants hardly ever wear anything beyond the plain, undyed yellowish-white, which, after all, suits them far better than any other colour. They look well though, on great occasions, in crimson, purple, or yellow, and they are wise when they stick to those warm colours, for blues and greens are fatally unbecoming to their yellow-brown skins, making them look heavy and dirty. They seem to have no natural taste for colour though, as they use some appalling aniline dyes, and make mixtures which set one's teeth on edge. They are only really safe when they stick to the red *sarong* and undyed *camisa*.

The *piña* is woven on hand-looms, which can be seen and heard clicking in almost every hut, and it is sent all over the Islands, and fetches enormous prices, but then it is practically everlasting, and when washed and done up with rice-starch, it looks like new.

They also have a muslin, much cheaper stuff, called *Jusi* (pronounced Hoosee), which is made from a fibre procured in China; and a third, and still cheaper one woven from hemp fibres and called *sinamay*—and the result of it all is that to the uninitiated the three materials all look exactly alike! On the *piña* the women do a very beautiful embroidery of graceful designs worked out in fine white sewing-cotton and marvellously shaded, mixed with drawn threads, and some of the antique pieces are exquisite. This *piña* embroidery is the only characteristic Filipino work I have been able to see or hear of, except the decoration of some weapons, and the grass mats with patterns.

The dress of the men I think I have already hinted at, and it, too, is the last word in simplicity (short of the loin-cloth, which costume is not allowed in the towns), for all the Filipinos wear in the house is tight drawers and a vest, and when they go out they draw on over those a pair of white or blue cotton trousers and a collarless shirt, rather like a Chinaman's coat, which I described to you before, I think. This shirt hangs outside the trousers, really looking much better than it sounds, and on galas and occasions of state they turn out in an ordinary European shirt, with a starched front, all pleated and embroidered, such as Frenchmen and Germans sometimes wear, and they look so clean and smart in them. In fact they look quite nice in their native costume, but unfortunately many of them now affect the white man's buttoned-up linen coat, with stand-up starched collar, and put on shoes and stockings, which subtly vulgarises the wearers at once. Like all coloured races and many white ones, as soon as they attempt modern European fashions the Filipino taste is villainous, and they look inexpressibly common and disheartening.

They are so clean—so scrupulously clean—all their clothes, even those of the very poorest, being spotless and fresh. They are for ever washing their bodies, too, or at least it is certain that the poor people are, for they may be seen at the wells and outside their houses tubbing ingenuously, the men with a single fold of stuff retained for decency, the women struggling inside a wet *sarong*.

We went yesterday evening for a walk along the beach, on the side of this spit where the view embraces the open sea and the end of the Island of Guimaras, the latter with a promontory of mountainous Negros jutting out behind and beyond it, and all the rest clear horizon. The tide was out, so we walked on the firm wet sand at the edge of the waves, little, flat waves which did not run up very far, as the beach is steep and shelving. Over the mountains, inland, the sky was a deep glowing orange and crimson, but from where we were on the beach we could not see the mountains, only glimpses of the gorgeous colour through the high palms that fringe the shore; while on the other side, out to sea, was a reflection like a delicate wash of pinky gold, set above deep blue sea and purple islands.

We walked a good long way, as far as the ends of the streets that come down on the beach, all dark with points of light, for the air was deliciously soft and the breeze almost fresh, and as the sunset faded, the stars came out and made quite a light upon the water, they looked so big and bright. We enjoyed the walk very much, and though we are too far this side of the town to be able to walk as far as the open country, we are very lucky not to be a long way from the beach, where we can always get a breath of fresh air and admire the lovely evenings.

LETTER VIII.

SOCIAL AMUSEMENTS

ILOILO, *January 8, 1905.*

This is my first letter to you in the New Year, and it does seem so strange to be writing 1905 already.

I wonder how you brought the year in. We were invited to a ball given by the Club Artistica, the Spanish Club, situated in a suite of very large rooms in the upper story of a big house in the Calle Real, the main street of the town, which I told you about when I was describing the amazing shops. The big basements are shops, but the long upper stories form large dwelling houses, very swagger ones, only the dust and noise are very disagreeable, and the rents about the same as flats in the best part of London, if not more. On these two accounts, most of them stand empty, displaying long rows of closed shutters, all the outside painted the prevailing bluey-grey. Some are used as clubs, however, one being this Artistica, and another, further down the street, the Filipino Club, which is called the Santa Cecilia—dedicated very appropriately to the patron saint of music, you see. These two clubs are very hospitable, and do nearly all the entertaining in the place, except for an occasional lecture at the Y.M.C.A., which, I daresay, is a wild revel, only I've never summoned up courage to go and see. The Swiss and Germans have a club, I believe, and the English Club has a beautiful house of its own, but neither of these institutions does anything towards the gaiety of nations, beyond playing billiards among their own members exclusively. It is a relief, however, to think that the poor fellows do not have such a very bad time as one might imagine, for they accept everything and go everywhere. The same comforting remark applies to the Americans, who have no club and don't entertain privately, except tea or Bridge parties amongst each other. So, as I said before, it falls to the Spaniards and Filipinos to keep the place alive, and very well they do it too, if the ball on New Year's Eve was a specimen of their average entertainments.

The Spaniards, Eurasians, and natives are all passionately fond of dancing, and *really* fond of it, for they do not make it a question of supper, as people do at home. All you have to do here is to clear the floor and get in some musicians (half the difficulty here is to keep groups of musicians out), and apparently your friends flow in. When we are coming home in the evenings, we often see the *salas* of quite little houses lighted up and full of people dancing, and I have seen small native huts having a *baile* of two couples jostling round in a space 10 feet square.

The chief room of the Spanish Club is a large apartment, almost a hall, where, on ordinary evenings, the members can be seen through the big lighted window-spaces, sitting about at little tables, with glasses at their elbows, playing dominoes; but for the *baile* the club was cleared and hung with electric lights in paper flowers, and decorated with flags and palm branches, while in a large recess at one side was a numerous string band of Filipino performers.

The music was excellent, but so slow that, as far as I was concerned, dancing was no pleasure, though that was not much of a grievance to me, as I was really far more anxious to look on than to dance.

We were invited for ten o'clock, but when we arrived at eleven the entertainment was only just getting into full swing. We had missed the opening *Rigodon*, a dance without which no Filipino *baile* could get under weigh at all, but the second half of the programme began with one, and I was very much interested to see it.

Everyone who wanted to dance the *Rigodon*, and there were only about three people who did not, sat round the room in an immense square, as for a cotillon, and the band struck up a very jolly old Spanish tune, to which the sides facing each other went through a few simple figures at a very slow walk. When they had done, they sat down, and the other two sides took their turn; and that, to different tunes, was the whole dance, which went on for an incredible length of time. The figures were a mixture of lancers and quadrilles, but the dancers never went out of a dignified strut, and though the first tune was followed by the inevitable Sousa marches and "Hiawatha," however lively the music became, the dancers continued to stroll and bow and shuffle about at the same slow pace. I am told that one becomes very fond of the *Rigodon*, but it seemed to me intolerably dull and listless as a dance, though as a spectacle it was vastly entertaining, and gave one a chance of really seeing the people, and they were well worth the trouble of turning out after dinner to look at.

The men wore white suits, most of them buttoned-up white coats of the every day sort. There were three Englishmen in evening dress, one or two in white mess jackets, and several advanced young Filipinos in grey tweeds. The American women wore every sort of outfit, from the missionaries and schoolma'ams in blouses and boots to the more exalted personages in evening dress; while the Filipinas, *Mestizas*, and most of the Spaniards had on the native muslin *camisa*, some of them exquisitely embroidered and hand-painted, and always worn with European skirts of appalling colours and cut. One little brown woman had on a long train of scarlet plush, with huge white lace butterflies fixed across and down the front, which made one burst into perspiration merely to look at; and another was in emerald green velvet, with straggling bands of gold braid meandering over it in such a queer way that I could not resist walking round her to see if any point of view would make the lines come out as a pattern, but they refused to go by any rule of any art—even the "newest."

As to the waltzes, which formed the chief part of the programme, they were very amusing too, for the variety of styles was infinite, though the universal pace was so slow. The Spaniards and *Mestizos* dance very well, and by that, of course, I mean Filipinos in general, for it is very difficult to distinguish between them, and to say where one race begins and the other leaves off. They are slow and graceful. The Americans are equally slow, but not very graceful, for they *walk* instead of dance, holding each other in such a peculiar way, sideways and very close, the man leaning very far back, with his partner falling towards him, and the hands that are clasped held very high, and swinging up and down.

At twelve o'clock everyone began to cheer and shake hands as the New Year came in; while the band played the American National Anthem, which is a most magnificent air, and then the Spanish Anthem, and then a few bars of "God Save the King," which did for us and the Germans equally well, and which we all thought a very nice little compliment. Filipino waiters came in, carrying trays covered with tall glasses full of some sort of champagne cup, and everyone drank healths, shook hands, and wished their friends a Happy New Year. We stayed on a little longer, and I danced a two-step with a very nice American, which was the best dance I had the whole evening, for it is one in which they excel, though they perform it quite differently to what we are told at home is "the real American way to dance it," as they do not plunge down the room in straight lines in the English fashion, but turn round more and make more of a waltz of it.

Suddenly, during an interval between dances in the middle of the programme, without a word of warning, a *Mestiza* sat down at the piano and played an accompaniment to which a young Eurasian, in a painfully blue satin dress, and with her face a ghastly grey-white with thick powder, sang a truly terrible song. She screamed in an awful manner, and I wondered that policemen did not rush up from the streets to see what was the matter, but she was perfectly self-possessed, and faced the audience with the aplomb and self-confidence of a prima-donna. I never heard such "singing" in my life—it was the sort of thing that is so bad that you feel all hot and ashamed, and sorry, and don't want to catch the eye of any relation of the performer. This happened not once, but several times, and is, I am told, a custom in Filipino *bailes*.

When we left at about half-past one, the ball was in full swing, and I afterwards heard that it went on till half-past four or five. Indefatigable people! I don't know how they can keep it up so, for, of course, the heat was very great—a temperature in which no one would dream of dancing at home, and not a breath of cool air anywhere, but I suppose they become accustomed to it.

One thing I have mentioned may strike you as odd, and that is the mixture of races and Eurasians, but there is socially no marked colour-distinction here as in every other country in the world, and this, I imagine, is because the natives of the civilised parts of the Philippines have been Christians for centuries, and intermarried with a Christian race. The fusion is not, however, really very complete, as one can see from a glance, at any gatherings, where the people of various shades of white and brown keep very much together. Some of the Eurasian women are quite pretty, but they spoil their little round faces with thick layers of powder over their nice brown skins, and use perfumes that nearly knock one down. The white men are friendly with many of the *Mestizos*, and dance with their pretty daughters, and are even occasionally foolish enough to marry the latter; but white women keep quite apart from the coloured folk, and it would be an unheard-of thing to dance with one; while as to marrying a

Filipino, no woman one could speak to would ever dream of such a horrible fate. That is where the real impassable gulf is fixed. The Americans profess not to recognise any distinction, however, for, as I explained before, they announce that they consider the Filipino of any class as their social and every other equal, and have the expression "little brown brother" (invented by Mr. Taft), which is supposed to convey and establish this generous sentiment. The sentiment, apart from any political utility it may possess, is a noble one, but it does more credit to the heart of the Americans than to their wisdom.

The Spaniards did not recognise the Filipinos as equals, but treated them with every courtesy, according to their degree, and I believe that whatever the political situation may have been in those days, society went peaceably enough, for every man knew his place and kept it; a system admirably suited to an Oriental people. Now, however, the *régime* is quite different, and the sudden glare of ultra-equalising views is what the Filipinos can neither understand nor profit by.

I wish I had been in the U.S.A to see many things for myself, but I have always read and heard much about the hard and fast line drawn in that country against "coloured" people and half-castes, and that the Americans have learned to adopt this custom from years of experience. This makes their professed attitude here very puzzling, and I can find no one who can even attempt to reconcile this extraordinary variation of opinion. Another unfathomable anomaly of American thought is that the "Equality," Nobility of the Human Race—Rights as a human Being, and so on, are for the *Filipinos*, but all these grand schemes officially take no account of the fierce, naked savages; the Mahommedan tribes; the negritoes, and all the other wild natives of the Philippines; though how, or where, or when, or by whom the line is to be drawn and the distinction made is another unanswerable problem.

New Year's Day being a holiday, we thought we would treat ourselves to a drive. So we sent one of the boys out for a *carromata*, which is a sort of tiny gig, with the driver sitting on a small seat in front of his fare, in fact almost on one's lap. Rain had been falling pretty well all day, and the *carromata*, when it arrived, was covered with mud, and looked such a disreputable turn-out that we burst out laughing when we saw it. However, there was no other to be had, and after all it was a very good specimen, so we climbed in over the wheel, and the driver, a boy of about twelve, gave the pony a chuck and a whack, and it turned round in the direction of the Plaza, and we stuck. Then the driver got down, and when he was out of the way and the pony became visible, we saw that we weighed the cart down so much at the back that as the little animal turned round he got his neck wedged under the shaft and was held in a rigid yoke. The youthful *cochero* shoved him down somehow, evidently both of them quite accustomed to the trouble, and, once righted, the little beast tore along, and we had a delightful drive in the cool of the evening, enjoying the air, which was so fresh after the rain.

We did not go far out of the town, as the sky was rather threatening, but kept more or less to the ever-amusing suburbs of native huts, which literally swarm with human beings, to every one of whom there is apparently an allowance of about six babies of under one year old, and on the roofs are cocks and hens clinging to the steep thatch; while under the hut lives the family *carabao* (a big grey water-buffalo) in his mudhole, along with stray dogs and wild pigs which eat up the refuse.

The number of children, very young children, is something astounding, but, according to statistics, I learn that 60 per cent. of the children born in the Philippines die under one year old, so that must help to keep the numbers of grown-up people down a bit. They are miserable little languid scraps, thin and solemn, but so supremely fortunate as to wear no clothes whatever, till they are about six, when a short muslin jacket is put on, which is more for adornment than anything else. The tiny ones ride astride the mother's hip, with little thin legs dangling, and round black head wobbling about, looking so uncomfortable, poor little souls. They are fed on rice, which they eat till their little bodies swell up to a certain tightness, when the food is taken away, and they are not allowed more till they have "gone down" again. This process results in a permanent "rice-tummy," which makes the babies look like air-balloons set on drumsticks; but, somehow, they lose that as they get older, and if they live, are generally very slender and well made.

There is a great fuss made now about this waste of infant life, much of which is ascribed to the horrible and unhuman practices and superstitions attending the birth of a Filipino child; but I imagine from the appearance of the children themselves, that the whole question is merely an example of the Survival of the Fittest, for of so many children born in such a delicate race there must be numbers who are unable and unfit to live. They are not a hardy people, these Filipinos, and the heat, fevers, and plagues of the country affect them even more than they do the white races, oddly enough. I believe that in the wild parts the natives are stronger, and sometimes live to a great age; but there the life is simpler; the cross-breeding less frequent; in the absence of civilisation of any kind the great Darwinian Law operates even more rigorously; and the young who are sickly stand no chance at all of growing up and transmitting their weakness. The skin of these people is not a healthy skin, not a warm brown, but of a greeny-yellowy brown; their fingers are delicate and weak, and their eyes not clear or bright, but like little bits of dull plum-brown jelly.

LETTER IX.

TARIFFS—INSECTS

ILOILO, *January 16, 1905.*

The day has come round for me to catch the mail, but I feel that I can hardly write calmly, as I am barely sane upon the subject I wish to tell you about, which is the Customs. I told you about the opening of our cases, and how we took them out of bond, as they were valued at £30? Well, a day or two ago the bill came in, and when we saw it we nearly fainted away, for the amount of duty came to 698 *pesos*—£70.

Of course we thought some mistake had been made, so C—— went off to the Customs officer and asked him what it meant. All the consolation we got was that they were very sorry for us, but the Appraiser had made a mistake, and classed some of our things under Class B instead of Class A.

So C—— said he could not afford this sum, which was far more than the whole of the contents of the cases were worth if they had been new. Of course it was impossible to send them back to Hong Kong, as we had taken them out of bond; but after a lot of talk, the officer said we could "abandon the goods" if we liked, which means refuse to pay the duty, when the things would be seized by the Customs and sold by auction to pay the Government; but we should be unable, by law, to buy them in ourselves. This seemed to be the only alternative open to us, and C—— came back and asked me what I thought of it, and asked the other Englishmen their opinion. They were full of sympathy and very kind, and at last one of them hit upon an excellent idea, which was to attend the sale and buy our things in for us as cheaply as possible. This, then, was arranged, but—"Oh no!" said the Customs, "you won't gain anything by that, because if goods, when put up for sale, do not fetch the price at which the Customs House has valued them, they are publicly burned."

So that is the end of our story. We have paid more than their value for our wedding-presents, which seems to me the meanest and cruellest imposition I ever heard of. But I won't say any more, for the subject can only be as painful to you as it is to us. We must just grin and bear it, I suppose, but good-bye to a pony and trap for a longer time than ever, and good-bye to any little jaunts in the hot season.

I must try instead to be more pleasant, and the only thing I can think of is a little lizard I have been looking at for the last ten minutes, while my thoughts roamed gloomily over each one of those seventy good golden sovereigns that have gone to help to teach the Filipino that he is my equal. A worthy cause, no doubt, but one that does not appeal to me—at any rate to the extent of 698 *pesos.*

This little lizard, which lives in the cornice above my writing-desk, has just come down on to the window beside me and nipped up a fly in the smartest manner. This is his hunting-ground, for the windows in the house only have sliding shutters, such as I described to you, like all the houses here. Glass windows are almost unknown, but this house happens to have them along the S.-W. front, where some former occupant has put in doors on to the balcony, with glass in the upper panels, because in the rainy season the Monsoon drives in on this side.

In all the houses here these little grey lizards abound, living in the cornices and corners of the ceilings, and feeding on flies, mosquitoes, and any little toothsome creature they can pick up. They must have plenty of supplies and wide variety, for one seems to come across some new sort of insect every hour of the day—and night. No fleas, however, I don't mean that, for Filipinos are clean and fleas are rare; but all sorts of queer insects crawl and fly and sit about, all of which I suppose the lizards enjoy; and I imagine they, in their turn, are having a good meal off some other still tinier creature.

The ceilings are made of bulges of canvas or matting painted white, pale blue, or green; or, in some of the old houses, with patterns, as in Italy. In one house in Jaro, a big building with long, wide-open window-spaces, there is a ceiling that is covered with some sort of shiny oilcloth stuff, drawn up by buttons at intervals, so that it looks like the seat of some giant padded leather chair—a most fearful looking contrivance, but, no doubt, a source of much pride to the Filipino who owns it. There is a wide space above these ceilings, for the corrugated iron roofs are very deep, and here live rats, mice, cats, cockroaches, snakes, all sorts of beasts, which come down into the house for plunder. The nicest are these dear, clean, bright-eyed little lizards, which make a funny and very pretty note, a sort of clear, musical chuck-chuck. Sometimes, but very rarely, one of these lizards is found with a forked tail, and this the natives look upon as an emblem of the most extraordinary luck, and they do all they can to catch the lizard and try to take off his forked tail, which they dry and wear for *anting-anting*. Any kind of luck, or lucky emblem, is *anting-anting*, and the mystical emblems, observances, and relics of Roman Catholicism, which appeal to the Filipinos with irresistible force, have but added to their original stock of superstitions.

In some of the houses there is a very *anting-anting* lizard, of a large size, which makes a loud, clear double note like a cuckoo, that can be heard a long way off. I have never seen a "Philippine cuckoo," as they are called, but have often heard them, and the houses that have this *anting-anting* are well known. There is one in the old belfry at Jaro, another in a house the other side of the Plaza there, and one in a certain bamboo clump on the road to Molo, and so on, all over the place.

A very general belief prevails that in the roof of each house there lives a big snake, which has a terrific meal of rats every now and then, and sleeps the rest of his time, coming down very rarely for water. I can quite credit this story, for the space between the roofs must be the very place for a snake, and many people tell me they have seen these creatures, but I don't suppose they are really in all the houses. Curiously enough, I thought there was a snake overhead before I had ever been told about such a thing, for one day, when I was sitting in the *sala*, I heard a most extraordinary noise in the roof overhead—a sort of heavy, dragging sound, and then a thump, and then the dragging sound again—and, somehow, the thought of a snake instantly came into my mind. When I spoke about it to some friends, half jokingly, they replied quite seriously that it probably was a snake I had heard, and then told me how they live in the roofs.

Talking of noises, one of the most curious sounds here is made by the crickets, the *cicadas*, which shrill night and day, ceaselessly and for ever. The ear becomes accustomed to the aggregate sound of their high, thin note, though I, for one, never get to like it, and sometimes it gets horribly on my nerves, so that I feel I must go anywhere to get away from it. At first when I heard it I was always having a curious impression of being in a Swiss field in the summer; but now that has worn off, and I think if I ever go into the Swiss fields again I shall think of nothing but Iloilo. When one of these *cicadas* gets very near the house, it drives you nearly mad, and when, as happened a few evenings ago, one is actually in the house, everything must be searched for the beast before anyone can expect sanity or sleep. This one that got in, stowed itself away in the writing-table, and we had an awful time, standing almost on our heads and streaming from every pore, before we found it in a tiny corner where one of the drawers does not run quite into place. When we fished the *cicada* out at last, or rather when one of the servants came in and took up the hunt for us and caught it, we found the disturber of our peace to be an ugly little browny-black creature, with a narrow waist, and the silly thing refused to give a single chirrup to show us how it was done.

Talking of insects, one of the things we are most fortunate about in this house is that we have very few of the black or red ants, which are a fearful plague in these Islands, so much so that one has to stand the furniture with its feet in small enamel bowls filled with water or paraffine to prevent the ants crawling up, for they eat everything; and besides that, they look particularly nasty when dead in jam or butter, or floating in tea or coffee. Some of these ants are a good size, but the common sort are very small, and many of the most destructive are simply red specks that run like lightning. They are terrible destroyers, and I can't think why ant-eaters don't start living in the roof menageries, for they would get on splendidly if they did not die of over-eating. However, the ants do scavenge to a certain extent, and the way a busy little mob can carry off a huge dead cockroach is a lesson in natural history.

The cockroaches, by-the-bye, are the size of mice. They are the most evil brutes I ever saw, besides being a constant source of terror and worry. You will hardly believe this, for you know that I never mind touching any animal—mice, worms, toads, slugs, earwigs—and how I have so often been laughed at, and even sniffed at, as rather an unpleasant young person, because I have no repugnance to taking them up in my bare hand, for, after all, they are only poor animals, and infinitely nicer to touch than many perfectly respectable human beings. Do you remember those people at Karnak who screamed when I brought them that lovely little toad with a speckled stomach? And the good folk at home who shudder if you pick up a poor slug out of a dusty road? Well, when it comes to these cockroaches, I confess that I have a genuine horror of the great red, evil-smelling brutes, with their horrible bulgy eyes and their long moving red antennæ. I can't tell you what it is about them—but I am not alone in this, for everyone has a horror of them. They breed in the cesspits, and prefer manure to any other diet, but will gladly supplement their *menu* with any form of food, as well as leather, paper, books, or clothes. The houses, the shops, and the steamers are full of them, and in the evenings they come out of their holes and run about. Ugh! they make one shudder. And every now and then they take it into their heads to fly about or into the lighted rooms, and I have even seen men who have been here for years turn quite sick when a cockroach lights on them, and as for the average woman, she screams outright, and many white women faint.

These horrible brutes are the curse of housekeeping, necessitating everything being kept in glass jars or tins, and cupboards and drawers being overhauled and searched every week or so. I must say, though, that we have not had so much trouble with them as most people, and so far I have never had one amongst the linen or clothes, and I believe this is because I hang cakes of naphthaline in the rooms, and put balls of it in all boxes, drawers, and cupboards, and they don't seem to like naphthaline, though they would come a thousand miles to eat ordinary insect powder, which is, apparently, just the very thing on which to bring up a nice little family of forty or fifty young cockroaches.

There are some pleasing spiders too, one of which I saw the other day, with a body nearly the size of the palm of my hand, sitting in a huge, tough web like a hammock, and looking exactly like those in Doré's picture of the Guest Chamber in the Castle Inn, in Croque Mitaine.

I said there were very few fleas, but the mosquitoes make up for any biting that has to be done. I am beginning to get more accustomed to their venom now, but at first I was quite ill and feverish from it, and many people suffer so that it amounts to an illness, and white men frequently have to be invalided home for nothing but mosquitoes. Nothing I have ever seen in any place round the Mediterranean approaches the Philippine mosquito for venom or ferocity, and here, too, their efforts are not confined to the night-season when lucky mortals are stowed under nets with no rents in them, but they bite relentlessly all day as well.

Well, I tried to leave harrowing subjects and tell you something more cheerful than the Customs woes, but I seem to have drifted into other griefs, and as my spirits are evidently damped beyond hope to-day, I had better leave off writing and end my letter.

LETTER X.

A FILIPINO THEATRE—*CARABAOS*

ILOILO, *January 22, 1905.*

We went a night or two ago to a performance at the theatre—a Filipino performance in a Filipino theatre. I daresay it sounds strange to you to hear of a theatre in Iloilo, but you see this is really a very large town, and then all the people are musical, and they have plenty of time to rehearse. They get together little dramatic clubs, the chief one of which is not far from here, "as the crow flies," though I think he would be a very keen crow for theatricals if he flew there as straight as he could. We heard this performance, an operetta, being rehearsed night and day before the performers considered it ready for the theatre. The rehearsals that went on until the early hours of the morning were those we cared least about; but we were really interested to hear them going on all day as well, for no one in the Dramatic Club apparently had any other occupation in life. At least, this seemed to me strange till I had become better acquainted with the Filipino character.

To get to this show, we set off after dinner, driving in a hired *quielez* with a disturbing cockroach somewhere about it, and soon came to a squash of all sorts of carriages and carts in one of the broader streets of the town—and a squash of vehicles driven by Filipinos is something no human mind can imagine without experience. We escaped alive, and went in at a big gateway into a courtyard, passing several stalls lighted with flaring naphtha, where native women sat behind flat rush trays containing cakes and sweetmeats, tumblers of coloured drinks, and ordinary ginger-beer and lemonade bottles. This, though I did not know it at the time, was the buffet.

Inside the courtyard another high gate, decorated at the sides with palms and paper roses, and very dimly lighted, led to the door of the theatre, a big, crazy-looking building, and here stood two inconceivably stupid and self-satisfied natives bullying everyone, and making a hopeless and baffling muddle of the tickets. Why they did this I can't think, as everyone passed into the place alike, whatever their ticket was, and scrambled up a broad wooden staircase, very steep and rickety, or else went about the ground-floor, every man looking for his own seat, and getting turned out of it by the next comer.

The "boxes" were little pens railed off, containing six chairs with no room for your knees, and in and out of these and up and down the precipitous staircase jostled a crowd of Filipinos, *Mestizos*, Chinamen, and Spaniards, with little dark women in gaudy *camisas*, wearing flowers in their hair and diamond brooches. Here and there an American was patiently and persistently trying to gather information in his own language, while he took some female relation in a white cotton dress upstairs and then down again, to keep her quiet.

I was so amused by these proceedings that I really felt as if it did not matter whether that was all we saw, but, nevertheless, we toiled up the staircase at the promptings of an obliging Filipino with one eye, very soon found our box, and settled down to wait for the friends who were to join us.

In about two minutes, however, we were engaged in an endless discussion with a little mob of "brown brothers," who declared quite politely that we had no right there, as the box was theirs. So we moved off and tried the ground-floor again; found another box with our number on it, empty; sat down again, put fans and programmes on the opposite chairs, and began to look about.

But we were shifted again, so this time we tackled a native selling programmes, and asked him where our box was, and why the little pens all seemed to have the same number; and he, in very broken Spanish, at last made us understand that the numbers were repeated six times, once on each side upstairs and down. This was a wonderful effort of lucidity for a Filipino, and really helped us a good deal. So we toiled upstairs again, feeling sure that we knew all about the theatre now, and determined on a shot at the sides. On the way there we were delighted to see that the people who had turned us out of our first box were being ousted in their turn, but by this time we had begun to giggle, and were too helpless with heat and laughter to take much notice of anything. At last we got into a box from which we were never evicted during the rest of the evening, though some people did come along with a programme-seller to back their claim, but we showed fight, and they went away again.

The theatre, a long, wooden building, appeared even more ramshackle from the inside than it had from the outside, and infinitely more dangerous, for the electric light was supplemented by Japanese paper lanterns, which looked the last word in incendiarism; and, when one considered the packed mass of faces all round, it was wiser not to let the imagination dwell on that steep wooden stairway, which was all there was between us and the next world.

The floor of the building was arranged with rows of chairs facing squarely, by way of stalls, surrounded by a row of the boxes I have described, where the chairs went sideways. Above jutted out a broad balcony with a similar row of boxes, and above that again, jammed under the ceiling, was a dense crowd of poor people, standing on what was really only a ledge with an iron rail; and they looked positively more like huge black and white flies clinging to the ceiling than anything else.

Everything looked as if it must fall down or break up, but no one seemed to be worrying about their doom, in fact all the faces were remarkably pleasant and jolly.

The stage was a fairly large one, with a row of electric footlights, which waxed and waned and waxed again at their own sweet will, and quite regardless of the needs of the performance. In front of the stage, on the floor-level, was an orchestra of natives who really played very well indeed, and they and all the men in the audience were in white, which looks very quaint until one's eye is accustomed to it.

The piece performed was an operetta called "La Indiana," a rather confused story about some old *Mestizo* with a white beard, whose son had secretly married an Indian, which is the word the Spaniards use for the Filipinos, and is employed by the Filipinos themselves as well, when talking Spanish. Well, the old father informed his son, an appalling, gawky, young *Mestizo* in a black morning coat, pepper and salt tweed trousers, and a very bright blue tie, that he must marry a white (*Mestiza*) girl of his, the father's choosing. On hearing which, the hero sang a song to the effect that he would abandon the *Indiana*, and had a long duet with that personage to explain that they would just say nothing at all about being married. Then all the chorus came in again, the old father blessed the hero and the "white" girl, whereupon the *Indiana*, a frightfully ugly Filipina with a fine voice, sang a long and frenzied solo with her hair down—and then the curtain fell.

I thought there must be another act, and was very much surprised to find that was the conclusion of the story. But evidently, to the native imagination, the plot was complete and the ends of poetic justice satisfied. They did not really act and sing as badly as I had expected, though, when one came to think of "La Indiana" as a public performance in a theatre, it really verged on audacity. No attempt at scenery or dress was made, the whole action taking place in a bare, worn, old "set" of a room, the usual stage room, unlike anything else on earth, and the only attempt at costume was the substitution of very ugly old European blouses for the *camisa*, which was a fatal mistake.

We left after the first piece, though there were to be two more of the same sort, for it was very dull and depressing. There is nothing in these Filipinos, you see, for they have not the melodious voices of negroes, nor the faultless ear of Spaniards, nor the fine physique of Chinese, nor the taste of Japanese—they are simply dull, blunt, limited intelligences, with the ineffable conceit of such a character all over the world, and when they break out into a display such as "La Indiana," all these deplorable qualities show up in the glare of the white light that beats even upon an Iloilo stage.

Yesterday we went for a delightful drive out along the Jaro road, off which we turned a little way beyond the town, and went down a rough, sandy track to the banks of a broad, half-dried-up river, not the Iloilo river, but another parallel to it, or a branch.

There we got out and walked down the steep bank on to the sandy bed, where we strolled about for a long time, watching strings of *carabaos* coming up from being watered, each herd led by a small boy, riding on one of the big old grey cows with a calf running alongside. They looked very picturesque, with the shallow river all the colours of the sunset, and the tall palms on the opposite bank standing in black silhouette against an orange-crimson sky.

The *carabaos* are big grey or reddish-grey water-buffaloes, with immense horns curving backwards, and a long, narrow, flat muzzle. They are used for every sort of purpose, the natives even riding and driving the great unwieldy creatures like horses, and guiding them by means of a single string passed through between the nostrils. If they want the *carabao* to go to the right they pull the string steadily, if to the left, they give a sharp jerk. Sometimes when the master is angry he will pull the poor *carabao's* nose, so that he tears the piece of flesh out altogether; not at all an uncommon occurrence, and nothing distressing to a Filipino.[3] In the days of the rebellion against Spain, a few years ago, when the Filipinos caught the hated Spanish friars, they ran a rope through the priests' noses, tied their hands, and led them about like the *carabaos*, so that people might spit upon the hated tyrants, and insult them at their own pleasure.

RIDING A CARABAO.

The *carabaos* are as gentle and amenable as horses with the natives; quite tiny children ride and bully the huge beasts, looking so comically small on the big backs, with their tiny brown legs hardly reaching to each side of the broad ribs, and driving whole herds with the most perfect independence and self-possession. The *carabaos* are not at all safe as regards white people, however, for they can smell and detect them at an immense distance; and they will occasionally charge them ferociously, so that they are very dangerous in the open country. I have heard some horrible stories of *carabaos* killing and trampling on white men in out-of-the-way places. They don't gore, I suppose because their horns are so flat, but they trample to death, which does just as well.

These great grey, lumbering animals are very picturesque, and redeem many a Philippine scene from utter dulness as they go shambling along, drawing the native two-wheeled cart, with its big hood of brown matting filled with bundles of emerald-

---

[3] Another method is to tie a rope round the *carabao's* horns, and it is so tight that it cuts into the flesh, so that the *carabaos* frequently go mad with pain and "run amok."

green *sacate* grass. They can shamble at an amazing pace, and that is their usual gait; but they can gallop, too, as quickly as a horse.

Besides the herds of *carabaos*, we saw several natives down in the bed of the river, going out to certain spots where the shelve of the sand was more abrupt for their supply of water. These were women, of course, for women do all the household tasks, even the most burdensome, their lords being busy standing about the roads or Plazas, or attending a cock-fight.

These women had long bamboo poles, with the divisions knocked out and the end closed up, which they laid in the running stream to fill with water, when they hoisted the long poles to their shoulders and carried them off like giants' lances. The slender little figures looked quaint and pretty as they came up over the yellow, sandy, shallows in their bright red *sarongs* and white *camisas*, walking lightly and gracefully, with their thin brown feet well turned out, the fading light of the sky behind them, and the outline of dark, fretted palms.

We walked through a little palm grove back to the place where we had left the carriage, driving back along the main road as the stars were coming out and the flaring naphtha lights appearing in the little mat-shed shops. There were a great many people about, and swarms of little children in fluttering muslin shirts, all enjoying the cool evening air, which was, as a matter of fact, the same temperature as an August mid-day at home. A lot of carriages and traps flew past, the little ponies tearing like the wind, amongst them the general's wife in her victoria, drawn by ordinary Waler horses, looking like prehistoric monsters amongst the little Filipino ponies; and we met our pet aversion, three young *Mestizo* "mashers," driving at a furious pace in a spidery buggy with huge acetylene lamps, and ringing a bicycle bell.

LETTER XI.

SOME RESULTS OF THE AMERICAN OCCUPATION

ILOILO, *January 22, 1905.*

Mail-day has come round again, but I don't feel as though I had much energy for writing, or anything else, as we are in the midst of a heat-wave, which means, in this part of the world, that the Monsoon has dropped unaccountably, and the heat is suffocating and appalling. Everyone is saying that such a temperature is quite unusual at this season, and some even go so far as to say they never felt it so hot here before; but this does not surprise me, as I have never yet come in for normal weather anywhere.

This heat comes in the middle of a drought, too, as we have not had rain for about four weeks—another phenomenon. Our rain-tank is empty, so we now depend on the supply of brackish water from the wells, and even that is reported to be limited, which is alarming, as one would commit almost any crime to get enough water for a bath. Even at times of plenty, however, one does not rejoice in the European style of bath, but an arrangement of a tub, the acquaintance of which I first made at Singapore, and I can't say I was much struck with it when I did see it.

The tub, of wood or china, is placed in a small room with a sloping floor of concrete or tiles, and the bather stands on a wooden rack; first using what soap he sees fit, and then pouring water over himself as best he can with a tin dipper. It is an economical method in countries where water is scarce and valuable; but it was a terrible disillusion to me, after the grand ideas I had always formed, when I read how every one in the Far East has his or her own bathroom. Don't you know how jolly it sounds in Anglo-Indian novels, or in descriptions of the world beyond Port Saïd? A dreadful disenchantment!

More than ever, in this heat, do we miss the dog-cart of our dreams, for we long to get out of the town on these hot evenings. Something to drive is a bare necessity of life out here, and even the humblest school-teachers and missionaries keep what the Americans call a "rig," such a queer word, which is made to signify anything from a four-in-hand to a *carabao*-cart. The Americans all drive in a very strange fashion, holding a rein in each hand, which looks awkward at any time; but is most comical in the case of the swaggering negro who drives the military waggons, holding in a team about as fiery as a couple of old circus-horses, with a rein twisted round each of his hands, body thrown back, and the gestures of a Greek restraining an untamed pair round a stadium.

The white man who drives the Government ice-cart amuses me too, for he is got up in full cow-boy pageantry—huge boots, loose shirt with broad leather belt, immense sombrero worn well over one eye, long moustaches standing out, and great gauntlets up to his elbows. All this to hawk ice about a dowdy little town.

When a soldier rides one of these quiet old animals, he sits in an enormous Mexican saddle, with a very high peak back and front, and his feet, clad in big boots with huge spurs, thrust into roomy leather shoe-stirrups. To the casual observer these horsemen would certainly convey the impression that they were venturing great deeds in a wild country, and one can't be anything but thankful to them for throwing a little picturesque relief into the humdrum life of the grey streets.

We have tried hiring carriages, but besides the terrible discomfort of all hired vehicles, their prices are more uncomfortable still. Fancy, in a place like this, having to pay as much for a little carriage for two hours in the evening as one would for a brougham in London for the day! Yet such is the case, and it is only an indication of the cost of living here, which is really alarming; as you may imagine it must be when I tell you that all the Americans I have met complain bitterly, declaring that it is more expensive to *exist* in the Philippines than to "have a good time" in New York or San Francisco! The only comfort is that we are not in Manila, which is a shade worse, I am told.

So, except for an occasional carriage lent us, we continue to walk about after sunset, but I find I can't get very far, for though exercise may not be very tiring at the time it is being taken, it makes you realise how the climate is taking it out of you.

There is no meeting-place like the club of an English garrison town, for the Americans seem to have no idea of anything of the sort; and I think this may, perhaps, be owing to their democratic principles, for, of course, it would be impossible to exclude the private soldiers from such a place, as in theory they are as good as the officers. I notice that in practice the officers don't think so at all, though most of them have risen from the ranks themselves. The U.S.A. have a sort of Sandhurst, called West Point, but I have been told, by highly-placed officers themselves, that the only way to get on in their army is to obtain a commission from the ranks through "pull" (political influence), and that "pull" is even more a factor in the army than in any other profession in America. This can easily be verified by reading the extraordinary cases that occur from time to time, when an officer with a "pull" gets the decision of a Court-Martial reversed without any further controversy, and, after an undoubted misdemeanour, is simply re-instated somewhere else, and often in a higher grade, by order of the Government at Washington.

This independence of military authority, together with the principles of extreme democracy which America professes, accounts, I think, for the curious behaviour of the private soldiers, who are really quite different from any others I have seen anywhere else in the world, for they lounge about when addressing an officer, and speak to him as an equal; which looks more than odd to anyone not accustomed to such ways. Men who were here during the American War have told me most amusing stories of the discussions that used to go on between officers and privates on active service; all straggling about anyhow, and men, with no notion of saluting, just giving their opinion with a drawling "waal" by way of preface. All the same, they fight well, and perhaps, in modern warfare, individual intelligence may be a very good thing, and it is only in peace time that a lack of smartness and discipline jars upon the faddy European eye. Perhaps.

But the oddest thing of all, to my mind, is to see officers in uniform salute ladies by taking their caps off. That I can't get accustomed to!

I call this a garrison town, though, as a matter of fact, the garrison is situated in the Island of Guimaras, at a place called Camp Josman, in the interior. This Camp, which is about 200 feet above sea-level, and possesses springs of good water, is supposed to be much healthier than Iloilo, where they only have the Hospital, Headquarters, and the Cavalry Barracks. It seems a strange and uncomfortable arrangement in a half-pacified country—the garrison half a day's journey away; though the real object is, of course, to keep the American soldiers out of the towns, where they are no end of trouble.

The town is well and even elaborately policed by the Constabulary, a Filipino corps of sturdy little "brown brothers" in dark blue linen suits. Each of these defenders supports an immense revolver in a leather case strapped to the back of his broad leather belt, and carries a short truncheon as well. I suppose they would fight all right, in reason, if there were a disturbance, and if the occasion were not of a patriotic nature. But that is not much consolation, as the occasion would not be likely to be of any character other than patriotic.

The Americans give out and write in their papers that the Philippine Islands are completely pacified, and that the Filipinos love Americans and their rule. This, doubtless with good motives, is complete and utter humbug, for the country is honeycombed with insurrection and plots; the fighting has never ceased; and the natives loathe the Americans and their theories, saying so openly in their native press, and showing their dislike in every possible fashion. Their one idea is to be rid of the U.S.A. to have their government in their own hands, for good or evil, and to be free of a burden of taxation which may be just, but is heavier than any the Spaniards laid upon them. The present burden is more obvious to the Filipino mind than the ultimate blessings.

They have no real say in their own affairs, you see, as the government of the Philippines is in the hands of a Commission consisting of five Americans, nominated by the President of the U.S.A. and three Filipinos, chosen by the Governor-General of the Philippines.[4] This body, however, does not govern the Islands according to what experience teaches, but is responsible to the Senate at Washington, whose members having their own interests to push or preserve, hamper the Philippine Commission at every turn.

---

[4] The actual numbers of the Commission have been changed several times, but the proportion of American to Filipino remains practically unaltered, as does the method of their election.

It does seem extraordinary to think that there is no Colonial Office, or Civil Service examinations, and that anyone in America who has a "pull" can get sent out here to fill any sort of post anyhow, anywhere. Tremendous salaries come out of the miserable Island Revenues to make these posts acceptable. So it is hardly surprising that, without the faintest glimmering of the language, customs, climate, or anything beyond their own State, these eager, well-meaning, bustling Americans tumble into pitfalls, and rub the Oriental the wrong way, and that the dislike and mistrust on both sides are about equal.

I did not mean to let you in for this political dissertation, but now I am on the subject I am reminded of a new tax, which has lately been levied, and is causing much vexation. It will give you a good idea of the methods in vogue. This is an order requiring every owner of a horse to take his beast to the Philippine Government, or rather its local and selected representatives, who will brand the animal on one flank with certain marks by which it may at once be known. Then the owner is to brand it twice on the other flank, and to find two sureties of 250 dollars gold (about £50) each, that the horse has not been stolen, and should the animal prove to have been dishonestly acquired, the sureties are to be held criminally liable!

SPANISH ARCHITECTURE IN THE PHILIPPINES.
An old church at Daraga.

This in a country where the crime of horse-stealing is entirely unknown! But it is believed that the Senators in far-off Washington have an idea that the Philippines are a sort of California, so they insist on applying exactly the same law here as obtains in that wide, wild State. It is hardly necessary to add that the examination, branding, papers to be signed, stamps upon same, and so on, cost the wretched owner a pretty sum before he is safe from the police with his poor, disfigured horse.

I have wandered away from a walk through the town, which I meant to describe to you—only I never seem to get ahead at all with descriptions here, as there are such endless mazes of side-issues to lure one from the track.

At the end of this street one comes on the Plaza, a very wide square bordered by odds and ends of houses, which include the Police Court, the Y.M.C.A., the Prison, and the Cathedral, the three former buildings being large, ordinary, two-storied houses, the latter a big, plain, grey stone front, with a belfry on each side, not unlike a miniature of the cathedral at Las Palmas, and, as far as I remember, in much the same style.

The town must have been quite handsome in the Spanish days, but during the Insurrection the Americans stood off and bombarded it from the open sea, while on shore the natives set it on fire. You see, when the Americans had conquered the Spaniards, and the Philippines had been handed over to the United States, the Spanish garrisons cleared out, leaving the Filipinos in charge to wait for their saviours. But the Filipinos beginning to realise that they had only sailed from Scylla to Charybdis, fought tooth and nail to prevent the American troops garrisoning their towns. So it came about that when the Americans had officially conquered the Spaniards, and *fêtes* and rejoicings were in full blast in the U.S.A., the trouble here was really only just beginning, for though they had managed to dislodge an alien race like the Spaniards with the full help and concurrence of the natives of the country, it was a very different task to conquer the disaffected people of the soil, even when it was being done "for their own good." When the American fleet came to take Iloilo, the Filipinos showed fight, and the American Admiral said they must give up the place or he would bombard it, allowing them so many hours to decide in—which hours, by-the-bye, were not unconnected with some complication regarding the Christmas dinners of the sailors, who insisted on eating plum-puddings they had brought with them, or had had sent from America. Well, the Filipinos replied that the Americans might come ashore and fight if they liked, but if the Admiral bombarded the town, they would set it on fire, and make Iloilo not worth the taking.

The end of this exchange of courtesies was that the Admiral chose the alternative of bombardment, whereupon the Filipinos promptly fired the town, and Iloilo was pretty well destroyed, and eventually taken for the Stars and Stripes. The loss of life was one mule and one old woman, neither of whom probably cared two straws who the Philippines belonged to, poor things.

One or two people were wounded, but this was only another instance of the extraordinarily small amount of damage done by a bombardment. I have heard many curious "yarns" about the bombardment and the fire, which took place on Christmas Day, 1899, but I have not time or space to tell you these legends now, even if I could remember them. I wish I could remember all the things I hear—though, I daresay, I remember quite enough for you as it is!

The chief feature of the bombardment stories is the terrible drunkenness and looting that went on; but even if those anecdotes interested you, they are all connected with personal adventures of people you have never met, and would not entertain you. I am glad I was not here though, for the anarchy and misery seem to have been terrible.

Many results of these stirring times still remain in the streets, for the top stories of the houses were knocked off and the stone foundations gutted, and when the people settled down peaceably again, there was no money to restore the buildings to their former state, so they just put rough rooms over the charred ruins, makeshift upper stories of Oregon pine with corrugated iron roofs, which arrangement makes the town look very shoddy and unfinished. In Jaro and Molo are to be seen many of the handsome old Spanish houses still standing, with carved wooden balconies and ornamented doorways, some of them still beautified by deep roofs of charming old red-brown hand-made tiles.

There is a *café* in the Plaza Libertad, in what was once a big, fine house, but now the thick concrete walls of the lower storey, with huge doorways and window-openings crossed by heavy bars, all blackened with smoke, end abruptly in a narrow-eaved corrugated roof, making a house like a misshapen little dwarf.

There are many buildings like that, and in the streets the jumble of different sorts of odds and ends is most curious, but not the least picturesque, for it is all grey and mean and squalid.

All the middle of the square, which, as I told you, is called the Plaza Libertad, is laid out as a pretty Alameda, with a low wall round it, and steps leading up on each side, the centre thickly planted with palms, bamboos, and various other trees of dark and light greens, intersected by four wide paths and a lot of little tracks, all bristling with seats. Some of the seats are of wood, broken and dilapidated, and others of iron painted to look like marble, which are quite warm to the touch hours after sunset. The first evening we were there, when I put my hand on one of the iron seats, thinking to touch cold stone, I got quite a shock on finding the surface warm.

This flowerless garden is a very pretty place, especially at night, when the big arc-lights shine on the very green trees, and throw lovely shadows of palm branches on the white paths, making quite a theatrical effect; but it is all overgrown, untidy, neglected, the steps broken, paths untrimmed—always reminding me of some place in a deserted city, or the garden of a house long uninhabited.

The Plaza Libertad has one resemblance to a real town park, however, in its rows of idle men; brown-faced, white-clad Filipinos in this case, who sit on the seats and low walls like rows of sea-birds, only, instead of making nests or catching food as birds would, they simply doze, and gamble, and talk, or, more often, sit about in the profound abstraction of the Oriental.

The "unemployed" has no grievance against society, however, in this country, if he ever tries to attempt one, for work is abundant and labour not to be had, even at the present scale of wages, which enables a man to work for one day and then keep himself and his family to the remotest scions, in idleness and cock-fighting for a week. You see in the Spanish days the Philipino labourers got from 10 to 20 cents a day wages but now the American Government, which sets the scale, gives a *peso* a day for unskilled labour, and that, of course, has altered the social conditions here, and, I believe, all over the Islands as well, for the same conditions prevail everywhere. A *peso* a day they get for loading and unloading vessels—just wharf-coolies; and as for carpenters and people like that who used to get 70 cents from the Spaniards and live well on it, they are now with difficulty to be caught for 2½ to 3 *pesos* a day. Of course this has enormously increased the cost of living without bringing any extra benefits, but that particular increase chiefly affects the white man, for I have asked servants and natives, who tell me the cost of *their* food, the eternal rice, fish, and bananas for them has very little altered, if at all.

The high rate of wages, far from bringing plenty, has caused great demoralisation and consequent poverty; and it does seem a pity that some one who understood Orientals and their ways could not have come and pointed out to the Americans how dark races differ from white men in body and mind. As it is, I should think that even if the well-meaning reformers do find out their mistakes, which is very doubtful, it would be very difficult, if not impossible, for the Americans to go back now.

On one side of the Plaza there stand a few specimens of the funny native trap called a *quilez*, which I have mentioned to you. It is very like the *tartana* of Spain, a sort of tiny wagonette on two wheels, and covered so that it is really a sort of miniature two-wheeled omnibus.

Such a cabstand! Such fearfully dilapidated old rattle-traps, with mangy ponies lashed in by odds and ends of straps and string, and the drivers dressed in dirty rags (the only dirty Filipinos I've ever seen) sprawling half-asleep on the boxes! This collection, as I have said, is by way of being a cab-rank, but there are always plenty of *quilezes* plying the streets for hire; their number indeed being at first astounding, till one becomes better acquainted with the laziness of the fares, coupled with the high rates of hire, which alone would make one job a day quite a good investment.

The discomfort and jolting of these conveyances is something which I can find no words to express —it is like one's first ride on a camel—like waltzing with a Sandhurst cadet—like—like nothing in the world! A drive of one mile inside a *quilez* is more fatiguing than a walk of two.

One thinks regretfully of the delightful luxury of the rickshaws and chairs of the real Far East, and I was very much surprised to see none of these luxurious comforts when we first arrived in the Philippines. It seems that a company was formed some years ago to introduce them, and got the concession to bring rickshaws and coolies from China, but as soon as these useful institutions appeared in the streets of Manila, the Filipinos stoned them, and at last forced the American authorities to banish the innovation altogether: "For," said the astute and progressive Filipino, "the next thing will be that *we* shall be made to draw these things about, and we will not be treated as animals."

Fancy giving in to them! And fancy thinking of a splendid country and people like Japan, "where the rickshaws come from," and listening to such preposterous nonsense from a Filipino! But these ignorant half-breeds got their way, and the only example they had ever had of energy or the real dignity of labour was promptly withdrawn to please them.

In the middle of the Alameda is a bandstand, bare and empty, with a big spluttering arc-light over it, shedding its cheese-white light on nothingness—for no band ever plays there, and the glories of social Iloilo went with the gay and courteous Spaniards. A few people go and sit about, however, in the evenings, and it is not a bad place to loaf in for anyone who can't drive out to the country and is tired of the beach.

One evening, as we sat under the trees watching a group of *Mestizo* children playing about some older people sitting on a seat, a little *banda de musica* came strolling by, half a dozen young Filipinos in white trousers and *camisas*, carrying mandolins and guitars. They stopped near to where the children were playing, and struck up a certain beautiful waltz which one hears everywhere here—the work of some native composer, I believe—whereupon the little things all danced about on the white path in the fretted shadows of the trees, making a perfectly charming picture, and all so happy and jolly it did one good to watch them, in spite of the excessive heat.

The *banda de musica* seemed to enjoy the fun too, for they smiled and showed their white teeth; speaking to the children and playing one tune after the other; and when we had to go home in time for dinner, we left them still dancing and playing under the trees, perfectly happy, even at that age, with anything in the nature of a *baile*.

LETTER XII.

CHINESE NEW YEAR—LABOUR CONDITIONS—A CINÉMATOGRAPH SHOW

ILOILO, *February 4, 1905.*

To-day is the Chinese New Year, and all last night the Chinamen were letting off crackers down in the town. All to-day they have been going on with them, too, and as the chief rejoicing seems to be to explode the fireworks under a horse, you may imagine—no you can't—what the streets are like. On an ordinary day there is a good deal of pretty wild driving and no small peril in getting about in a vehicle or on foot, but the frightful risks one runs on every other day of the year are mild adventures compared to this Chinese New Year.

There are a great many Chinamen, you see, for they continue to come into the Philippines in spite of the heavy tax against them; and besides that, so many are left over from the Spanish days that Celestials are still the principal shopkeepers of the Islands. They make large fortunes here, I believe—the fortunes that are ready waiting for anyone who is as clever and industrious as a Chinaman—and so good a speculation do they think this country that they are constantly arriving, whenever they can get permission, paying the heavy tax, and then beginning by working for a year or two with some friend or relation for no pay!

Of course, the Filipinos hate the idea of being cut out by strong, hard-working, clever rivals, who make fortunes under conditions in which they themselves starve, so they have forced the hand of the American Government in abolishing foreign labour, which measure, so the business men say, has been the ruin of the Philippines. They say that such a law is wise enough in a country like America, perhaps, which is teeming with a busy population of its own, but here it is quite different, and "Philippines for the Filipinos" would be all very well if these people wanted their country, which does not seem to be the case. Moreover, if they did want it, it is too large for them, for there are 75,000,000 acres of cultivable soil in the Philippines, and the population *all told* is barely 7,000,000. Suppose one calculated one in ten of the natives of all ages as a capable tiller of the earth—a *most* unlikely average—and *if* three Filipinos could do the work of one Chinaman or white man (which they can't), even then one would think there would be room for competition and other labour.

The magnificent forests of priceless woods simply fall into decay; the gold and all the metals with which the country is filled, lie untouched; the marbles are unquarried; the rich soil is uncultivated; and so these riches must remain as long as it pays no one to work them. Men often come to the Philippines to "prospect," but when they find out the conditions of labour and the rate of Export and other Duties, they go away and are no more heard of; for, though you may run a sort of Government with philanthropical ideas, you won't get business to flow in on the same system; and business men don't care two straws if a labourer can read Latin or understand mathematics, so long as he will work well for low wages; but this latter ideal is the very last one the American Government appear to encourage or aim at.

Well, we went last night to a cinématograph show, which has established itself in a big empty basement in the Calle Real, with a large sign outside, made of glass letters lighted behind with electricity, all in the most approved European style. The "show" lasts for half an hour, going on from six in the evening to about ten o'clock at night, and the proprietor makes about 300 *pesos* a week out of it, for he has very few expenses, and it is the sort of thing these people love. They come out when the show is over, stand about and expectorate for a few minutes, and then pay their cents and go in again and enjoy the same thing about five times running, probably without the faintest idea what it is all about from start to finish. You remember the dreadful extent of the habit of expectoration in Spain? You have heard about this failing in America? The Filipino is the epitome and concentration of the two.

Everything in the hall was boarded up to prevent any stray, non-paying enthusiast from getting a free peep; but all the same I saw several little brown forms in fluttering muslin shirts, outside, where the wall formed a side street, with eyes glued to the chinks of a door in rapt attention; though I don't suppose the little chaps could really see anything but the extreme edge of the back row of benches.

In the hall we were saved from suffocation by two electric fans, and kept awake by a Filipino playing a cracked old piano with astonishing dexterity, rattling out the sort of tunes you hear in a circus and nowhere else on earth. I could not help wondering where he had picked them up, till it suddenly dawned on me that one, at least, gave me a faint hint that perhaps the performer might once have heard "Hiawatha" on a penny flute; so I concluded that he was playing "variations." Pianos never sound very well out here, and I am told it is difficult to keep them bearable at all, for the chords have an unmusical way of going rusty in the damp season, or else snapping with a loud *ping*.

The moving pictures were not at all bad, rather jumpy at times, but the subjects really quite entertaining, and all the slides, from the appearance of the figures on them, made in Germany, I imagine. The series wound up with an interminable fairy tale in coloured pictures, really a sort of short play, and in this one could see the German element still more apparent, in the castles, the ancient costumes, and the whole composition of the thing. I don't suppose the natives in the audience had the wildest idea what it was all about, or what the king and queen, the good fairy, and the wicked godmother, were meant to be, probably taking the whole story for some episode in the life of a Saint.

The audience were really more amusing to me than the pictures, and I was quite pleased each time the light went up so that I could have a good look at them. In the front rows, which were cheap, as they were so close to the screen, sat the poorer people in little family groups, with clean *camisas* and large cigars, the women's hair looking like black spun glass. Our places were raised a little above them, and were patronised by the swells who had paid 40 cents—a shilling. Amongst the elect were one or two English and other foreigners; some fat Chinamen, with their pigtails done up in chignons, and wearing open-work German straw hats, accompanied by their native wives and little slant-eyed children; a few missionaries and schoolma'ams in coloured blouses and untidy coiffures *à la* Gibson Girl; and one or two U.S.A. soldiers, with thick hair parted in the middle, standing treat to their Filipina girls—these last in pretty *camisas*, and very shy and happy. A funny little Filipino boy near us, rigged up in a knickerbocker suit and an immense yellow oil-skin motor-cap, was rather frightened at old Tuyay, who had insisted on coming to the show and sitting at our feet. When she sniffed the bare legs of this very small brown brother, he lost all his dignity and importance, and clung blubbing to his little flat-faced mother. Poor old Tuyay was dreadfully offended; she came and crawled right under C——'s chair, where she lay immovable till the performance was over.

To watch the people here is an endless source of amusement to me, and I only wish my words could be more photographic, or our photographs more pictorial, so that I could convey to you a real impression of this queer end of the world. That is what it is—I feel as if I had arrived at the end of the world, where nobody cares or knows or hears or thinks of anything, and where the inertia that is in the very air of things will at last wear down even the vitality, pluck, and good intentions of the Americans themselves.

I have arranged to go to Manila on the 28th, to-morrow three weeks, by the *Butuan*, the weekly mail. We heard fearful reports of these steamers, as I told you, when we were leaving Manila, but unfortunately there is no other means of getting to Manila from here. I am very glad it is arranged that I am to go, and I am looking forward very much to the change of air and scene. C—— is very anxious for me to take a servant to wait on me, for ladies generally take a native retainer with them when they travel about; but I won't hear of such extravagance, and think I shall have far less trouble with only myself to look after, and without the extra burden of a bewildered Filipino. A friend of ours came from Manila the other day on a visit, with one of these appanages of state in her wake, and he seemed to me to be more trouble than the whole journey was worth.

À propos of servants, we had an amusing and very characteristic adventure with the cook a day or two ago, when it occurred to us that for some time past we had not seen what we thought was the worth of a *peso* and a half of food appearing on the table, and nearly all the dishes seemed to be concocted from ingredients out of the *dispensa*; and eggs which, tiny though they are, cost the same as fresh-laid ones of ordinary size at home. What is more, they go bad so quickly that the price is really more, because so many have to be thrown away. Well, C—— said to the cook quite amiably that that functionary must revert to his original plan of giving us a daily list of his expenses, and the cook replied, very sulkily, "*Si señor.*"

Next morning, when I was giving out stores, the cook said:

"I should like to leave the *señora's* service to-morrow. I can't read or write, as the *señora* knows, and the cook downstairs, who used to do my list for me, has gone away."

Of course I knew every word of this to be an utter lie, and that my wily friend was only "trying it on," as they say, because he knew it would be very inconvenient for us to dismiss him before I went to Manila. But I did not flatter him or "play up" to him by looking the least surprised or put out; I merely answered, very gravely and politely: "Certainly, *cocinero*, that will suit us perfectly. I will see about your wages."

Such a look of utter disgust and surprise came over his monkey-face—exactly like Brookes' monkey with the frying-pan—but I said nothing, and went on serving out potatoes and tinned fruit, and giving orders as to how I wished to have the things cooked.

When C—— came home and heard this domestic history, he wanted to go and find the cook, and call him and his ancestry every name under the sun; but I implored him not to pander to the creature's vanity by such a compliment as letting him think for one instant that we wished him to stay. So no words were said; but we observed that the *menu* was immensely improved.

Next morning, when Domingo came for the cook's marketing money, instead of sending it out, I went out myself and said: "Well, do you want the *gastos* money or your wages?"

"Oh," said the cook, with a regular sort of rogue's way he has of looking you straight in the eye, "I will take the *gastos*. I will remain with the *señora* to-day, as I see she has not been able to get another cook."

Inwardly I gasped; but I thought it better not to take any notice of such impudence, so pretended I had not understood what he had said, and replied that I was very sorry he had not been able to find another situation, and that the *señor* would permit him to stay on. He opened his mouth as if he were going to answer, but evidently changed his mind, for he said nothing, but just held out his hand for the money.

Since which skirmish he has given us better food, and better cooked than we have ever had from him, and a daily list of expenses is handed to me without comment.

I hope I don't bore you with my simple domestic stories? But this one I felt I must really tell you, as it is so absolutely characteristic of the half "cute" Filipino.

Talking of native characters, there is a strange but very typical hairdresser along our street, with one poor-looking little room opening on to the road as his whole shop. All the barbers here do their business in the evenings, when their saloons may be seen brightly lighted, with men inside being operated on, while others loaf and gossip, but we have never seen a sign of a customer in our neighbour's little shop. Perhaps he does business in the day time, and though we doubt it, we always hope this is the case. In the evenings his door stands wide open, and inside, the barber is to be seen lying back in an old armchair, with his bare feet on the basin, playing an old fiddle in absolute peace and contentment, while he watches his reflection in a big looking-glass.

In a sort of wild and whimsical way he makes me think of The Lady of Shalott, and I fancy that some day a real customer will come riding by, when the mirror will "crack from side to side," and the hairdresser will look out and see the world as it really is, and just die of misery.

But I am sure that as long as he sits and plays like that, it would be a thousand pities if anyone came in with foolish and mundane ideas about shaving chins or cutting hair.

The burst of heat I told you of, is over, and the days are cool again, by comparison. Also, last night rain fell, and we got some water in our tank, after the preliminary excitement of diverting the pipe to let the dirt wash off the roof. This is a most important consideration, and as the servants are very apt to leave the pipe over the cistern, instead of moving it, so that when rain comes the first dirt will run away, one has to turn out at any hour of the day or night, when rain begins to rattle on the roofs. And how these tropical showers do rattle and roar, so that one cannot hear the other speak without "hailing the main top," as papa would call it.

LETTER XIII.

SOME INFLUENCES OF CLIMATE, SCENERY, AND RELIGION

ILOILO, *February 18, 1905.*

You must excuse my writing still being rather bad, as my illness has left me so weak that I shall not be out of bed for some days longer, in fact I am beginning to be fearfully afraid that I may not be well enough to go to Manila on the 28th after all. However, I have ten days to get well in, which gives me hope, and my progress so far has been simply wonderful, which is due to the extraordinary luck I have had in finding such good doctors and such a charming and clever nurse.

I am much disappointed in having missed the visit of a U.S.A. man-of-war, the *Rainbow*, which is on a cruise through the Islands, and has come here for a couple of days. She is the flagship of the squadron the Americans keep in the China seas, and a very fine ship, I believe.

Last night her crew gave a sing-song in the theatre, to which I persuaded C—— to go, and was very glad I had done so, as he enjoyed it immensely, and says it was a very good sort of Christy Minstrel "show." It ended with a small play, done by real "American Negroes," as they are called. The *Rainbow* gave the same entertainment in Hong Kong, just before we arrived, and I heard then how good it was. This afternoon we have been invited to a reception to be held on board, but, of course, that also is out of the question for me, and C—— will be busy at the office till very late.

There is a great deal of work at the office now, as the chief business in this island is sugar, and this is the height of the "season," when great loads of thousands of sacks go out every day to be put into steamers and sailing vessels off the estuary. They have a rough factory here where the cane is crushed, and the stuff exported is a thick, brown sort of sand (*don't* make a joke about sand and sugar!), a great deal of which goes to Europe and America, but most to Hong Kong, where it is refined in great factories. The refined sugar that comes back from Hong Kong is what we buy here; and, though an English company has started a sugar refinery in Manila, they find that the conditions of trade in the Philippines are such that they can only *just* compete with the stuff refined elsewhere and imported subject to the export tax and the enormous duties.

I think I am very lucky in having such a nice room to be ill in. It is very large and shady, with three windows and two doors, and I look out on a bright garden belonging to the house opposite, and a green field and trees, which is charming. Through the trees are glimpses of the grey backs of the houses in the street parallel to this, and then a thick, high belt of palms, which hides the open sea.

This is the S.-W. side of the house. The back, to the N.-E., looks out across a rough garden of fresh, thick grass to half a mile or so of shallows, where the tide fluctuates, and beyond is the strip of blue river, which looks so narrow seen from here that the big steamers which go by seem to be sailing on dry land. Beyond, again, comes a fringe of bright green palms, and then the open sea—a stretch of darkest blue—and a bit of hilly, verdant Guimaras.

I think one of the great beauties of the views here is that the sky is never quite cloudless—there are always very white clouds somewhere in the dome of intense blue, which give relief and value to all the colours below.

On days when the Monsoon is not too high, we open the shutters looking towards the river, but these open wooden slats keep the houses quite cool, even when the shutters are closed. I wish there were something like the *tatties* of India; but no one out here has ever heard of such a thing. The open shutters are very nice though, and the view framed in the dark opening which faces us at table is like looking at a large, bright picture. Sometimes the tide is right up to the garden wall, the sky cloudy, and the water like slate. At other times, when it is far out, the shallows turn into mudflats, with groups of native women wading about in their bright red clothes, looking for mysterious fish which Filipinos alone dare eat and live.

Some friends from Manila were looking out of the hall window a little time ago, and said, "What a lovely view. I should never tire of that." I said we never did, which was quite true.

When I am well again, and if C—— can get away, I hope to be able to go beyond the roads to Jaro and Molo, though they are beautiful and inexhaustible. With all the beauty, however, I begin to have the same sort of feeling about this country that that old friend of ours, General R——, had about the girl at the Aldershot ball. You remember the story he told us of how he saw her exquisite face across the ball-room, and insisted on a common friend introducing him to her? And when he and the friend had got half way across the ball-room, the old general said: "Stop! Take me away. Get me out of it. Her face has never changed and never can change. It isn't a face. It's a mask, sir, a mask! It is not a human being. Come away!"

Well, I feel like that about Philippine scenery, which can be dark or light according to the reflections thrown on it, but it has never changed, and even if there is a slight change, when that has passed it will always and for ever be the same greens and the same blue. No alternation to red and yellow autumn, no brown and purple winter, no delicate spring—nothing but perpetual, chromo-lithograph mid-summer, which has always seemed to me the least beautiful season of the year.

When the wet Monsoon blows, I believe that season is counted as a sort of spring, for various trees then come into bloom, but, for the great part, everything just goes on growing and dying, and growing and dying in dull routine, like the natives. In fact I often think the much-abused Filipino is only a prototype, as it were, a sort of reflection, of his country. It seems as if this were so, too, for those who go away to Hong Kong or Japan to be educated, and come back full of civilisation and enthusiasms, soon cast off their energy like a slough and return to the shiftless, slouching habits of the land where it is "always afternoon." For them such habits are natural, and perhaps necessary, but a worse effect is that white men get like that too, in time, and though they may work well enough at the business by which they live, they become indifferent, shiftless, careless about dress and the niceties of our civilisation; everything is too much trouble, and they just jog along in a half-animal routine. The young ones still fret for the world they have left, which remains fresh in their memories; but this life takes hold on men, and they become so rooted in its ways that they deteriorate and can never live happily anywhere else again—in the same way that a mind deteriorates on the slip-shod mental fare of magazine-reading, and cannot be happy with anything that requires more effort to assimilate. This, then, I find is the secret of that "nameless" fascination of the Far East that one hears and reads so much about—it is the secret of deterioration which is so easy, and elevation which is so hard, so useless, so unnecessary—let us lie in a long chair and drink one whisky peg after the other—who cares what the home papers say—what rot it is to bother about anything but poker and shooting, or why old Wing Chang bought Brown's pony.

And when you think of the *real* meaning of "Ship me somewhere east of Suez"—well, you can't think of it till you live there yourself for a month or two. My refrain is, "Ship me somewhere west of Suez," where there is health for body and soul—the west of the exquisite thrush and the lilac bush, instead of the empty, gaudy parrot and the flaming, scentless canna.

Heavens! What a tirade!

One woman have I met who likes the Philippines; though many, as I know, love India, and the Straits, and Ceylon. But then those are generally people who go away to "hills" and so on, or take trips home. Here there are no "hills," and a trip home is a serious life-problem. Just so, this one woman who has been found to like the Philippines happens to be the wife of a missionary, so, of course, she goes every hot season for a "nice long holiday" to Japan.

It occurs to me that you may imagine we have savages here when I speak of missionaries, but that is not the case, in this island at any rate, for these good people are here—oh such a lot of them!—to convert the Filipinos from Roman Catholicism. This is really a work of supererogation, for, though the Spanish priests did ill-treat the Filipinos, the natives are free now from that terror, and this religion, with its mysteries and pomp, appeals to them, and suits their dispositions perfectly.

I am afraid the unbiassed observer would find the missionaries far more convincing in their enthusiasm, if it led them to give up the beautiful houses and comfortable carriages they enjoy here, their tea-parties, lectures, and so on, and go and rough it in some of the other islands, where there are plenty of savages, Mahommedans, devil-worshippers, cannibals, and all sorts of unreclaimed sheep.

Before I left home, I remember a very enthusiastic but woefully ignorant old lady being filled with excitement when she heard I was going to the Philippine Islands, and showing me missionary journals with a great deal written in them about "the good work" being done out here. At first I very naturally thought it was the savages who were being tackled, but—"Oh dear no!" she cried, quite shocked. "The poor Filipinos are being saved from the dreadful influence of the Roman Catholics."

I said: "But surely they are also the followers of Christ? Only they do not interpret His sayings quite as we do ourselves."

"No, *no*, they are *wicked* people! The Filipinos *must* be saved! Do, *do*, when you are out there, interest yourself in this noble work. I will send you little books———"

Strange, isn't it? And of course about the people, the laws, the climate, she knew less than nothing, though I am sure the poor old soul gave many a shilling out of her miserable income towards the fund that gives the missionary's well-dressed wife a "nice little holiday in Japan."

In these civilised (?) parts of the Philippines there is a good deal of religious trouble and dissension already, without missionary enterprise to stir it up, as a very determined patriot of the name of Aglipay has cut himself adrift from the authority of Rome and started a church called La Iglesia Filipina Independiente, which title, I am sure, needs no translating. His followers are numerous, in fact it is generally believed that they now out-number the orthodox; and the whole movement is known to be the outward and visible sign of inward and hidden fires of Insurrection and Independence. The *Aglipayanos*, as these independent thinkers are usually styled, have churches of their own, and processions and ceremonies almost indistinguishable from those of the Papists. Do you remember a procession I described to you when we were in Manila? The bringing down of the Virgin of Antipolo? I now learn that that was all to do with this quarrel amongst the followers of the gentle Christ, though to which side the Virgin of Antipolo belonged, and who was to be galvanised into loyalty by the contemplation of her journey, I am not quite clear, and do not much care, for the fate of the little old wooden doll is uninteresting—it is only the people who are ready to fly at each other's throats about it who are remarkable. What poor "worms that bite and sting in the dust!"

LETTER XIV.

VOYAGE TO MANILA

S.S. "BUTUAN," *March 1, 1905.*

I am launched, you see, and on my journey to Manila after all, though I do not feel at all well again yet; but that is not surprising, as it takes such a long time to pull round in this climate. It is not that the climate is so much worse than any other, as long as you keep well, but as soon as you get ill you go all to pieces, and the first thing to be done is to ship you off to Hong Kong or Japan as soon as possible. The climate of the Philippines is very much abused, more than it really deserves, I think, for the chief causes of all illness are anæmia or liver, both arising more from the dreadful food and the lack of fresh vegetables, fruit, milk, and good meat than from the actual climate; though, of course, the illnesses arising from each bad diet are aggravated by the heat. The amount of tinned things the people eat would be trying in any climate, but out here they must be simply deadly. I have just been reading a book by a traveller, who announces that there is nothing the matter with the Philippine climate at all, because he tore round the Archipelago in record time, crossing the islands on foot at astounding speed, and living on native food—and he was not ill. Naturally, he was not ill; but then his experience is of little value to men who have to work for their living, sitting in offices for eight hours a day on six days of the week, whose food is the sort of provisions one can get in the towns, and their houses rooted on ill-drained mud-flats.

Everyone would like to rush about and live a free, wild life, and, no doubt, if they did, there would be fewer illnesses and less human wrecks; but the trouble is that no one would pay them for doing it; and men must work out here just the same as in other climates—in fact they seem to me to work longer hours and harder than anywhere I ever saw; and the wonder to me is, not that they are ill, but that so many of them survive at all. Undoubtedly the only billets worth having in the tropics are those of a tea-planter, a British officer, or a professional traveller.

I am in the regular mail steamer, you see, as I told you I should be, and we were certainly not given to understand more than the truth anent her shortcomings, for she is about the same size and class as those pestiferous little nightmares which run between Gibraltar and Ceuta. There is no deck but a plank or two outside the saloon, the latter a sort of excrescence on the ship, leaving just room to squeeze a chair between its sides and the scuppers. The space in the bows is thickly occupied by marine wonders covered with tarpaulins. What these may be, as they are not deck cargo, I can't think, but they are evidently important enough to want all the fresh air in the ship.

Aft, the galley treads upon the heels of the saloon, its fragrance extending still further, and the strip of deck outside it is completely blocked by dirty little tables, where frowzy men of the crew seem to carry on a perpetual March Hare's tea-party.

Beyond that, again, a half-clad native is for ever killing hens, and all in a muddle with a couple of terribly mangy but very kind dogs nosing about for snacks.

She is a Spanish steamer, and the officers all Spaniards, very polite, but unkempt, unshaven, and dressed in soiled white linen suits with no attempt at a uniform.

It is astonishing to think that this is the mail between Manila and the chief town of the Islands, and I can't understand how it is that in six years no American enterprise has stepped in to do something better. I have asked Americans about this, but they tell me the question does not affect them, for they can always get permits to go in their own transports, and then, besides that, there is nothing to tempt American capital in so slow and jog-trot a fashion of making dollars. As we went out of the river, I tried to see our house in the estuary, but all the blue-grey houses, and corrugated roofs, and green trees and palms look so exactly alike that I found it impossible to distinguish ours from amongst the jumble.

While I was looking over the side, a Filipino passenger, a middle-aged man, came up and said something to me, waving his hand towards the shore. I daresay he took me for his equal and meant no harm, but I thought it very cool of him to speak to me, so I simply drew myself up and said that I did not "habla Castellano," whereupon he shuffled off and has not been seen again.

Luckily the weather was very calm, and is so still, so I was able to appear at the evening meal, which came off at six! A deadly hour—when you have not had time to get up any interest in food since lunch, and yet if you don't eat you are starving before bed-time. The dinner consisted of a thick meat-and-drink soup, such as one might imagine Russian convicts yearning for in the depths of a Siberian winter, but for which it was hardly possible to return thanks in a stifling cabin in the tropics. After this nice, comforting brew followed a procession of eight courses of thick and greasy fried lumps or appalling stews, each one more fatal and more full of garlic and spices than the last. I thought that even if I had been feeling fresh and hungry on a winter's day at home I could hardly have faced the *Butuan menu*, but, as it was, the mere sight and smell of the dishes made me almost hysterical.

The polite little captain pressed me to eat, and I did not like to hurt his feelings by refusing what he thought was excellent fare; but I escaped alive by waiting till his head was turned, and then dexterously passing lumps down to one of the kind, mangy dogs until the poor beast was detected by a *muchacho* and kicked, howling, on to the deck. After that I assured the skipper that I had had quite enough; an excellent dinner; I positively could not eat any more. He bowed and offered me coffee. I took a cup, and with that and dry biscuit made a tolerable meal.

About eight o'clock I went below, as I felt very tired, because it was almost my first day out of bed since my illness. Besides that, even if I had been in keen and robust health there would have been nothing to tempt me to remain on the narrow deck, which was pitch dark, or in the stuffy saloon with a couple of guttering candles in tall stands on the table by way of sole illumination.

The accommodation below is of much the same type as the luxury above, below decks being just of the build of one of the old penny steamers that used to go up and down the Thames—you remember the sort of things—a very low roof supported by small iron pillars. Off a narrow passage open seven small cabins, with four berths in each of them, but they are really not so bad when you get one all to yourself, and I have the best one, at the end of the ship. I caught the fat *Mayordomo* (chief steward), and after endless trouble, managed to get a key for my cabin door, though the choice lay between having it open or dying of asphyxiation; but I preferred the latter risk of the two, as at least I could be certain what to expect if I kept it locked.

One look at the mattresses was enough. I slept, or rather lay awake sweltering, on all the coverlets piled on the least filthy of the upper berths. The cabin smelt horrible, and the only light there, as in the saloon, was a candle in a bracket, the glass of which was so grimed with dirt that it gave hardly any light at all. No water was laid on to the filthy basin, and it did not do to let one's mind dwell for one instant on cockroaches—like a child who tries not to think of some horrible ghost story in the dark.

About six this morning the *muchacho* (they have no word for steward apparently) woke me by rattling at the handle of my door, when I climbed down and held parley with him through the crack. He said something in English about "washing," and I thinking he had brought me water to put in the unspeakable basin, said: "No, not yet," and tried to shut the door.

However, he was not to be ignored, for he shoved the door open, apologising as he did so, came in and shut and fastened down the scuttle, and then backed out again with many more bows and excuses. Then I understood that it was not I who was to be washed, but the decks! Somehow, it had not occurred to me that the decks of the *Butuan* ever could be cleaned like those of other ships!

All day long we have been slipping past these Dream Islands, sometimes so close that one can see the waves breaking on the rocks and the blue sea running up into fairy bays, and I should so much like to go ashore in some of them, and see the negritos and savages, and the beautiful jungles where monkeys swing about on great flowering vines. That is always the Tropic Island of one's dreams, is it not? But now I begin to think that possibly life is not all a transformation scene in the lovely jungles, where there are doubtless deadly snakes; poisonous, scentless plants; swamps, and malaria, to say nothing of the fatigues and difficulties of getting there. On the whole, for beauty of scenery, health and comfort, I think I would rather live in a glen on a Scottish moor.

My luggage is rather on my mind, as I found I had to bring such a quantity, for muslin and cotton frocks take up so much room that I was compelled to abandon my first plan of one moderate trunk, and am now engineering what looks like a family "flitting." Talking of frocks, you once asked me to tell you if those I had brought out were all right. They are quite right, thanks, at least the muslins are and the very thin cottons, but anything thicker, even print, is too warm, and the very thinnest of stuff skirts or coats are stifling and impossible. I always envy the lucky women in Hong Kong whom I left going about in white serge and grey flannel, and even being compelled to put wraps on in the evening!

Another thing I find about clothes is that every one wears white, and though one gets rather tired of it, still it is the best thing for the fashion of washing clothes by pounding them on boulders, and then drying them in this terrific sun will evaporate the strongest colours in an incredibly short time. Clothes don't last long here anyhow, colour or no colour, as there is something in the water that rots material, so that it goes into holes and tears if you look at it, and something in the air which rots silk even more disastrously and quickly, and turns all white silk and satin quite deep yellow.

I have been writing this at intervals all day, and now it is six o'clock, and the meal is due. I can see the polite skipper standing waiting for me to enter and take my seat, and the mangy dog trying to squeeze himself in under the bench where my place is. So I will leave off and finish this in Manila, where we are to arrive in the early morning.

MANILA, *March 2.*

I thought a mail would be going out the day I got here, but I find it does not go till to-morrow morning, of which I am rather glad, as it gives me time to let you know I have arrived safely. Yet when you get this—oh what a long way off—the trip to Manila will be a half-forgotten thing of the past!

The *Butuan* (by-the-bye, she has taken that name from a town in the big southern island of Mindanao) anchored off the mouth of the Pasig at three o'clock this morning, and deck-washing began at four. So at about five I opened my door a little bit and roared for the *muchacho*, till someone else in another cabin got tired of hearing me, and took up the cry, and it spread through the ship like the cock-crowing in the dawn. By-the-bye, I got away from the shrill of the crickets for a few hours, but did not, as I had hoped, escape the eternal cock-crowing, for those fowls on board the *Butuan* which had escaped death began to crow at four o'clock for all they were worth, poor things. Well, at last the *muchacho* came along and brought me a perilous candle and some hot water, and I dressed and packed up the few things I had out, and went up on deck at about six.

At sunrise—a thick, pink, hazy sunrise—we steamed up the river, but I was *blasé* about everything but food, so I stayed in the saloon and managed to get some biscuits and coffee, and to avoid a plate full of deadly-looking ham and eggs.

There was no room to anchor at the quay, which was fringed with a close line of steamers berthed stern-first, so she anchored in the stream; and until I was "fetched," I amused myself watching the blue-green water-plants go trailing past, and trying to observe life on board the big, covered, brown lighters. No life was to be seen, however, except the natives wielding immense punt-poles, who walked along the sides of the barges on a platform one plank wide.

At about seven the company's launch came for me, and she made quite a long trip, down the Pasig and all along outside the breakwater, as the shorter way through was blocked by a dredger. A tremendous new harbour is being built, which bids fair to be a very fine concern, and the Americans think a great deal of it, and say it will enable Manila to compete with and eclipse the shipping of Hong Kong. This is a difficult piece of reasoning to follow, for a glance at a map shows how out of the stream of the world's traffic Manila lies; and then, besides that, there are the tariffs and customs, and all the vexations of the American system of government, which will make it impossible to compete with the traffic of a free port like Hong Kong. Moreover, it will never pay anyone to shift cargoes in a port where the coolies are so lazy and labour so expensive as in Manila.

It is the American go-ahead, run-before-you-walk way, too, to build great docks and harbours costing millions before they have spent the necessary thousands in constructing roads to bring the merchandise from inland, or sacrificed the hundreds required to encourage trade.

The same thing is being done down in Iloilo, where two millions are being spent on a harbour, when there is not one tolerable road across the island, and all the revenues that choke agriculture go to pay the officials and the school-teachers, conditions which prevail throughout the Archipelago. The Americans mean well by the Philippines, that no one can doubt for an instant, which makes it all the more sad to see them wasting magnificent energy, and earning nothing but failure and unpopularity, by going dead against everything that has ever been discovered about the successful government of Asiatics. But then, is this real government? It is very difficult to know what to call it, as at one time the venture is referred to as a "Colony," at another as "The youngest of the United States," and yet again as "A Sacred Trust." I mean they use these terms indiscriminately and officially, which is very puzzling.

But I am wandering away from the trip in the launch, which went all round these same harbour works till it came right in front of our friends' house, where a boat came off and took me through the shallow water to the steps at the end of the garden.

It was then nearly eight o'clock, so the day was getting very hot, and the cool house seemed delicious. Breakfast—nice, clean, ungreasy breakfast!—and the joys of a bath. There was a "bathroom" on the *Butuan*, but in a state of dirt that would have made bathing impossible, even if the bath itself had not been full of old lamps, boots, tin cans, and dirty clothes.

I have spent all the day resting in the house, to save up my energies for an entertainment which I should be very sorry to miss. This is a public reception to be held by the Governor, Mr Luke E. Wright, at his palace on the river, where one will see, as a compatriot informed me, "all Manila at a glance." I don't think a glance will satisfy me though, for I want to go and have a good long look. I feel better already for the change of air and scene, and am sure I shall be quite equal to the reception, besides, I would rather be ill than miss such a party!

I say I spent all the day in the house, but that is not quite accurate, for we went for a drive at sunset to a library in the town, in a Spanish book-shop; and on our way back took a turn round the Luneta, the promenade by the sea, which I fancy I may have mentioned to you already. The band plays there every evening, and everyone drives or walks about. It was a very pretty sight to see the people in white dresses, all moving about in the radius of the electric lights on the bandstand, the lights looking like spots of white fire against the yellow sunset.

LETTER XV.

AN OFFICIAL ENTERTAINMENT

MANILA, *March 3, 1905.*

I sent a long letter to you by the mail, which went out this morning; but I must begin another at once, as I want to tell you about the reception last night. Indeed, if I don't keep a letter always going on while I am here, I shall not be able to tell you half what I want to say about Manila.

We dined at half-past seven last night, and then, with a small party of friends, drove through the town to a wharf in front of the large Cold-Storage buildings by the river. Here we had to pass over some large, flat lighters, on the decks of which the moonlight revealed myriads of enormous cockroaches hurrying about in all directions, which made us catch up our skirts and run for the launch lying alongside the lighters, and all decorated with palms and Japanese lanterns.

At the wharf some more friends had joined us, so we were quite a large party in the bows of the launch as she steamed up the Pasig, and the cool, or comparatively cool, night air was delicious. The river looked quite pretty in the moonlight, and though it was only a small, rather new moon, the light was quite strong, and the green of the trees was quite perceptible, for there is colour in the moonlight in this part of the world, where the moon does not make mere black and white outlines, but you can distinguish colours quite plainly. The Palace of Malacañan soon came in sight—a big building blazing with lights, and adorned by rows of little lamps in festoons all along the water's edge, like Earl's Court Exhibition.

We landed at a low stone wall, outlined for the occasion with red and yellow electric lights. The launch immediately in front of ours was that of the Chinese Consul, very profusely and beautifully decorated, and filled with Celestials in bright silk dresses. We stepped at once into the gardens, which come right down to the water's edge, and found ourselves in the *fête*—all in full swing, with crowds of people walking up and down paths covered with sailcloth to protect the dresses. Of course everyone was going about in evening dress, as if in a ball-room at home, and feeling very hot, and looking for cool places. The idea of this perpetual heat soon becomes familiar, but sometimes it strikes the imagination, on occasions of this kind, with particular insistence. In my letters to you I can't go on saying "It is very hot," "It is very sultry," and so on, and yet I know that you reading them at home, can have no idea of the *setting* of all I tell you; of the terrible blazing sun all day long; the hot nights only bearable by comparison with the day; of one's skin always moist, if it is not actually running in little rivulets, as in a Turkish bath; of even the dogs and cats spending all their lives trying to find draughts to lie in. And this, I am informed, is the "winter."

MANILA.
Malacañan Palace.

Well, this entertainment, which was very well done indeed, reminded me more and more of Earl's Court, as we passed under arcades of coloured lights, and the Constabulary Band played selections on a grass lawn under the trees. There was a huge open-air ball-room, built over some lawn-tennis courts, raised up and approached by a little flight of steps, and with seats all round inside a rail.

Our first duty was to present ourselves to the Governor, Mr Luke E. Wright, and his wife, who stood under a canopy of white silk, on which were embroidered the Arms of the Philippines. This coat of arms is a new invention, and this was its first appearance. It was designed by an American called Gillard Hunt, and its heraldic description is very complicated, and would probably convey as little to you as it does to me. It happened to be on the front of the programmes as well as on the canopy, so I had a good look at it, and the gist of the design is that it is all red and silver and blue, and the symbols are the Castle of Spain and a sea-lion, with a background of the stripes of the American flag. Above is the crest, which takes the form of the American Eagle, and the inscription written below is "Philippine Islands." It makes a very pretty crest, but it is difficult to understand why the Philippine shield should be quartered with the Arms of Spain any more than if the American flag should have the Lion and the Unicorn in the corner. In fact the latter device would be far the more reasonable of the two.

Well, as I say, the Wrights and their party stood under this white silk canopy, and the aide-de-camp introduced those whom they did not know already; whereupon our hosts shook hands, repeating each guest's name, and adding "Pleased to meet you" in kindly American fashion.

This little ceremony, the American introduction, always appals me, because I never know what one is supposed to say in answer. I am afraid I smile helplessly and murmur, "Thank you so much!" but I am sure that is not the right thing to do.

Having passed what the Manila papers call "The Gobernatorial Party," we proceeded to drift about the grounds, which were really charmingly pretty. I met a good many people I knew, and enjoyed the evening immensely. After a time I began to feel very tired, and Mr P—— took me to the ball-room, where he managed to find places, and we wedged ourselves into the row of people sitting all round. I did not dance, but I found quite enough amusement to compensate me in looking on.

The crowd was pretty mixed, of course, but "Manila at a glance" included one or two who looked like gentle-folk, and there were certainly a great many pretty dresses, which, I am told, the wearers import from Paris recklessly. Some of the *camisas* worn by the native ladies were quite lovely—beautiful, delicate fabrics exquisitely embroidered and hand-painted—and in the Official Rigodon, with which the ball began, I noticed how well the wearers moved.

As a contrast, one of the most remarkable spectacles of the evening was the Gibson Girl, of whom there were several specimens to be seen strutting about. All Americans, men and women, as I have noticed at home and on the Continent, have something of this type about them, and I often wonder whether Dana Gibson has discovered the essentials of the American type, or whether he has invented a model which they admire and try to copy. Whichever it is, when it is natural it is pretty enough in moderation, but some of them have, as they would express it, "got right there," and they may be picked out of any crowd of ordinary human shapes at a glance. Of course no human being really could have the proportions of the Gibson Girl as she is on paper, for no living thing ever had such length of leg and neck but a giraffe; only so many Americans have that type of face, with a low, pretty square forehead, thick, round nose, heavy jaw, and arched eyebrows. Corsets and high hair-pads can help towards the rest of the design. I can't think how anyone wants to be a Gibson Girl, unless for twenty guineas a week at a theatre, as the pose and the untidy hair is inexpressibly common and shop-girlish. Moreover, I don't see how anyone can expect to ape anything and avoid being vulgar. The Gibson Girl does not escape this latter calamity. She "gets right there just every time."

After watching the dancing for a good while, I was taken round the grounds and given refreshment at one of the little buffets in the garden. A most amusing episode occurred at the chief of these buffets, where a big bowl of punch was being administered by the Chinese servants, who opened everything they could lay hands on—whisky, port, claret, soda, liqueurs, brandy, champagne—and poured it all into the punch. You can imagine what ludicrous stories were afloat about people who had taken one sip of this fire-water, and were reported to have been carried off half-dying, and shipped home down the river.

About half-past ten the crowds began to thin, and we left the palace, getting upon our launch again at the same place where we had landed. There was no more moon, but the stars made quite a bright light, and the air was so fresh upon the water at that hour that one could actually stand the extra warmth of a chiffon scarf across one's bare shoulders.

March 4.

I found myself very tired yesterday after the *fête*, so I stayed in the house all day, except for a drive in the evening to the Escolta, which is the principal street of shops. When we came here in November, fresh from palatial Hong Kong, I thought this town the most shoddy and hideous place I had ever seen, but now I find it really difficult to recall my first impressions, for it seems a gay and handsome metropolis to the provincial from Iloilo!

MANILA.

The Escolta.

At Iloilo our streets consist of ruins hastily patched up, and great fire-blackened gaps in the rows of houses, but in Manila, though there has been apparently just as much hasty patching, there are comparatively few ruins to be seen, and perhaps a trifle less string used in the harnesses of the horses. White women and *Mestizas* go about in hats too, which is a superfluity we do not affect in the provinces, and after so many weeks of not wearing a hat, I find it very irksome and hot to have to put one on. However, in Manila one must do as Manila does, I suppose, though the fashion, which did not obtain in the Spanish days, seems a foolish and unnecessary one, and the people who were here under the old *régime* rail helplessly against the innovation. Certainly it is no gain to the coloured ladies to hide their nice, thick black hair with the frightful "Parisian" confections which appeal to their exotic taste; but, of course, it would never do for them not to follow the fashions set by their American equals. They have, however, that strange and subtle way of the Oriental all the world over, of setting a seal of their own upon even the most slavish imitations. One feels in this, as in everything else in Manila, that if the American influence were withdrawn, in twenty-four hours all trace of that busy, kind-hearted, bustling, incongruous people would begin to melt steadily away, and in a month would be wiped clean out.

There are big, or comparatively big, shops, with a great display in the windows, and huge signs, and hurry-up-its-your-only-chance notices, and conversational advertisements in the American fashion. But when you get inside the shops there is the familiar barrenness, and there are the same half-asleep or half-drugged Filipinos and yellow *Mestizos* yawning and trimming their nails with the same vague indifference, and nothing to sell that any human being ever wants. And the prices of the things you buy, instead of what you wanted, are enough to make your hair turn snow-white on the spot.

One fact, striking fact about the shops in this country is that the largest and most important are those of the jewellers, and the reason of this is that the Filipinos and Eurasians have a mistrust of banks and investments for their spare cash, with which they buy jewels partly for love of the glittering ornaments, and partly from some muddled idea of having their money safe in a portable form. I was talking about this to a very civil Frenchman in one of the biggest jeweller's here this morning, while I was waiting for a ring they had been repairing, and he was very interested to hear I had come from Iloilo, for he told me he had travelled all about Panay selling jewellery a year or more ago, and that he knew that island quite well. I asked him if he had done well there, and he said yes, very good business indeed; and when I asked him what sort of things he sold, he showed me beautiful diamonds set in rather red gold, and said I would be astonished if I saw the "*types*" who could buy such ornaments. He said he rode a horse, as the roads were only rough tracks with broken bridges, but I don't suppose he really did go all over the island, and fancy he must rather have gone in coasting steamers and ridden about the suburbs of the towns, for there are no inland towns in the Philippines, and no market, even for the best diamonds.

Talking of *Mestizos* reminds me of an account I heard, from a friend at the reception, of an English-*Mestizo* wedding, which may amuse you, and is extraordinarily characteristic of these people. The bridal party assembled in church in the orthodox fashion, but the bride's Filipino and Eurasian relations, instead of remaining in their pews, all crowded up to the altar and stood in a mass amongst the wedding-group and bridesmaids; and after this astonishing ceremony, the happy couple marched down the aisle to the strains of "The Washington Post."

LETTER XVI.

MANILA AND ITS INHABITANTS

MANILA, *March 5, 1905.*

I wrote in the morning yesterday, and after the heat of the day we drove outside the town to a nursery garden. To get there we passed through long streets of untidy suburbs, not of palm-thatch huts and bamboo groves like those in Iloilo, but very broad and treeless, with mean, low houses at intervals, and bits of waste ground strewn with lean dogs and rubbish. There are not scavenger pariahs here as in Turkey and the Near East, and I suppose they could not exist in such a climate, where the rubbish would be too putrid even for their savoury taste. There are a good many hawks about, but they don't scavenge either, like the hawks in Egypt; all they seem to do is to hover over poultry, and every now and then get away with a young fowl or chicken. When we were driving round between Molo and Jaro a week or two ago, near the village of Mindoriao, we heard a great squawking and a scream, and looked round in time to see a hawk rise up from near a *nipa* hut with a fair-sized hen in his claws. The people rushed about the plantation and sang out, and the hawk staggered once or twice, and nearly fell with the hen, which was very big and heavy for him; but he got away at last, and the people were left gazing after him into the sky, like in the picture of "Robert with his Red Umbrella" in *Struwwelpeter*. But the scavenging is, or should be, done by the half-wild pigs with which the native quarters teem—lean, rough, black and white animals, generally very mangy, and with long legs and snouts.

A STREET IN MANILA.
Showing Electric Tram.

A great deal of the way to the nursery we followed the route of a new electric tram, which is to be opened in the course of a few weeks, and is to connect all the suburbs with the main town. Manila is immensely proud of this tram, which is such a token of progress that it somehow or other makes up for the lack of paving and other primary symbols of civilisation. There is a railway here too, the only one in the Philippines, which goes about 150 miles inland to a place called Dugupan. There is constant talk of railways to be built all over the islands, the concessions for which are being granted, of course, to American speculators; but those who know the islands well say the railways will not benefit anyone, even the speculators, for what are wanted besides labourers are roads, just good traffic roads, kept in good repair. However, it sounds imposing to talk of so many millions of dollars to be spent on railways "to open up the Philippines," and a great deal of philanthropic energy is, somehow, inferred.

The entrance to the nursery garden was up a narrow, sandy lane, where a lot of little, half-clad, brown children ran out after us and offered small, tousled bunches of faded flowers. Queer little souls, these Filipino children, with thin limbs and fluttering muslin garments.

On each side of the sandy lane was a field planted with rose bushes; in the garden itself nothing appeared but rows and rows of flower-pots containing green plants and ferns—the sort of plants and ferns one only sees in conservatories at home. The garden was laid out in formal earthen paths, bordered with tiles, but the gardener was anything but formal—a huge, fat, old native with Chinese eyes, got up airily in white bathing-drawers and a muslin *camisa*.

We went about, and my friend chose ferns and plants, some of which were lovely, and I very much wished I could have taken some home with me to Iloilo, but for the difficulty of transporting them by the *Butuan*. There was a charming old grey stone well in the garden, with steps leading up to it, some of them formed of beautiful old blue and green Chinese tiles, the whole shaded by big, drooping trees, which made that corner of the garden quite dark. Overhead, along the greater part of the paths, was a pergola of orchids, while all sorts of orchids grew from bundles of what looked like dried sticks tied to the posts. The sight of the orchids made me realise once again the temperature we live in, for I thought of how, on a summer's day at home, one would find the outside air quite cold after an orchid house. It also occurred to me that it sounds all very fine to think of orchids in cheapness and profusion, but I have never yet seen an orchid that could compare as an object of beauty with a dog-rose out of a hedge.

On the way back we halted to hear some jolly tunes played by the band on the Luneta. Again there was the blue dusk; the orange and saffron horizon; and the moving crowds in white on the bright green grass plots round the bandstand. We stayed in the carriage, which moved slowly round with hundreds of others, all going in the same direction. I believe the only carriage that has the privilege of moving the other way is that of the Governor.

Going in and out of the crowd, everywhere, were two little American girls, seated astride on a bare-backed pony, with their hair floating loose behind, and tied with an immense bow of ribbon on one side of the forehead in American fashion; their thin little legs dangling side by side on each flank of the pony. They looked very happy and solemn, and the way they stuck on was simply wonderful.

MANILA.
The Luneta.

The Luneta is a pretty sight in the evening, and even amusing, but I must confess I was very much disappointed in it, because I have read so much about Manila in American magazines, in which the Luneta is described as "an evening assemblage where all the nations of the world jostle one another";—or phrases, more lurid, to that effect; followed by "word pictures" of Jew and Moor, Chinaman and Turk, Cingalee, Slav, and Hindu, all rubbing shoulders in their respective national costumes. So I looked out for this sight particularly, but have never seen anything but men of varying degrees of white and Malay in linen suits, and women and Gibson Girls in the last scream of Paris-Manila fashions. I have asked people about it too, in case I should have been to the Luneta only on days when the Jews, Moors, etc., were unavoidably absent; but I only got laughed at for imagining such nonsense, and when I said, I had read accounts by American eye-witnesses, my friends only laughed the more.

March 6.

I am afraid I am not seeing as much of Manila as I had hoped, after all, for I find I am not well enough to go about a great deal, but what I do see I try to remember in order to tell you. Having these letters to write is an amusement in the long, hot hours in the house, so don't think that I am giving up delirious joys to find time to write to you! All the same, if I did go out more into Manila Society, I should not have any more to tell you, for there would be nothing to describe but Bridge. That is the only thing anyone ever does. Manila was pictured to me as a very gay place, in fact the

Manila papers even go so far as to label it the "Gayest City of the Orient"; but it is really a dreadfully dull little town, with a very occasional dance to enliven the interminable round of dinner and Bridge parties, and those curious and costly luncheon parties which American women give to each other. So much I had already inferred from the Society Columns of the Manila papers, which come to us in Iloilo as a breath from the wide world! When I arrived here and saw the place, and asked some questions, I found my worst fears realised, and that far from being the gayest city of the Orient—think of Cairo, Calcutta, Colombo!—Manila is probably the dullest spot of the East or West, and any gaiety or intellect it might have is choked and strangled by Bridge and Euchre. In a country like this, where there is little or no housekeeping and no shopping to fill the minds and time of the average women, card-playing seems to attain colossal proportions, for they actually go out of their houses at eight in the morning to meet and play cards till lunch (the Americans do not use the word tiffin), and after a siesta they begin again, go home to dinner, or out to a dinner party, and probably play half the night.

The Americans in Iloilo are just as keen, however, and the first question they ask you is if you play Bridge; and if you don't they take no further interest in you, and never dream of inviting you to their houses.

The Americans are fearfully down on the Filipino national game of *Monte* about which the natives are infatuated, and over which they ruin themselves, but the indignation of the ruling race carries very little weight, as it is all precept and no example.

I went for a little drive yesterday evening, through the old Spanish Intramuros, the Walled City, within the high old walls, which stand in a neglected moat, and are all covered with moss and grass and trailing weeds. The narrow streets are cobbled, and the quaint houses, with deep, barred basement windows, have a delightful air of repose, after the half-finished, skin-deep, hustling modernity of Americanised Manila. The whole quarter seems a far more appropriate setting than the rest of the town for the "mild-eyed lotus eaters," which the Filipinos really are by choice, nature, and instinct. I think that if I lived in Manila (which heaven forbid should ever be my fate!) I should like to live in the Walled City—that is, if I survived the awful smells—and imagine myself in an East where there were no arc-lights, no electric trams, no drinking saloons, ice-cream sodas, "Hiawatha," or Bridge, and where the natives would be humble, civil, prosperous, and happy.

There are some fine old gates to the Walled City, but the Americans whose idiosyncrasy it is not to reverence antiquity unless it has cost fabulous sums at Drouot's or Christie's, are pulling them down for no reason at all.

A great many natives bustle about American Manila in European or white linen suits, and it is a very exhausting place; but one can't quite see the good of it all. I asked an American official (what they call "a prominent citizen"), whom I met at dinner the other night, how the Filipinos were to profit by all this bustle and book-learning.

"Why," he said, "I guess they will learn to appreciate our civilisation and then want it, and want all the things that civilisation entails, so there will be a demand, and trade will come right along, and these islands will wake up *and* flourish."

I wanted to argue, however, so I said: "But why should the Filipinos wake up? Why not give the poor creatures lots of cheap food. If they have a little rice, and a banana patch, and a *nipa* hut, and no priests to bother them, that is all they want, and there will always be an inexhaustible market for the produce of the islands. It seems such a pity to daze their poor brains, and hurry them about like this." But he said it was no good trying to talk about this to me, as I evidently could not understand the American Ideal.

So I dropped the subject, for when it comes to the American Ideal, I am hopelessly at variance, and think it better to say no more. The Ideal is this, you see, that every people in the world should have self-government and equal rights. This means, when reduced from windy oratory to common-sense, that they consider these Malay half-breeds to be capable, after six years of school-teaching by the type of master I described to you (about which type, by-the-bye, experience has given me no reason to change my mind), of understanding the motives, and profiting by the institutions which it has taken the highest white races two or three thousand years to evolve. They are supposed to be so wonderful, these flat-faced little chaps, because they have shown a sudden aptitude for the gramophone and imitation European clothes, a free and abusive press, and unlimited talk—endless talk. But it seems to me that these are the traits one is accustomed to in the emancipated coloured person all the world over. In fact, when I come to think of it, America with this funny little possession of hers is like a mother with her first child, who has never noticed anyone else's children, and thinks her own bantling something entirely without parallel or precedent; quotes it as a miracle when it shows the most elementary symptoms of existence, and tries to bring it up on some fad of her own because it is so much more precious and more wonderful than any other child any one else ever had.

March 7.

Yesterday we went to buy prison-made goods at Bilibid, which is the big jail of Manila, and of the whole Philippine Islands. When anyone has committed a serious crime, he is sent up to Bilibid to eke out the period that has to elapse before he is carted back to his original island to be executed. The prison is a mass of half-finished-looking grey stone buildings, where prisoners in yellow-striped jerseys, like gigantic wasps, were going about behind iron railings.

We went into a huge stone hall, where there were quantities of all sorts of basket-work furniture on show; a row of carriages, all prison-made; and at the farther end a white man standing behind some glass-covered tables containing little objects for sale. I wanted to get some small souvenirs to send home, and examined carefully all the little trifles and curios in black wood, bone, and silver, with which the cases were filled; but I could not see anything that was uncommon or characteristic, or even worth buying at all. All the things looked to me as if someone had been to Naples or Colombo, and come back and told the Filipinos what to make, for here were souvenir teaspoons, paper knives of black wood, bone hairpins, and so on, and not one of them of a pattern one has not seen prepared for the traveller in every city of the world. I hunted all through the cases, and amongst the furniture in the hall, but could find nothing distinctive—everything was well made, but utterly *banal*. However, this did not concern me much, as what I had really come for was ordinary furniture, and this I managed to get to my satisfaction, and a little cheaper than in the Chinamen's shops in Iloilo, which is to say exactly double the prices of Hong Kong.

Amongst a great many things stored in a corresponding hall upstairs were some basket chairs of an uncommon pattern, with a back like a huge spreading peacock's tail; but, though they were pretty, these chairs did not strike me as characteristic of a people living in *nipa* huts, but much more like the suggestion of a wandering admirer of *l'art nouveau*.

Besides the chairs, I noticed some small columns of hard Filipino woods, intended for flower stands, but the price asked for them was 10 *pesos* (one guinea) each, which I thought ridiculous for plain, flat, polished wood. It appeared that they were derelict from the St Louis Exhibition, or, as it is called, "Exposition," and on each was resting, temporarily, a little figure carved in wood and painted in bright colours, representing a Filipino man or woman—the woman in red skirt (not *sarong*) and *camisa*, and the men with their shirts outside, and carrying a fighting cock under one arm. By-the-bye, there is fierce indignation and terrible offence taken by the Filipinos about that same "Exposition," as the Philippine section was got up attractively barbarous, with too much of the savage element, wild-men-of-the-woods in fantastic hovels, and so forth, to please the educated and high-class natives and *Mestizos*, who want independence, and think *they* are more likely to get it than the prehistoric savage.

On the way out here I met a German who had been to St Louis, and who told me that the two chief exhibits were the Boer War and the Philippine section, and that the latter was nearly all savages in huts, with fish-*corrals* in artificial ponds, and all that sort of thing. I remember he was quite surprised to hear that there was any other town than Manila, or any civilisation in the Philippines except the marvellous dawn that rose with the Stars and Stripes. I believe that was very largely the impression produced in America, and not quite ingenuously—that the inhabitants of these islands were a race of naked cannibals and savages who were suddenly being transformed into the educated *Mestizo*, who goes to college in America and returns here to write seditious articles and talk his head off. Well, whatever the impression desired or produced, the way it was brought about has caused endless anger amongst those Islanders who would rather be thought civilised than picturesque.

March 8.

I have been out shopping this morning, going out at such an unusual hour because heavy rain had fallen in the night, and the air was fresh in the morning. It is nice to have a fresh morning, for the early part of the day here is heavy, and day dawns thick and foggy. At least, the mornings are thick and foggy in comparison with the exquisite clearness of the dawn and early hours of the day in Iloilo. Talking of that, I am much struck by the colour of the sky here—all over the Philippines, I mean, or rather, all over where I have been—for though it is very blue, it is a whity-blue, a thick sort of colour, not a bit transparent like the sky of Southern Europe or North Africa. I can't quite describe it, but when one looks up at the zenith one does not seem to be looking into illimitable spaces of transparency, and the thick white of the horizon stretches far upwards.

On this shopping expedition I went to buy some things for the house that I thought I might be able to get cheaper and better here than in Iloilo. The principal street of shops is, as I told you, the Escolta, and the next in importance is the Calla Rosario, where the shops are kept by Chinamen and one or two Japanese.

BIRD'S-EYE VIEW OF INLAND SUBURBS OF MANILA.

On the way there I saw a steamer on fire, which was a great sight, but rather alarming. When the carriage was passing over the bridge spanning the Pasig, I saw crowds running and looking down on the river, so I told the coachman to stop, and stood up and saw a fairly large coasting steamer drawn out from the other vessels at the wharf and pulled across the stream, where it lay in a huge wall of flames like Brünnhilde in the opera of *Siegfried*. When I first caught sight of it, there was a complete steamer, but it burnt up with amazing rapidity, and as I looked, the machinery suddenly sank through the hull, the bows and stem rose up to meet each other, and the whole thing doubled up and vanished beneath the water. Of course there was no one left on board, but all the same it was a gruesome sight, and one I know I shall think of all the way back to Iloilo in that fearful little *Butuan* with its wobbly candlesticks.

In the evening we drove out to pay some calls, and then took a little turn out beyond Santa Mesa, which is a big residential suburb on some low hills inland. The people living there have told me that the air is appreciably cooler than down in Manila, and there are far fewer mosquitoes. The latter alone would be sufficient reason for living there, as the mosquitoes here are awful, and always hungry night and day.

We drove a little beyond Santa Mesa (which is, being translated, The Holy Supper) over abominable roads through little scrubby coppices. At one place we saw a most curious sight of hundreds of white-clad native people, in the sunset light, passing along a broad field-path bordered with trees; and I at first thought we had come across a religious procession. But when we got nearer, I saw that it was a crowd returning from the cock-pit; for every second man carried a cock under his arm; some sitting comfortably; some draggled with blood, wounded and miserable; some limp and dead.

I can't tell you what a feeling of sickness came over me, for I thought it one of the most horrible sights I had ever witnessed; and I was glad when the procession was out of sight, and I could no longer see the animal-like, degraded faces of the men and their miserable, blood-stained, dying birds.

I suppose the good folk in the towns and little villages in the U.S.A., the electors who control Philippine affairs, would rise as one man if a bull-fight took place in these Islands; but yet a bull-fight, horrible though it must be, is not so bad as these cock-fights, for at least the toreadors and matadors risk their own lives to a certain extent, and run an equal chance with the animals they torture; so it cannot help being a more noble, or less ignoble sport than this sickening cock-fighting. But so much has cock-fighting become the national "sport" of the Filipino that, as I have shown you, he is always represented, typically, with a fighting cock under his arm. But the significance of that also, and all its natural consequences of brutality, gambling, and cruelty, I suppose, escaped the attention of the benevolent elector, who visited the "Exposition" at St Louis.

One thing I can never understand, and that is why people make less fuss about the cruelty towards an animal in proportion to its size. This sounds ridiculous at first, but when you come to think of it, it is absolutely true; for if horses or tigers were set to fight like these poor fowls—one fight in one palace!—there would be a howl all over the civilised world, would there not?

March 9.

We had tea yesterday afternoon at four as usual, and then drove out to Malacañan for me to call on Mrs Luke E. Wright. The grounds of the palace looked even more beautiful by daylight than they had when lighted up at night, and the house is very fine, with huge rooms like halls, and floors polished into brown looking-glass, all crowded with big pictures, arms, and handsome furniture.

Mrs Wright received us on a big open balcony-terrace overlooking the river, with a fine view; and here we sat and had tea and talked. Some other people came before we left, for it was Mrs Wright's At Home day, amongst them one of the prettiest women I have ever seen, wife of some young man in the American Diplomatic Service, a tall, dark girl with an exquisite face, and perfectly dressed in something very filmy and floating, of delicate mauves, with a big black hat. Her walk, her air, her dress, made one suddenly feel how far away Manila is from all the world one is accustomed to, and what a small, dull, back-water of the stream of life this is.

We went on to call on the wife of Commissioner Worcester, a scientist as well as a politician, and, as his title implies, one of the Americans on the Philippine Commission. The Worcesters' house was a little higher up the river, and again we sat on a balcony-terrace, but this one was all hung with plants and creepers, and overshadowed by dark green trees, through which could be seen the blue-green soapy-looking river swirling past, and the opposite bank with flat fields of emerald grass and bits of bright blue sky. The rail of the balcony was bordered with plants in pots, while all sorts of queer orchids and things grew on the over-hanging branches. It was like a scene in a play, I thought, and the shade of the deep trees was delightful, though they made the balcony rather steamy and airless. Mrs Worcester showed me some of the most lovely needlework I ever saw; all this native embroidery on *piña* muslin, of which she is a keen *connaisseuse* and collector. Some of the pieces were as fine as the most delicate lace, and one large shawl, in particular, was a marvel of embroidery on what I took to be very fine net, but discovered to be drawn threads!

I have been finding out about prices here, in case we are sent to Manila later on, and the result of my investigations is that I pray we may be kept in the Provinces! Rents are appalling, the equivalent of our £100 a year being quite a modest rent for a small unfurnished house, and wages are more than double what is given in Iloilo. You can't get a cook to look at you here for less than 40 *pesos* a month, which is £48 a year! Most of the cooks are Chinese, I believe, as it is considered rather common to have a native cook, though why this is I am unable to find out, for the Filipinos are excellent cooks. But that is just where the American Ideal of Philippines for the Filipinos begins to fall through, and I noticed at Malacañan Palace that all the servants were Chinese, and was told that they were an institution of Mrs Taft, the wife of the last Governor, the man who, as I told you, I think, was *the* original pro-Filipino. One hears a good deal about this Governor Taft, who is now Secretary of War in the U.S.A. He was the first American Civil Governor of the Philippines, and seems to have a very strong personality, which he flung into the pro-Filipino cause for all he was worth, on which account he has become a sort of patron saint, rivalling Dr Rizal, with the natives, who believe he is working tooth and nail in the U.S.A. for the independence he promised them.

It is as impossible to get a clear idea of Mr Taft as of any other public personage, for while some people tell me he is a high-souled, disinterested philanthropist, who will live up to every word he has uttered, others vow that he is only an American politician with a skin-deep catch-vote policy, and that having got the billet he wanted in America, he is quite capable of turning imperialist if it suits his book. What is one to believe?

One thing they all agree in, which is that he has personal magnetism and a great deal of social charm, which great gifts have stood him in very good stead, I have no doubt, with the Filipinos, and have more to do with his vast popularity with these Orientals than any vows and protestations; and, perhaps helped to make up for the *faux-pas* about the Chinese servants, which still rankles in the native mind.

LETTER XVII.

DEMOCRACY AND SOCIETY IN MANILA

MANILA, *March 10, 1905.*

I am still in Manila, you see, but am going home to-morrow, so I will write a line to go out by the next mail, which I should miss if I waited till I get to Iloilo.

I rambled off so in my last letter that I quite forgot to tell you about a party we went to at the house of some very rich *Mestizos*; a sort of reception, with desultory dancing, but in the afternoon, or rather, the evening hours before dinner.

When we arrived, at about six, the party was in full blast; rooms cleared for action, blaze of electric lights, string band, crowds of pretty frocks, and grounds all lighted up with arcades of paper lanterns. This climate lends itself particularly to such entertainments, with the warm evenings, and there is not much trouble in the way of preparation, with big, open houses and polished floors.

Our host was a small man, Filipino altogether, but his wife, a tall and very pretty Mestiza, "had fewer annas to the rupee," and was exquisitely dressed.

I walked about the pretty rooms and met many friends, besides recognising many of those I had seen at the Malacañan *fête*, and saw again the pretty young woman who had charmed me so at the palace, when we were calling there. She looked prettier than ever amongst a crowd, though they were all very smart, and some of the American women really well dressed with nice hats.

This is such a small place, and so few travellers ever come here that everyone knows everyone else, which makes parties very pleasant, though I noticed, again, that the Americans are not really democratic a bit, and there is a great deal of social distinction made, and people do not recognise others whom they really know perfectly well.

The army is just as superior as the soldier set in any garrison in any kingdom; and if a man is a merchant, unless his business happens to bring in a large income, it would be absurd for him or his family to expect to be asked to the exclusive dinners and parties at which the administrative, military, and millionaire set congregate. I don't think I am at all keen to be a democrat, even a theoretical one, for it must be very tiresome to have no real social position of your own, but to depend on some one else's recognition of your claims to a certain income, an appointment, or who you are seen with, and what you wear—and then, when all is said and done, to be the social equal of your workmen and servants. Not that I suppose for a moment that anyone is really a democrat, for I have never yet read or heard of such a being, and certainly I have never seen one.

I have discussed this subject, in all good nature, and generally half in fun, with nearly all the Americans I have met, for it is one that interests me enormously; and the gist of all they tell me—or imply, which is better—is that all Americans are the equals of those above but not of those below them. If I suggest a social distinction between *any* citizen of the United States and the King of England, the mere idea of such a proposition makes these democrats go into fits of laughter; but when I ask them if they, personally, would consider it an indignity to be sent to dine in the King's kitchen with his scullions, they generally get quite offended and can't see that at all. I think, too, that these subtleties of democratic etiquette must be even more distracting to the simple Filipino brain than they are to persons like myself, for though the "little brown brother" is now being taught that all men are equal, he can see without doubt that a native or *Mestizo* with plenty of money can get the wives of the highest American officials to visit his house, whereas the poorer relative is not even recognised.

Emerson told his countrymen the truth once for all when he said that "humanity loves a lord,"—and it will have "lords," and must make "lords," and the best-intentioned Americans in the world will no more make these half-bred Malays equals of each other, or any one else, than *they* are of each other or negroes.

You will laugh at me for my vehemence, I expect! But you can't think how aggravating it is to have a principle for ever forced down your throat by the good folk who blatantly and utterly disregard the practice. So the end of my reflections is that I am quite content to curtsey to a king—*and* to make my Filipino servants call me *señora*, and put on a clean *camisa* when they come into my presence.

I have wandered away from the *Mestizo* party, but not so very far in reality, for it is at such gatherings that such reflections occur to me, along with speculations about the floor, and the refreshments, and how much duty that woman paid for that frock. The refreshments, by-the-bye, were very well done; and indeed, so was the whole party, and the charming manners of the host and hostess did a great deal towards making everything go off well.

Yesterday I spent a harrowing morning trying to buy some vests for C——. Perfectly ordinary white cotton vests, such as the men wear here under their white linen coats, but more difficult to track and procure in Manila than so many birds of paradise. When I told my friends I was going to get vests, they were amazed and asked me why I did such an eccentric thing, instead of sending to Hong Kong for them like everyone else. But I was rather on my mettle about it, and said I would get them in Manila in one of the Chinese shops, for people in Iloilo had done this thing, and why not I?

At one shop, where I had been told to go, a weary-looking Chinaman was sitting in a chair at the shop door, and first I tried Spanish on him, but with no result, not even a flicker of intelligence on his face. I might have been talking in Pekin. So I said, "Do you sell cotton vests?"

"Wests? No. No have got wests." And he spoke in a tired, helpless drawl, as if his soul had been deadened by a life of trying to get "wests."

But I was not to be put off, as I had been to six other shops and was getting tired. So I said, "But I was told you sold vests. I don't mean waistcoats," which I know *they* often do, "I mean things to wear under a coat. Vests."

"Oh, yes. Allitee wests. Mellikan-Filipino store on Escolta. Oh, yes; me savvy all about wests." And he looked beyond me as if he had been marooned in mid-ocean. I think it was really opium, which one gets accustomed to in the Filipinos as well, for sometimes they are simply maddening when they speak as though in a dream, staring with dull eyes.

The end of the vest story was that at last I tracked what I wanted to a Chinese shop, where the display in the windows consisted of tin pans, sausages, bead curtains, picture postcards, and things like that. After a tour of the Escolta, I had arrived at this shop by the advice of the coachman, to whom I managed to explain my wishes by a lurid pantomime in the middle of the street. When the coachman at last understood that I wanted to buy vests, and not to make him take his off, we went, as I say, to this Chinese shop with the unpromising window-decorations. When I entered and asked for vests, everyone brightened up, and a very yellow old man took an opium pipe out of his mouth, and said something in guttural words to a fat youth in the comfortable *négligé* of a pair of blue cotton trousers and a jade bangle.

This person evidently understood English, for he waived my Spanish aside and began to talk very fast in *pidgin*, which, when you hear the real thing, and not on the stage at home, is very difficult to understand. However, he seemed to bring the word "wests" in pretty often, so I began to feel hopeful, and made the old man draw a chair up to the counter for me, and sat down.

Presently, after a fearful lot of talk with several other fat, yellow youths, and a great deal of hauling down and putting away again of bales and boxes, and sharp rebukes from another old Chinaman with a bead counting-board, who was doing his accounts in a big book with Indian ink and a paint brush, the boy who was attending to me came back to where I sat, and threw down a pile of big, flat bundles with a triumphant air, exclaiming "Wests!"

No such luck, however, for the bundles contained coloured furniture cretonnes. So I set to work to explain again, but it was not so easy as it had been in the Spanish shops, for no one, as far as I could see, had on such a thing as a vest, an open coat being the most they wore above the waist line. I did not dare to go out and make a demonstration with the coachman, so I just struggled along with pantomime and bits of French and German, which really did just as well as English or Spanish; till at last a light dawned on a Celestial brain, and they all said some word in Chinese to each other, and nodded and grinned and replied: "Allitee, Mississy. Have got."

And at last a box was opened, inside which were really and truly white cotton vests. But the size was unfortunately intended for very small and consumptive youths, so I had to begin another long and troublesome explanation that the person they were intended for was forty-two inches round the chest, which was conveyed by calculations and juggling with a metre tape.

"Ah," said the two old men. "Can catchee flom Hong Kong. All same steamer. You waitee two tlee days."

I said I knew that already, and explained that I was going to Iloilo to-morrow.

"Velly good," said one old man. "Mollow can get. Catchee flom one piecee Chinaman in Manila."

"Can't I go to the other Chinaman myself?" I asked.

"Me catchee wests. Mollow can get number one size west."

However, while this was going on, a bright idea had evidently occurred to one of the shop boys, who had been looking so hard at me that I thought he was ill; but he suddenly left the shop, going out of a doorway with big Chinese letters in gold on a red placard over it, and came back, just as I was leaving the shop, with the very things I wanted—a dozen of them in a big cardboard box.

Such, then, is shopping in Manila, and it is only the replica of how I tried to match embroidery cotton in the Spanish shop it had been bought in; and the other despairing adventure I had when I went in search of fruit dishes. So I now understand why everyone said it was absurd of me to think I could "go shopping" in Manila, and I wished I had done as everyone else does, and got the things direct from Hong Kong, and saved all the trouble, as well as the annoyance of paying double; for, duty and all, it is cheaper to get things in oneself.

I am glad to be going home to Iloilo, as the weather is beginning to get pretty hot, and Iloilo is much cooler than this. Of course in Manila one has the advantages of the Australian provisions from the Cold Storage, which means fresh meat, vegetables, and fruit, besides being able to get any amount of ice, all of which luxuries are a great aid towards bearing up in a hot season; but the air at Iloilo is so much lighter, and the fresh mornings and evenings down there are wonderful tonics.

As to the social attractions of Manila, they are no better than those at Iloilo. Bridge! How one gets to hate the very sound of the name of the game! And now when I see a group chained silently round a Bridge table, I can only think of the Souls tied to their Vices in the Frescoes of Hell in the Campo Santo at Pisa.

I met at dinner the other night the wife of a very "prominent citizen," who was a source of infinite delight to me in an elaborate defence I drew out of her by pretending I knew nothing about the game. I find this is the only safe course, by-the-bye, as, if you admit any knowledge of Bridge, you are forced to play whether you like it or not—or whether you can afford it or not, which is more important!

This good lady told me that it was quite true that she and the other American ladies play cards all day, informing me that every morning she, herself, played Bridge from eight to twelve, either in her own house or in that of a friend. I said:

"But how about your housekeeping?"

"Why," she answered, "if you have a good Chinese cook that don't amount to anything."

"But it must be an awful bore," I said, "in this climate to put on a dress and a hat and go out in the hottest part of the day."

To which she replied that if I would let her teach me Bridge I should understand why she did these things. She was very amusing, in her dry, American way, and made us all laugh very much at the comical things she said. However, she was really in earnest about her offer to teach me; but I said I was very grateful, only I thought I would rather remain ignorant as long as I could if it "took" so badly as she described.

I feel much better in health for the change; and everybody here, both my hosts and others, have been so kind to me that I am quite sorry to leave them all. There are several pleasant people down in Iloilo, but I think a change of society does one as much good as anything else, don't you?

This will go out by the Hong Kong mail to-morrow, and I will catch the next one by writing as soon as I get home, and sending the letter by the *Butuan* when she returns.

LETTER XVIII.

THE RETURN VOYAGE AND MY COMPANIONS

S.S. "BUTUAN," *March 12, 1905.*

I will begin a letter to you now, as I may not have much time for writing just after I get home. Not that there is really any fear of my letter to you coming off second best in any case! You say how much you like my letters, and what a pleasure they are to you, but they can't be half such a treat as yours are to me. I can't tell you what it is to hear all the home news, and about the frosty days, and the Christmas shops, and the cold, jolly winter, and all the things one longs for out here with a longing that is absolutely painful in this everlasting, sweltering heat.

Talking of heat, I don't think I told you about a place above Manila away inland, called Benguet? It is nick-named the Simla of Manila because it is a cool region, high up in the mountains, where there are pine trees, and frost at night, and fireplaces in the houses. This resort is not much good to the average person, however, for it is three days' journey from Manila by rail and road—when the said road is not swept away, which is its usual condition—and the trip costs more than to go to Japan. The governor and the whole administration move up *en masse* in the hot season, and they have very nice houses, but there is not much in the way of accommodation for mere mortals. This is the only attempt at "hills" in the Philippines, which is a great pity, but then there are no roads, and the places away from the big towns are not at all safe. Even round about Manila the country is infested with what are officially called *Ladrones* (robbers), who are really Insurgents, and quite recently the wife of a Filipino official was kidnapped, and there was a great fuss about it.

The *Butuan* is, on this trip, even less of a floating paradise than when I came in her, for, on arriving on board yesterday, I found to my horror that she was simply swarming with a Filipino boys' school going on an Easter outing to Iloilo. I wonder if you can even faintly imagine what that means, or even dimly picture the condition of the ship, when I tell you that there are seven four-berth cabins and we carry seventy-two first-class passengers!

I consider myself fortunate in being in the best cabin again, with nothing worse to put up with than the company of a pleasant native and her little maidservant. She, the mistress, is a full-blooded Filipina, and fearfully indignant at any insinuations to the contrary; a fat, swarthy person, with a good-tempered, flat face that is probably handsome according to its standards, and she wears a costume reduced to the last limits of propriety, in the form of an untidy skirt, a spotlessly white loose linen jacket, and slippers—which, I must say, is a most enviable get-up in this temperature.

She tells me she was first married to a Spaniard, who left her very well off, and her present husband is a German-American in the coastguard service in Manila. She is now on a visit to her brother in the Island of Negros. I took this person to be about thirty; but she tells me she is forty-three, and that her good temper has kept her young looking, which I can quite believe, for she takes the most "unpleasant episodes" with the greatest amiability, and is really quite a charming companion. She says that her husband is of a worrying nature, so he looks forty——

"Which is a very good thing," she says, laughing all over her jolly fat brown face, "as he is only twenty-eight. Did you see him when we left Manila? He came to see me off."

But unfortunately I had missed this individual amongst the seething crowds that pushed about the deck till we started, and were then bundled over the side and down a plank like so many sheep. I can't think why on earth none of these places have a gangway for the steamers.

She has told me endless "yarns" about the Philippines and the Filipinos, the chief points of interest being emphasised by a bang of her fan on my knee, which conveys anything to me from her views on the Papal Supremacy to her opinion about the sanitation of this ship, the latter subject taxing even her powers of pantomime.

We have so far had the marvellous luck of coolness, a clouded sky, and wind. The wind, however, is a mixed boon, for it means waves—waves which would hardly count on the Round Pond, but make the *Butuan* roll heavily, and prove too much for the Filipino boys and youths, who are thick on the ship as swarming bees. They must be thankful to get rid—on the deck, by-the-bye—of the fearful, greasy meals which they stow away with horrible greediness. Knowing that the Filipinos eat lightly and sparingly, I remarked to my cabin mate, who came to sit next me at table, about the diet of these young countrymen of hers. She, herself, like the other native passengers, only eats very little—some chicken and a few vegetables, rice, and fruit. The gesture she made as she looked at the schoolboys was most expressive.

"*Babuis!*" she said, which is Visayan for pigs, and as bad as calling a Frenchman *cochon*. "*Babuis!* These Government Schools are ruining my people. I thank God that I have no son who will be taught to be insolent and unclean, and to eat like that."

I asked her what she meant by "unclean," and she said that the Filipinos wash a great deal, which I knew already, and are very careful in certain small details of cleanliness and sanitation, but that all the new schoolboys were little better than animals.

Opposite us at table sits a very good-looking American officer in khaki uniform, who is evidently not a keen advocate of equality, as he does not open his lips except to the captain, and even omits the little bow which the other passengers make on taking their seats at table. Moreover, he does not pass things, which is not a pretty example to the very polite Filipinos and *Mestizos* at the table. All the Filipinos I have ever seen have those beautiful gracious Spanish manners which may mean nothing beyond mere politeness, but they do help to grease the wheels of life a great deal. The contrast to the older people of these horrible, noisy, ill-bred young "yahoos" is heartrending,—the first-fruit of the American ideal, dressed in appalling variations on the European costume; cheeky, gluttonous, self-important—just what one would expect of a mongrel Malay who is told he is the social equal of white women.

As I write this to you I am sitting on the narrow deck, trying to get as far away as I can from the schoolboy crowd, whose portion of the deck is unspeakable, apart from the fact that they think I am an American, and spit on my chair whenever they get a chance of approaching within range of it.

At the end of my chair (I brought my own with me) sits my cabin mate, looking at a lot of illustrated English papers which I have with me; and I am afraid my letter must read very disjointedly, as I am constantly leaving off to answer some of her endless and very intelligent questions.

Near us are camped a Spanish *Mestizo* and his fat little wife, who wears a great deal of sham jewellery and a cotton dressing-gown—a very superior person, with no pretence at veiling her scorn of my Filipino friend, nor of me for talking to her.

The Filipina laughs very good-naturedly, and says the *Mestizas* think themselves very great *señoras*, but she herself does not find their snubs humiliating, "For," she says, "I behave as I should, and we all come from *el buen Dios.*"

She is great on *el buen Dios*, and one of the first of her innumerable questions was to ask about my religion. When I said I was a Protestant, she hastened, politely, to assure me that she was very broad-minded on the subjects of heretics, and refused to believe that they were all devils.

I remarked that I thought we were not much worse than anyone else.

"Oh," she said, "I quite think you are no worse. Once we had a young man to board in our house, who was in my husband's business, and he was a Protestant. The *padre* used to come to me very often and tell me the young man was a devil, and that I must send him away. But I would not do so, for I am broad-minded, and I said he seemed as good as anyone else, and, though he was a good man, *el buen Dios* had made him a heretic for His own good reasons."

I complimented her upon her breadth of view, and asked her if she were an Aglipayano, but at this she very indignantly declared she thought it very wicked to side against the Holy Father, and one would surely be punished for such heresy. "They are worse than the heretics," she declared, "and besides that, they are all *Insurrectos.*"

"But," I said, "if you don't sympathise with the *Insurrectos*, then you like the Americans?"

"No," she said, "I hate them," and she made an ugly grimace.

I asked her why.

She got quite excited, and exclaimed, "Why? Why, what are they doing here? Who asked them to govern the Philippines? Who wants them?"

"Oh," I said, "but they are a very civilised people, and are going to do you such a lot of good."

She simply laughed, and pointed with her fan at the schoolboys in the bows.

After a little while she said, "*Paciencia!* In a little time they will go. I hear all my people saying that the Americans will go."

"You want to govern yourselves, then?" I asked.

"Yes, but I don't think we shall be able to. Some other nation will come and take the islands when we are left alone. The Japanese, many say; but we do not want the Japanese."

On the whole she has made the voyage much more pleasant for me, for she interests me so much to talk to, and though it is uncomfortable to be at such close quarters in the cabin, nothing could exceed her kindness and good breeding, while the little maidservant is attentiveness itself.

At night I wanted to have the door open, but they were both very frightened, and implored me to shut it and lock it as well, which I readily consented to, as they were so timid, and I thought it a shame to make them uneasy, though I felt quite brave now I was no longer alone.

I daresay you are surprised at my accounts of these and other conversations in Spanish, but the fact is, though I have not tried to learn the *patois* that obtains in the Philippines, I find it impossible not to pick up a good deal, partly from knowing Italian, I suppose, and partly from having to talk it occasionally in spite of myself. They speak badly, though, and the accent does not sound a bit like what one heard in Spain, besides which, there are so many native and Chinese words in current use. Instead of saying *andado*, they say *andao*; *pasao* for *pasado*; and so on, with all the past participles, besides other variations on the pure Castilian tongue. I found that the Spanish grammars and books I had brought with me were of so little use for everyday life that I gave up trying to learn out of them, and just get along on what I pick up—though I am very shy of it, and would not for the world let any other English person hear me trying to talk! The native language is a queer, guggling noise; when written it looks all g's and b's and m's, and full of uncouth combinations of hard consonants. Some of the names of places are native, but many are Spanish, and the Filipinos themselves all have fine, rolling Spanish Christian and surnames, which were dealt out to them indiscriminately by the priests.

ILOILO, *14th.*

Now I am home again, you see, and delighted to be back in my own house, though I had a very good time while I was away. The *Butuan* got in at four yesterday morning, anchoring off the mouth of the river, and deck-washing set in at once—never was it more needed!

Oh, the scenes, the sights, the noises on that foul steamer! At the best of times she is dirty and uncomfortable, but no words of mine can convey her unspeakable condition with those awful Filipino boys on board—at least, no words that can be set down on paper.

The air of the morning was fresh, when we dropped anchor off the mouth of the river, and a nice cold breeze blew from the shore, which at first only showed as a black line in the dark, with one or two points of light where the town lay. Gradually it became more and more distinct in the dawn, till we saw the outline of the corrugated roofs, the palm trees, and the shipping on the river, while a faint, steady crowing of cocks could be heard.

Have I told you about the cock-crowing? It is one of the features of Philippine life, and one of the things you must get accustomed to, or lie down and die. It begins before daylight, and goes on till after the sun has set—the screaming of innumerable cocks, for every living Filipino keeps one, and most have two or three.

We got a candle, and I dressed first and went on deck, where I was eventually joined by a tremendous swell in a trailing silk skirt, French blouse with lace yoke, long gold chain, white canvas shoes, and so on, whom I just managed to recognise as my cabin mate.

While we leaned over the rail waiting for the *Sanidad* (the port doctor's launch), she told me she thought she should be able to get away that afternoon for Negros, but she hoped she should see me again, and said I must be sure to come and pay her a visit if I went to Manila again. To which end she proceeded to write down her address on a crumpled bit of paper which she pulled out of her pocket, handing me half of it to write mine on. I saw my piece had writing on it, and I said: "But is this not something you want to keep?"

"No," she said, "it is only a note of my home accounts for last month."

I looked at the accounts and saw the first item was: "To the *padre*—for a mass—two *pesos*;" then some vegetables and meat, and more *padre*; then cigarettes, and again *padre*, and lower down, yet again *padre*.

"You seem to pay a lot to the *padre*," I said.

"Ah," she answered, "for my mother's soul." (*Por el alma di mi madre.*) "One must get to heaven."

"But the missionaries tell you that you need not pay money to go to heaven."

"Perhaps," she said. "But with them one is certain to get to hell."

If my cabin mate was a swell, she was completely eclipsed by the brilliant appearance of the fat little *Mestiza*, who came up on deck and leaned over the rail not far from us with a really heroic effort to appear unconscious of her gorgeous clothes. Her husband was very waxed about the moustache, and thin and pointed about the boots, and he kept shifting his sombrero with a fat hand, which displayed one very long little finger nail and a huge diamond ring. The Filipino schoolboys were got up in all sorts of suits, some in tweeds, some in linen, and one in bright blue striped silk, which had shrunk a good deal, and a straw hat with the brim made in a pattern like an ornamental cane chair-back. The little chaps were showing each other their clothes, and the older boys, of fifteen and sixteen (or that was the age they looked), were fearfully busy and important, smoking cigarettes, giving orders, and switching their legs with little walking sticks.[5]

About six o'clock the *Sanidad* came and gave us *pratique*, though I think if he had come before the deck-washing he must have put us all in quarantine for the plague. Apparently, too, there was no objection raised to the number of passengers in proportion to the accommodation, so we got ashore. Long before this the company's launch had come fussing down the river and out to the *Butuan*, with C—— standing in the bows; and as soon as the doctor's tour was over, I was conducted across the *Sanidad* launch into the other, and we went straight to the wharf, and home in a *quilez*, leaving my luggage for the shipping agent to tackle.

When I arrived at our house, old Tuyay flung herself down the staircase into the road with screams and yells of joy, wagging not only her tail but her whole body; and when I got into the hall there was the cat from downstairs squeaking, and telling me some long story about all she had noticed while I was away, and following me from room to room.

This cat has established herself with us for the last few weeks, and now thinks it her right, not to say her duty, to smell everything that comes into the house. She was fearfully agitated about the furniture I brought from Manila, and while it was being rigged up, and other things shifted, and so on, the poor pussy went nearly wild with excitement and curiosity, to say nothing of laying herself out to be tumbled over and half killed.

---

[5] In the Spanish days, no Filipino was allowed to carry a walking-stick, except the *Presidente* of a town, which distinction was jealously preserved.

LETTER XIX.

A *BAILE*—A NEW COOK AND AMERICAN METHODS

ILOILO, *March 20, 1905.*

I am sure you will be glad to hear that I feel much better for my Manila trip, and able to go for our evening walks again, which we still enjoy very much, though the season is getting rather hot for moving about with much comfort.

While I was away, there was an outburst of Carnival gaiety, and C—— went to a ball at the Spanish Club, which seems to have been a very good one. It was fancy dress, many of the costumes were beautiful, and there was a big supper laid out at little tables in the open air, with decorations and paper lanterns. They danced till five in the morning, when the more enduring and merry spirits drove round the town in open carriages; so they seem to have had a very gay time, and I was rather sorry I had missed it, as a fancy dress ball in Iloilo must be a rare and precious experience.

So Lent has begun, but apparently it is not going to be made too strict, for last night we were bidden to an amateur theatrical performance at the Santa Cecilia (the Filipino) Club, which was a very festive affair. The big room of the Santa Cecilia, which is upstairs, like the Spanish one, but with a stage at one end, was very gay with festoons of pink and white muslin, and chains made of little hoops covered with tinsel paper. Nearly the whole audience consisted of Filipino women, in skirts of screaming reds, blues, greens, and yellows, set off by bewildering *camisas*, their black glossy hair adorned with many combs, and everywhere whiffs of penetrating cheap scent.

The hall is so large that the two or three hundred people present did not nearly fill it, though little groups of men hung about the side that opened, with spaces between columns, on to the staircase and outer hall.

We sat for a long time past the normal hour for beginning, staring at the drop-scene, which displayed a large picture of Saint Cecilia playing on a piano, and looking up to heaven; and had plenty of time to take in the paintings all round the room of Magellan, Rizal, Washington, and other heroes, which were stuck high up in frames, or frescoed on each side of the stage, while the band gave us waltzes, Sousa, and "Hiawatha." This latter tune seems to have become a sort of Filipino National Anthem, for no entertainment of any sort can come off without it, and even a *banda de musica*, playing in the street in the evening, won't go away, even after they had received money, before they have gone through "Hiawatha." I don't think I ever described to you a launch party we went one evening, on the occasion of a *despedida* (farewell), to a departing American official? We were a large party, English and Americans mixed, and filled up the bows of a fair-sized launch, while abaft the engines a Filipino string band clung on and played as best they could as the launch rolled about in a choppy little sea off Guimaras. As we left the *Muelle* (the quay) these musicians struck up "Hiawatha," and when they had got through it they began again, and again, and again—and I have no doubt they would have played that air contentedly the whole way out and back, and probably fully intended to do so, if they had not been implored to stop. It is not a bad tune, though, and went remarkably well with the clicking of the launch's machinery and the motion of the waves.

But, to get back to this theatrical performance—though I don't think there is much to say about it, for it was a very ordinary amateur show, and except that the skins of the performers were naturally darkened and not artificially white, and the language they spoke was Spanish, it was indistinguishable from the same sort of thing at a charity bazaar at home. Not musical, like the performance I told you about at the theatre, but a playlet of a strangely exotic type that must have been rather unintelligible to most of the brown brothers and sisters, for it was a sort of French farce about a man and his wife living in a flat below another couple, with the usual complications that apparently inevitably result from such a dangerous experiment in Paris. One man acted well, and was now and then really funny; but the humour was *not* the most refined fooling I have ever heard, as you may judge when I tell you that the chief source of jokes was that one of the husbands was represented as insinuating himself into the other household by pretending to be a doctor, and there was no bowdlerising of his interviews with his lady patients. The few things he left unsaid were reserved for another character, who came in as a house-agent with the most extraordinary fund of questions imaginable. But the entertainment hit the popular taste, evidently, for the more broad the remarks, with no attempt at wit, the more the "little brown sisters" laughed, in true Oriental manner.

I got very bored and tired, but did not like to go out till the first playlet was finished, for fear of hurting our hosts' feelings. We afterwards heard from a friend that when the second piece was over, the floor was cleared for a *baile*, which was kept up till quite the early hours of the morning. In the middle of this dance, however, "a strange thing happened," as a certain number of the hosts suddenly appeared with little plates to collect money for the expenses of the production. This manœuvre, as our friend expressed it to us, "knocked many of the guests completely out of time," for the average person does not take much money to a dance. Some wrote little *vales*; but our friend was rather sharp, for when a girl held out a plate to him, he bowed very politely and took it from her, saying, "Pray let me help you," and so became a collector instead of a contributor.

We went a new walk through the town a few evenings ago, on a lovely night, when the grey streets were all black and white in the moonlight, but the shadows quite luminous and the sky a real blue, dark and velvety. We strolled down one or two streets and through a group of native huts by the shore; but that part of the shore is some way from here, as, you see, we were walking across the spit of land formed by the estuary and the open sea.

In our walk we came to a walled-in graveyard, with an open grille in the great doorway, through which one could see a little chapel and green trees, looking very dark green in the moonlight. On the opposite side, across the rough, sandy road, was a high, broken wall of concrete, with a big iron gate, and apparently nothing but the sea beyond it. We wondered what the gate could lead to, and thought there must be some garden on the shore; but when we went up the one or two crumbling steps, we found ourselves at once on the beach, and at our feet a quantity of ruined graves, some half-opened, some newly-covered, all jumbled up in the moonlight, and strewn with rank grass, sand, and pebbles. It seemed so weird and uncanny, the great, strong wall shutting in nothing; and the tall gates leading to nothing; and we afterwards learnt that this was the Chinese graveyard, which is always being destroyed by storms, and the wall had suffered in the bombardment. I don't suppose the Chinese use it much, as they always get their bodies sent back to China if they can, in huge, gaily-painted coffins, for burial in their native soil.

I forget if I told you about the trouble we have been having with our cook—the voluble person I described to you when he was new and interesting. Now I know that type of Filipino so well! As time went on the cook's easy flow of talk became less interesting, especially as it took the place of cooking, and I got tired of always telling him to do his best, for he was one of those half-clever people who always do things just not as well as they could do them. Whenever I reproved him, too, I found a stranger in the kitchen next day, who told me that he had been sent to take the place of my cook, who was ill "with his leg."

Always his leg. Though no human ingenuity could find out what he was supposed to have the matter with his leg. I was inclined to think it was a "sulk leg," but C—— observed darkly that he had heard before of fellows getting "drink legs." On these occasions the cook's wife was generally to be found—a pleasant-faced little woman, in a bright, clean dress, and wearing long, gold earrings—squatting on her heels, outside the hall-door, smoking a huge cigar. The moment I appeared she always repeated the information about the leg, with apologies, and vanished.

When the cook had recovered from his indisposition, he would take up his place in the kitchen, affable and fluent as ever, and no remarks would be made by anybody, for I put up with him as long as I could on account of his generally being sober—a rare and precious virtue. At last, however, when I was ill he surpassed himself in crime, sending in uneatable food to poor neglected C——, and giving me the same soup and rissoles every day, twice a day, for a fortnight, till I could not even bear the smell of them.

When C—— remonstrated, the cook instantly became impudent, and as impudence is where C—— draws the forbearing line with Filipinos, he gave the cook one good kick that sent him sprawling out on to the Azotea. C—— observed that if the cook summoned him for assault, he would half kill him next time, but our friend did not resort to Law. He gathered himself up and went off, and was no more seen again, though he sent the usual stop-gap to do his work next day. However, we had no intention of letting him farm our kitchen, so we asked the stop-gap, who was an excellent cook, if he would like to stay on permanently, and he said he would, and there he is "to this very day," as they say in books.

The change has made a great difference in my housekeeping, both socially and materially. By socially I mean that I now have a quiet, silent, intelligent man to deal with instead of a chattering, cunning monkey; and by materially, that this man caters for us infinitely better for a *peso*, including firewood, than the other gem did for a *peso* and a half a day. He is willing to learn—real learning, not jabbering "*mi sabe, mi sabe*," and then sending in the things all wrong—so I have got out my English cookery-book and explained many of our ways of preparing various foods, which he has grasped with intelligence and admirable results.

We are in great tribulation about ice, as a deadlock has occurred by which we are without any in this hot season—a most serious and horrible discomfort. From the beginning we, like everyone else, got our daily ten pounds of ice from the Government factory—the military supply—which came round every morning in the cart driven by the Stage Cowboy whom I think I described to you. When this cart pulled up and the handsome driver sang out "Hielo" (Ice!), servants flew out from all the houses and presented a ticket, each man secured his nice cold lump and rushed upstairs again to put it in the ice-chest.

But a month or more ago an American with a "pull" (political influence) got the municipal contract to supply this town with ice, to be worked in connection with the electric lighting of the streets, also placed in his control, on which the Government withdrew their supply so as not to interfere with private enterprise.

So far, so good. But the "'cute" financier had got an old electric plant, which works so badly that the arc-lights are extinguished and the streets are pitch dark at night. The ice has given out altogether. The financier, still being paid out of the rates, has gone off to Manila, and there is no redress anywhere, for he has a relative high up in office, is received everywhere, and—in fact he has a "pull."

The Government won't renew their supply of ice except to the Americans and the clubs. A few other people who have influence have managed to get a lump now and then, but for the greater part we struggle on, at 90° in the shade, with tepid water to drink, food decaying before the evening, and butter—even tinned train-oil butter—a thing of the past.

Such a state of affairs is not so astounding out here, however, as it may sound to you, for though you may have heard of the corruption of American political life, it does not strike one with such force when read in papers as when it comes home to you in daily life like this.

Even out here there seems to be no sense of that *noblesse oblige*, which alone can keep the ruling race upright before the eyes of the "little brown brother," for one cannot take up a Manila paper without seeing the case of some Provincial Treasurer, or someone tried for official swindling.

Each town or district is controlled by a *Presidente*, a Filipino, something like a mayor, who, in his turn, is under the guidance of an American, called a Provincial

Treasurer. Far from being an example of integrity, the Provincial Treasurer is very often anything but proof against the temptations that beset him financially. It is not hearsay; there are the actual police reports in the papers. And if those found out and brought to justice are so many, one can only speculate in amazement upon the numbers who escape, or are sheltered by influence or a "pull."

It does seem such a pity that a great and noble nation should not be better represented in the eyes of another—and, when all is said and done—an inferior race.

LETTER XX.

FILIPINO INDOLENCE—A DROUGHT

ILOILO, *March 31, 1905.*

Many thanks for your letter of February 23rd. We were greatly interested in your description of the radium baths, though it seems difficult, out here, to imagine that there is anyone anywhere taking so much trouble to get hot! I must say, though, that I don't feel this heat quite so much as one might imagine, at least, as far as actually feeling hot goes. For an evening or two ago I was quite surprised, when we were in Hoskyn's stores, to notice that the thermometer was marking 92° Fahrenheit. Of course that was in the cool of the evening, but I had not noticed any particular heat during the day. I thought how much it would interest you to get some idea of the temperature we live in, so we bought a thermometer and have hung it up in the *sala*. In a way, I am sorry we have done this, as we did not know before how hot we really were, and did not mind the heat half so much.

A watering-cart has begun operations, and as I write, it is passing down the street. It is a most amusing contrivance, consisting of a *carabao* waggon with a cask laid longways on it, and a native sitting astride the *carabao*, guiding with a goad and one string. The water flows out of a bamboo pole at the back of the barrel, and a spray is produced by means of a circle of holes, through which the water squirts uncertainly. The only result, as far as the roads are concerned, is a long narrow puddle and a great waste of precious water, though I expect it is sea water they use. The whole contrivance is so amusingly extravagant, shiftless, inefficient—so characteristically Filipino!

À propos of the ways of the natives, a Spanish friend of C——'s, who was here the other day, told us a long and harrowing story, which was to him somewhat of a tragedy, though to me, I am afraid, it was only a source of amusement. This man tried the venture of keeping a small stable of *quilezes* for hire, which is a favourite speculation with young men who want to play with a little capital, either with the idea of trying to keep body and soul together in this expensive country, or else with the perennial hope of being able to get away from it. One of the Englishmen professes to have made a good thing out of it (*quilez*-hiring), but when we told our Spanish friend this hopeful news, he refused to be comforted, and hunched up his shoulders and spread out his hands, saying, "Horses are cheap enough, and fares are high, which is very well from our point of view; but you have the eternal Filipino to deal with."

"What does he do in this case?" we asked.

"He does nothing," said the Spaniard. "In this, as in every other employment, he does not think it necessary to learn, or to know anything at all."

We said we had observed this trait, and that anyone seemed to be confident in signing on for any job, anyhow.

"They do," he said, "and this is the sort of conversation I have with every man who represents himself as a driver. 'Where were you *cochero* before?' I ask.

"'With *señor* L—— at B——.'

"'How long ago was that?'

"'Five years ago.'

"'Where were you *cochero* after that?'

"'Oh, I was not *cochero*. I was cook to *señor* S——.'

"'And then?'

"'Then as *muchacho* with *señor* C——, and then as cook——'

"'And you are a cook, not a *cochero*!'

"'Oh no. *Mi trabajo* (my job) is really a *cochero*, but I went as cook to *señor* L——, and as *muchacho* to *señor* C——, and as——'

"'Yes, yes. I heard what you said.'

"Then, as this is as good a man as you may hope to get, you engage him, and it is a great piece of luck if you get half your fares, and the pony not killed."

This story, and many others I have heard to the same effect, account, in some measure, for the marvellous and eccentric driving one sees going on—one can hardly call it "driving," though, it is simply a rough and tumble with destiny, and there are more street accidents in Iloilo in any given number of hours than in the same time in the whole of London.

It is so Filipino to be content with make-shifts—the same thing, the same lazy Malay, and Spanish *Mañana* in their food, their music, their houses, their work—nothing thorough, nothing complete, no heart put into anything but cock-fighting and talk. I don't suppose any influence could alter these racial faults, certainly not the hasty assimilation of mathematics, electric trams, and ice-cream sodas. They are stupid, too, these people, with the malicious cunning of all stupid people, and cruel—sickeningly cruel.

A night or two ago we went again to the cinématograph, but the evening was rather spoilt by an unpleasant "incident." While C—— was getting the tickets, I sat on an empty bench by the wall, whereupon a common native boy came and sat down beside me.

I got up and walked away, for there were plenty of other benches empty, and I knew this was only an act of impudence. When C—— came back with the tickets and saw what had happened, he was simply furious, wanting to kick the fellow out of the place, and pretty well out of the world too! "You should have sat there," he said, "and beckoned to me to kick the brute out."

But I implored him to let the thing pass unnoticed. "For," I said, "if you touch him you know he will summons you, and the case will go against you. Besides, according to the customs of the country, the man was not doing any harm, for he thought I was an American, and his equal."

Whereupon C—— exploded; but luckily the door of the show was just opening, so I got him to hurry in to secure good seats, and the "incident" passed off. But when one thinks of the social status of the coloured person in America!—Words fail me!

We are having more drought now—the rain-water tanks empty, and the well-water brackish. We filter the latter, even to make tea with, which makes the tea more palatable; but for washing, it is like using sand-paper on the skin, and after soap has been used the water remains perfectly clear, with the soap in a woolly cloud at the bottom. I wish some millionaire philanthropist would take it into his benevolent head to help his country with this "Trust from Heaven," as they call the development of the Philippines, and begin with building an aqueduct from the hills into its second largest town! However, the 40-acre law would stop any extensive enterprise of that or any other sort.[6]

Water is being brought over from Guimaras and sold in the streets at fabulous prices, only I am happy to say we have been lucky enough, so far, to secure a daily supply out of a friend's well, sufficient to get along with if we are careful.

All this time I have not told you our great piece of news, which is that we have bought a horse and trap—or rather a pony and a *calesa*—a sort of small dog-cart, with big, spidery wheels, to seat two, which tips up unless a third person, generally the groom, is sitting on a small perch behind. This is a very light and comfortable trap, and the pony an exceptionally good one, both being the property of an American officer we know who is going to Manila and selling off his effects. It is a great stroke of luck to get hold of such a turn-out, and we are to enter into possession in ten days or so, or possibly longer. I shall be glad to drive, as it is not very pleasant for ladies to walk about the town, owing to the way the Filipinos have of shoving white people off the footpath, when there is one, and expectorating as close as they dare.

---

[6] The Government owns 60,000,000 acres; but no non-Filipino can obtain more than 40 acres, and no corporation may hold more than 2500 acres. Five years after the passing of this law, that is in 1907, all corporate lands owned in excess of this amount and under cultivation must be disposed of or forfeited.

LETTER XXI.

THE WHARVES—AN OLD SPANIARD

ILOILO, *April 9, 1905.*

Many thanks for the book about carpentry, which arrived quite safely by this mail, and is a treasury of delight to C——, who has got all sorts of ideas out of it. One of the first things he did was to swarm up the box-room door, getting through a flap in the matting ceiling and up into the roof, to see what hold there would be to fix up a punkah over the dinner-table. All the English people, and many of the Americans, have punkahs in the dining-room, but we have not troubled about one so far, as we are so lucky in our splendid draught through the hall, right across the dinner-table. Now, however, the Monsoon is changing, and with the wind this other side of the house, we want a punkah badly, for, you see, if you get out of a draught here you nearly suffocate.

A PHILIPPINE PONY.

C—— said it was like a huge hall up in the roof, and fearfully hot, which I could quite believe, as the thermometer in the dark, airy rooms below stood at 91°. Many of the houses have a sort of small top roof, like a little hat, with a wide gap, which acts as a ventilator, and lets off this heat out of the space above the ceilings; but, of course, the corrugated iron always makes a dreadfully hot roof, however it is treated. The only cool, healthy, and reasonable houses are the native ones of palm thatch, but they are so very inflammable and dangerous that no company will insure them. Though the way the native huts are lighted with naked, flaring lights or rickety lamps, and remain unburnt for two hours, is a marvel and a never ceasing source of interest to us when we go about after dark. In each grass-covered *carabao*-cart, too, there is a flaring torch by way of complying with the lighting regulations, and when one sees them jolting and swaying along, it is impossible to imagine why the regulations are not exceeded by the whole cart going along in a blaze.

We went a walk last night, down this street, through the Plaza Libertad, and down two more streets to the Muelle Loney, the quay along the estuary. As C—— had come back from the office late, we did not have tea till sunset, and by the time we went out it was nearly dark, and the moon had not risen. The Muelle was all deep shadows and spots of light, and the lamps in La Paz, the suburb the other side of the river, made long reflections of yellow light in the dark water, while the masts and sails of the ships at anchor stood out like Indian ink-drawings against the deep blue sky. All along the quay are offices of business houses, stevedores, customs, etc., and vast *camarins* (warehouses) with low, corrugated iron roofs, and open in front with iron bars like colossal menagerie cages. Inside the *camarins* could be seen shadowy piles of sacks of sugar, which is to be detected by a certain heavy, sweet, nauseous smell.

The quay itself is a very wide road, with a stone wall going into the river—the latter deep enough to allow steamers of a fair size, such as the *Kai-Fong* and the *Butuan*, to come up and lie at anchor opposite the wharves and *camarins*, as I told you when I went to Manila. There are a lot of curious, rusty old steamers huddled together at the side of the quay, with open decks and fixed iron awnings, which ply between here and Negros, and other neighbouring islands; little launches belonging to the offices; and the big steamers that go to Manila and Hong Kong, which all look quite commonplace by daylight, but seemed very mysterious in the darkness, with a light burning here and there, and always the tinkle of a guitar, and a voice singing softly in a minor key.

There was one big, dark bulk, larger than the others, which was a Hong Kong steamer, and we heard the funny, quacking jabber of the Chinese crew on the fo'c'sle. They can't get ashore in the Philippines, as a guard is placed on the gangway, and the captain is liable to a fine of 2000 dollars if a Chinaman escapes ashore. Now and then one reads in the Manila papers about a Chinaman without a passport having been caught, sentenced to a few months of Bilibid prison, and returned to Hong Kong. As we passed the Chinese steamer, I could not help thinking how tantalising it must be for such keen, industrious men to be almost on the soil of this Eldorado of lazy natives and high wages. The few who do enter, as I told you, make fortunes very quickly, or what is a fortune to them, as well as the fortunes of those who employ them. It is most unfortunate that popular opinion in the far-away U.S.A. is so dead set against this source of prosperity and revenue.

At intervals along the Muelle, with its jumble of dark buildings on one side and jumble of dark ships on the other, in front of the offices and *camarins*, and at the corners of the little dark alleys that turn off into the town, were numbers of little stalls, each with a flaring naphtha light, round which natives were sitting about laughing and talking, and chewing betel-nut, and haggling for hours over the price of some little bunch of eggplant, or a tiny, insanitary fish. The wares were laid out on flat rush trays—bananas, maize, horrible-looking toffee, native fruits, and tumblers of pink *tuba*—a drink made of the sap of the palm tree coloured red. The stall-keeper was invariably a little brown native woman, with a huge cigar in her thick-lipped mouth—not such cigars as are sold at home, but a loose bundle of tobacco leaves about four times the size of the largest cigar you ever saw, and tied round with cotton or fibre. The way their mouths stick out beyond their noses when they are pulling at these big "weeds" makes their flat faces look very funny. I saw a native girl the other day, walking round the Plaza at Jaro, in a very tight *sarong* and freshly-starched *camisa*, puffing at a big black cigar all coming to pieces and tied up with white cotton, and her swaggering gait, and the way she looked to right and left for admiration, displaying a profile with absolutely no nose, was one of the most comical things I have ever had the luck to see.

There are always any amount of natives along the Muelle in the evening, for it is a favourite lounge, and they make such picturesque groups, loafing about the stalls or lying against the walls in deep thought or opium. Their voices are subdued, and they are all perfectly good-humoured, and another point about such a crowd here is that there is no smell from them, for the clothes of the poorest Filipino are spotlessly white and clean, and their bodies carefully washed. One or two costumes made up from empty sacks amused us very much, and they are really very effective, for the wearers imagine the names on them to be a pattern, and arrange the rows of letters quite carefully, generally across the back and chest. Beyond the offices and ships we came to immense mud-flats, which are partially covered at high tide, and look quite nice when they are a sheet of shallow water, but appear depressing, and smell nasty when they are bare. The tide was far out, and the rising moon showed up a lot of curious tracks and channels, with planks across them, and in the distance the backs of some of the houses in the town. Such a desolate place! The spot to which one would think sick animals would crawl when they feel they are going to die.

A lot of little native boys were rushing and screaming about in a remote corner, their short shirts fluttering behind them, playing some mysterious, meaningless game, revolving round certain heaps of manure and dead dogs. The little chaps seemed happy enough, but they looked so uncanny, like little black and white imps in the moonlight.

In time, I daresay, all this desolate waste will be reclaimed and built over, for someone told me that the Harbour Company are filling it up with dredgings. In Manila I saw a vast mud-flat being reclaimed in the same way by harbour-dredging, and the flattened, finished part had lines drawn on it, which I was told were the ground plans of streets and houses. It seems so strange to go on building the towns out on the mud-flats in a climate like this, when there are acres and acres of native huts standing on sound land a few feet above the sea-level. I asked a man who has lived here many years why this was done, and he told me that it was because of the great cost of transport, owing to the high rate of wages, which would take away all profit if one had one's shops and *camarins* far from the water's edge. I said I thought it must be very unhealthy on the mud.

"Absolutely fatal," he said. "But then, you see, it is a toss-up between a chance of fever on the mud and a certainty of starvation in the town."

I enjoy the walks about very much, or rather, I am more interested and amused than exhilarated; but all the same I am looking forward so to having our trap and going for drives, and even though there are only two roads, still we shall be able to get out of the town. I keep thinking that it is spring at home—or rather, I try not to think of it! How one longs to see a bunch of daffodils or a snow-drop; to hear a blackbird sing; to see beautiful oaks and elms coming into leaf instead of these eternal green palms, and to feel fresh and invigorating air instead of this everlasting swelter and sun!

We have a queer old neighbour here, an ancient Spaniard, who lives on the ground-floor of a house, in two rooms which are, so C—— tells me, hung with pictures of Isabella and the King; medals on velvet, framed and glazed; and certificates and memorials, for he was once some official in the Royal Household of Spain.

He is a courtly and dignified old person, though about 4 feet 6 in height, and as broad as he is long. He is very poor, and when he can sell some piece of land, he is going back to Spain to die.

This personage came to call on me a few evenings ago, on account of having on a black evening suit, as he had been to a funeral. We stumbled along in Spanish, and would have done better if my guest had not persisted in trying to remember French so as to convince me that he really had been in Paris. However, we got on very well, and I showed him some of papa's sketches of Spain, which enchanted the poor old thing. Over the Alhambra he waxed quite sentimental, with his head on one side and one podgy hand raised to heaven. Of course the fact of my having been in his native land made me quite charming, and compliments bloomed like spring-flowers in the gardens of the Vega.

He had told C—— that he wished to come and pay his respects, as he had heard that the *señora* had good *custumbres*, which is a Spanish word for good breeding and good manners—not that I mean the two can be separated, but that the expression conveys those two, in a sort of way. This fact he repeated to me again, with much decorative compliment, and many assurances that I did not look the least like an Englishwoman—and oh, no! not a bit like a Frenchwoman—and still less like an Italian! Anyone would know at once that I must be a Spaniard—and from the southern land, where the women are elegant as flowers, and their eyes speak of love.

At last he backed himself out, still showering compliments, and offering to teach me "*la lengua Castellana.*" His Spanish was beautiful to listen to, so round and full and correct, and he implored me, with his hands clasped, not to learn the language of "*los Indianos,*" as I told you the Spaniards call the Filipinos.

All the Spaniards here long and yearn for Spain, and everything Spanish, which is only natural, I suppose. They hate the Archipelago, as they call it, but confess that the prospect of continuing to earn a living here ties them by the leg.

Another old Spanish friend of C——'s, a man in business, amused me very much one day, by giving me, as one of his reasons for disliking the Philippines, that he was in constant terror of "*los Indianos*" coming and "click"—he drew his finger across his throat.

"Really?" I said. "But you don't, honestly, think that, do you?"

"*Señora*," he said, "I *know* it will happen some day. There will be such an uprising as will wipe us all out. *Mi corazon*" (my heart) "beats perpetually with terror."

I thought, however, that this life of secret anguish could not have done much harm to the old fellow's system, for he looked remarkably flourishing after thirty years of life in the tropics, without any idea of panic at all.

As to this panic, I am surprised to find how prevalent is this notion of a general uprising, for though the Philippines are full of Insurrection, and many of them in a state of open warfare, still one can hardly believe that a reign of horror could sweep over these slow little towns. Not that the Filipinos are not capable of any atrocities when roused—and in the War many terrible and horrible things happened, which are not printed in newspapers or found in books.

LETTER XXII.

A TRIP TO GUIMARAS—AN ASTONISHING PROPOSAL—HOUSEBUILDING

ILOILO, *April 14, 1905.*

Yesterday, Sunday, we had the launch offered us, so we arranged a little trip in the cool of the evening.

We drove down to the Muelle Loney (too hot to walk at five o'clock), and when we had got on board the launch and seated ourselves in basket chairs in the bows, she steamed down the river and the estuary, and out into the channel. There was a fresh breeze blowing, and the air was delicious. As to the scenery—words fail me! The blue and green of the sea, and the mauve and rose lights reflected on Guimaras from the brilliant sunset behind us over the Panay Mountains, were like some wonderful picture wrought in amethysts and sapphires and exquisite enamels, while all along the shore line the groves of palm trees glowed in the strong light like a border of emeralds set in golden sand.

We crossed over, going close to the opposite shore, with the object of visiting an old steamer which lies over by the quarries from which they are getting the stone to build the harbour. This steamer used to be a French packet, and was bought cheap by some Spaniards for inter-island traffic, but the owners soon found she burnt her head off with coal, and did not pay for her keep, so now they are trying to sell her, and she has lain out there at anchor for a year or more; a fine old boat, with splendid saloons and cabins all rotting away.

We climbed up the rickety gangway and came up upon what looked like the ship of the Ancient Mariner or the Flying Dutchman, all still and silent, everything ready as if for use, but worn and rotten with the sun and weather. We went all over her, into the saloon with its long table of handsome, polished wood and ghostly chairs with high, carved backs; and into the cabins where the closed scuttles were dark with dirt, and there was a musty smell like bones, and our own reflections in the cracked green mirrors made us jump. C—— said he was sure there must be a forgotten skeleton of a pirate in one of the dingy bunks hidden by close-drawn curtains of faded green cloth, and really, the prospect of something of the sort seemed so inevitable that I did not dare look in one of them!

We came out on the deck again, which looked quite a cheerful place after those spectral saloons and cabins, and we saw the galley, with dead fireplaces, and wandered on the bridge, up a very unsafe companion. Old Tuyay had scrambled off the launch after us and followed everywhere, struggling and slipping up and down stairs and ladders, smelling about, and getting stuck somewhere every now and then, and having to be helped and hauled by the collar.

When we got back to the launch, there was still enough daylight to make a *paseo* along the coast a little way. We went so close to the land that we could see right into lovely little bays, where palm-thatch huts stood amongst the groves and the white sands, and tiny figures were walking about or wading in the shallows for fish. It all looked exactly as it must have appeared on some fine evening, when the first Spanish navigators or Captain Cook came sailing along in their big three-deckers, while the people ran away into the jungles and began sharpening their arrows at the sight of a white face.

We said to each other how much we should like to be Navigators, and go about in fine ships and land in undiscovered islands, and, if we escaped the arrows, fire a rifle or take a photograph, and be made kings for being so clever. Instead of doing that, however, we steamed back to Iloilo when darkness fell, and on landing, went to the Plaza Libertad, where a band was playing a two-step.

This band which performs twice a week, on Thursdays and Sundays, from about half-past five to eight, is a new and delightful institution. It is not due to any enterprise on the part of the authorities, military or civil, but is a purely native enterprise, consisting of a number of Filipinos who have collected themselves together under the title of *La Banda de Musica Popular*. They started the notion of playing in the Plaza twice a week if they could raise enough subscriptions, whereupon we all paid up at once, promising to make the same contribution every month in so good a cause. I think our share, personally, comes to about 2 *pesos* a month, and it is really well worth it, for now the band is an institution, and a very good one too. They have not got a very extensive programme—some marches, a few "coon" tunes, an overture or two, and some dance music—but they play with spirit, and with the marches they are particularly successful. It is very creditable, too, when one thinks that this is a brass band, for the only instruments the Filipinos are really proficient with are the mandoline and guitar.

It is a great pity that the American authorities left this very important affair to drift so that the natives themselves, in sheer desperation, started a band depending upon public charity. I am not exaggerating in calling it important, for the Filipinos, like all other Orientals, can understand and be ruled by tangible and visible signs of the ways of a ruling people; but the empty bandstands in the towns, and the dull, colourless lack of ceremonies or ceremonial of the American *régime* have had an extremely bad effect, though the Filipinos are laughed at for wanting the gay, courteous Spaniards back again. Not only is this fact patent, but I have heard the people say so, and they are accused of being unreasonable about wanting the Spaniards back again after having got rid of them; but really, quite apart from their not having courted foreign rule at all, and loathing the usurpation of the Americans, the Filipinos have something to complain of in the lack of all that pomp which an Oriental loves and understands. The American Ideal is noble, grand—but it cannot be compressed into an Oriental brain. I can't make myself better understood than by asking you to picture what India would be if the durbars were stage-managed by Americans!

We delight in the band evenings, when we sit and watch the groups of natives walking about under the pretty trees; the fat mothers with coveys of slim, dark-haired daughters in fresh muslin frocks; the young Filipino "mashers" in white suits with straw hats worn daringly on one side, and long, thin, tight boots, trying to hide their shyness by a lot of swagger with a walking-stick; and all the little comedies and flirtations that go on. I have hardly ever seen any white people there except ourselves; a newly-married American couple who sit in the dark shadows very close together, and some American soldiers in khaki and turned-up *sombreros*. The programmes always end with "The Star-Spangled Banner," on which we stand up and C—— takes his hat off, but the American soldiers unfortunately seldom trouble to salute their Anthem—and as to the Filipinos, they remain truculently seated with their hats on. It makes one feel rather foolish to be the only ones to take any notice, but C—— insists.

We have now entered into possession of our trap and pony, and have had some blissful drives along the eternal roads to Jaro and Molo, out in the sunset and back in the starlight or moonlight, skimming along on rubber tyres. Tracks that we used to *tear* down when anyone lent us a carriage are now rigorously tabooed! Everyone here drives top-speed, and the Filipinos all crawl about the roads, and never dream of getting out of the way unless one shouts out a native word—"Tabé!"—when they just move enough to avoid instant death like a clever matador in a bull-fight. The curious thing is we have more trouble with the natives who are walking *towards* us instead of those going the same way. That may sound strange to you, and even incredible, but if you knew the Philippines and the Filipinos you would understand that it could not be otherwise. This element is very exciting, and makes an ordinary evening-drive to Molo rather better than a trip on a fire-engine in Piccadilly.

I quite forgot to tell you that some time ago an unknown man was announced and walked into the *sala*, in the evening, just before C—— came home. This person was an American, of about thirty, with rather a good-looking face and the usual thick, long hair parted in the middle. He bowed and said:

"Mis' Darncey, I guess?"

I said Mrs Dauncey was my name.

"Is your husband to home?"

I said he was not, and began to get alarmed, for I thought the man had come to tell me of some accident to C——; but he soon reassured me by telling me he guessed I could tell him what he wanted to know, which was whether we had a spare room, as he was looking for a family for himself and his wife to board with.

I nearly fell down flat with amazement, but I managed, I hope, not to show my surprise, for I remembered that the Americans live out here in "messes," often several families together, and I reflected that this touting must be some curious custom of which I had not heard. So I said, quite politely, that I was very sorry, but I was afraid this house was only large enough for ourselves.

"Oh," he said, with a great deal of bowing, but no intention of going away, "I heard this was a big house and reckoned you didn't fill it."

"We have a room empty," I said, "in fact we have two, but I am afraid my husband would never *hear* of such a thing as anyone we did not know, or any friend, either, coming to live with us."

"Oh, that's all right," he said. "My wife is in a *quilez* downstairs, and I can fetch her up to see you and look at the rooms."

At this fresh and astounding announcement, I gasped. But I kept my temper, and replied that I thought he need not disturb his wife, for we had really no intention of taking anyone to live in our house; but the man would not be convinced, and argued the point, saying that he had been to six other people, and he was "fair tired of going around."

I was wondering how to get rid of him, for he was so remarkably oily and polite, and kept on saying ma'am every two words. But just then C—— came home, and when the visitor introduced himself, with explanations of his mission, C—— flushed up, and I began to be afraid he would kick the man out. But luckily the American was quick enough to see there was no mistaking the few words C—— said, nor the manner in which he said them in, and he bowed himself out in a about two seconds.

A strange story? But stranger still is the fact that this was not a common man—I mean his position was not what we call common—as C—— has found out that he is an official high up in the Customs service, and lately married to a schoolma'am. And stranger still is the fact that the Americans to whom I have told this story can see nothing odd in it at all.

I can't suppose that such peculiar customs really prevail in the United States, and that if C—— were to call on the President's wife, as they are all equals, and leave me in a cab below while he asked her if she took in boarders, that he would not get into trouble. Fancy if this man made a big fortune out here, and we called on him in his mansion in New York and insisted on taking rooms in it—the idea is preposterous—but *why*?

After this person had departed, we soothed our excited nerves by sitting on the balcony and watching one of the eternally beautiful sunsets. I will describe it to you, for it is very much the same every evening, with varying shades of intensity. The sky behind the palms in the distance was deep orange, fading into rose, and overhead into apple-green blue. We went through the house and out on to the Azotea, and all the sky on that side was like a radiant, pale amethyst, with a big bright moon rising—a great silver shield—through the lilac and rosy mist; the water a deep sapphire blue; and Guimaras a brilliant green outline dividing the sea and sky. The tide was in, and the water came up to the wall at the end of the garden, where a sheep was nibbling grass at the end of its tether, perfectly indifferent to a fool of a puppy, which ran backwards and forwards barking at its heels. In the empty stables on each side of our own is a regular camp of poor people, who were lounging by the well, watching one or two naked brown babies playing on the ground. They all looked so peaceful and happy and so picturesque in the sunset and moonlight, that we agreed with each other that perhaps life in the Philippines might be quite pleasant if one only lived the right way and had a brown skin covered by a minimum of clothes.

They are a singularly happy people, these Filipinos, when they are unspoilt by the advantages of civilisation. One never sees or hears people quarrelling, and they are so kind to their children—always laughing and chattering and showing their fine white teeth, so that to watch a group of poor people is always a pleasure. We have been amused for a long time by the spectacle of a house that is being built in the suburbs, a stately go-as-you-please undertaking that is being gone through in an amusingly characteristic manner. They begin a house by constructing the roof, all lashed with *bejuco*, and very neatly put together, which sits on the ground an indefinite time. Then the *arigis*—the posts of bamboo or hard wood—are put in position, and a floor is made about 15 or 20 feet from the earth. Our friends on the Molo road got so far, and then started to live in the bit that was finished, camping in a sort of tent on the split-cane floor, with the roof lying alongside on the ground. I daresay they were "out" of *nipa* thatch, and did not dare to trust the building out of their sight, for the town-dwelling Filipinos are shocking thieves and burglars. Whatever their reason was, there they lived for quite a long time, till at last we were quite relieved to see them begin to put thatch on the framework. Then, one day when we passed we saw that the roof had also been thatched and hoisted into place, though how this latter feat was brought about I don't know, as we unfortunately missed that part of the operations; but I have been told that, when the roof has been thatched, it is raised and put in position by sheer human force and much advice and swearing.

LETTER XXIII.

A TROPICAL SHOWER—OUR SERVANTS—FILIPINO CUSTOMS

ILOILO, *April 27, 1905.*

Nothing from you by the mail to-day. The forwarding from Manila seems to be so unsatisfactory that we think you had better begin sending letters straight to this place. The address for the future, therefore, will be to us to—P.O. Box 140, Iloilo. You have to put this, as there is no delivery of letters—a most strange and tiresome system. In the outside wall of the post-office is a recess with a number of pigeon holes, some glazed, some shut with a flap, each with its own lock and key, of which the owner keeps a duplicate. On the wall outside is a blackboard where the arrivals and departures of mails are chalked up, and when you see a mail has come in, you go off and do a sort of "bran-pie" dip in your pigeon hole to see what you get out.

To-day we have had a very heavy thunderstorm, which has filled the tanks and cooled the air, the thermometer having gone down from 90° to 82°. The rain came on just as I was dressing after my *siesta*, so I hurried on a dressing-gown and went out on to the Azotea to see about the pipe, as it was no good blowing my whistle for a servant in the noise of the storm and the terrific din of the rain upon the iron roofs.

I found Sotero having a glorious time with a petroleum can, which people use here for all water-carrying, like we used to see them do in Palestine. This can was fixed to a line, and the *muchacho* was risking his neck to let it down so as to intercept the overflow of a roof gutter belonging to the people below, and filling every tin, jug, and bath the house possessed, all spread out on the Azotea; giving the concrete floor of the Azotea itself a liberal wash-down at the same time. He was hopping about the balcony, face beaming and clothes dripping wet, and I laughed as I thought of the conventional idea of an English butler! He is a very good butler, all the same, or has learnt to be one, for when he came to us he did not know how to lay a table; while now, if we give a dinner, he insists on arranging everything himself, and does it perfectly, even to folding the serviettes in fancy shapes, which he has got some other servant to teach him.

All round I hear stories of the miseries and terrors people go through with their Filipino servants, and "the inevitable *muchacho*" is a standing joke in the American papers. But our retainers just jog along in perfect peace, always in the house, always clean and tidy; and as to their work, not only not shirking it, but improving every day, and always ready and willing to give any help in the stables, or anything they can think of. I agree with my friends that we have been very lucky in finding such excellent "boys," but I must take a little credit to myself too, for having treated them with the utmost consideration and politeness, showing them things patiently over and over again, and never once speaking sharply or angrily. I am sure they appreciate such treatment instead of the way in which I see people scolding and cursing their *muchachos*, and that our having such good and trustworthy servants is not entirely due to random luck in choosing them.

Now the rain has come. We shall have mosquitoes again—they had almost disappeared in this long drought, but an hour or two after a shower the place is humming with them again.

Yesterday was Palm Sunday, on account of which a procession was going about of all sorts of people carrying palm branches, headed by a *banda de musica* playing "Hiawatha," and in the midst a large cart covered with coloured paper, bearing an image of some sort; all very tawdry and crude, and not in the least picturesque.

In the evening, when we drove into Jaro, we saw some Negritos from the mountains inland—the aborigines who sometimes come down into the towns on such occasions of *Fiesta* to do a little trading, and beg and pick up what they can. These people are very small, much smaller even than the Filipinos, who are so little; and they have quite black skins, irregular faces of real nigger type, with big heads of fuzzy black hair, like Bescharins. They were all very dirty and ragged, and looked very skinny and miserable beside the plump Malay town's-people, and those we saw were begging from door to door, and from everyone they met, poor souls.

Sometimes in the Filipino race a child is born with curly locks instead of the usual black, straight, Chinese-looking hair, and this curliness is considered a great beauty, and tremendously admired; which is very strange, as, of course, such a trait is only a reversion to some strain of the despised Negrito; but the Filipinos are far too stupid to know that. In fact, if the hair is so curly as to be positively woolly, they are more pleased than ever.

On *Fiesta* days, too, certain beggars appear, sitting by the roads displaying horrible deformities, and praying away at an amazing rate, sometimes with a child to run out and beg for them. It is a simple, unsophisticated idea, that of having your begging done for you, but I don't know that the custom is confined to Filipinos.

A day or two ago an American described to me an incident of Filipino life, which I thought very characteristic of this people. She told me that after she first came here, she was sitting in the house one day, when she heard a band coming along the street playing a rattling two-step march, so she rushed to the window and pushed the shutter aside to see the fun, which turned out to be a funeral, with a pale blue coffin, decorated with garlands in carved wood painted pink.

I asked her if she thought the people imagined the occasion to be a festive one; but she said no, that they simply did not know one sort of tune from another, she thought, for they were walking along in the most approved mourning style, and as to the coffin, it was only the Filipino idea of taste. It is curious to think what a very thin veneer of our civilisation these people have acquired, and how they would shed it all as easily as my little lizard has cast off his old coat; and would probably, as he does, feel infinitely lighter and jollier in the primitive covering underneath.

LETTER XXIV.

EASTER FESTIVITIES

ILOILO, *April 24, 1905.*

This is Easter Monday, and since Thursday the town has been crammed full of people—natives—and alive with processions. We got a double allowance of the latter, as the Aglipayanos turned out in full force—fuller force, in fact, than the Orthodox, and their marching and counter-marching was most interesting, even if a little confusing.

We are having holidays, of course, but a holiday here is never very complete, as the different religions go their own way, and now, for instance, the Chinese shops are all open; but the Spanish and *Mestizo* establishments are shut, while the Englishmen have all gone away, except a few juniors left in charge. One party has gone shooting, and they were very anxious for C—— to accompany them, but he did not like to leave me alone here, and refused. There is plenty of good shooting—wild duck, snipe, etc.—but some way inland, and the difficulty is to get there, when you are a busy man, with only forty-eight hours to spare at rare intervals.

À propos of shooting, C—— has only *now* got his gun back from the Customs! It was detained by endless dilatoriness and delays, and the finding of the sureties, which I described to you. There was more trouble and fuss and worry about that gun and my little revolver than you, who have not been in this country, would believe. Such a lot of signing of papers, taking of oaths, and so forth! all of which precautions seem remarkable and rather superfluous in a "perfectly peaceful and contented country."

Well, C—— tried to console himself for not going shooting by playing lawn-tennis at the Bank, where a very good court has been marked out in a field at the back of the house, by the estuary. That gives you a little hint of the climate, does it not? A grass lawn-tennis court in the hot season?

We walked to the Bank and back, as the pony had gone to be shod, and on our way home we were stopped in the Plaza by crowds of people evidently waiting for a procession to pass. We got across the road as best we could, and up into the garden in the middle of the Plaza, where we managed to get a foothold amongst a line of people—all natives of the poorer classes—standing on the low wall. Just as we got there the procession began to come past—a long double file of women in black skirts and black or white *camisas*; the men in mourning, which is an ordinary swallow-tail evening suit. This was Good Friday, and the Emblems of the Passion were borne aloft, draped in black, while the Madonna, carried shoulder-high on a big platform, had on a stiff, black robe; and the whole company was moving slowly along to a guitar and mandoline *banda de musica*, with big crape bows on their instruments, playing slow tunes in minor keys.

What do you think this procession was?—Christ's Funeral! The whole parade was a real funeral procession, and the last thing of all, preceded by acolytes in black, swinging censers with large crape bows on them, and followed by priests in black vestments saying (not chanting) prayers, was a huge black and gold catafalque—the coffin made with glass panels—through which could be seen a wax figure of the dead Christ lying swathed in an embroidered white satin winding-sheet, with a last touch of realism in His head, bound with a blood-stained handkerchief where the Crown of Thorns had rested.

We waited long on the wall of the Alameda while this weird and gruesome procession trailed past, dwindling away down a long, straight street to the right, with its files of bowed figures and its great, black, swaying catafalque.

When we turned to come away, C—— drew my attention to the curious fact that the Cathedral door was shut—a most extraordinary spectacle—which struck me as peculiar at once. At first we could not understand the reason, and thought it must be part of the solemnity. "Perhaps," I said, "they go so far as to take the procession to a cemetery."

"I know!" said C——. "They've shut the doors because these fellows are the Aglipayanos!"

Then it also occurred to us that of course this procession had had the native music, whereas the Orthodox go about to the strains of a brass Constabulary band to show that they are all right with the Government. I must tell you, too, that on these, and all occasions, fights are so frequent between these sects of the followers of Christ that the processions go about with a strong escort of police.

As the tail end of the procession passed, we looked up our street from our vantage point on the wall, and C—— said: "What a pity we are not on our own balcony, as they have made a round, and are coming past the house."

But I thought they could not have had time to do that, slow as they had been, and was sure that what we saw must be the head of the procession passing the other side of the square. It was quite dark by now, and all the mourners carried lighted tapers. The crowd in the square and the procession all seemed hopelessly mixed, but when we at last made our way to the end of our own street, we found that we were both right about the Funeral, for there were two of them—the tail of the Aglipayanos was passing the end of our street, while away up, beyond our house, the road was blocked by the Romanists waiting to let the others go past.

We tried to get up our street, but the R.C. procession had started to come down it, so we took refuge on a flight of stairs through an open doorway. We had a very good view of this Funeral too.

It was just the same style of thing, only with more Spaniards and Eurasians amongst the mourners; and, following the bier of the Christ, a dozen or so of converted Chinamen with their pigtails lopped off. In this procession, too, the priests were white men, but on the other hand, the Aglipayano *padres* are all Filipinos, only we had not been near enough to the first procession to see their faces, which would have shown us at once which sort they were.

The Papists had their drums and trumpets tied with huge black bows, and their catafalque was a still more gloomy erection, set round with large oil lamps in frosted globes, and topped by great bunches of nodding black plumes, like the old prints of the funeral of Wellington.

About midnight we were awakened by the sound of a slow, muffled band and feet shuffling along the road, so we went out on to the balcony, and saw the R.C. procession go trailing past, very solemn and uncanny in the moonlight, with their yellow taper-flames looking like little bits of gold paper in the strong white light. This time they had not the great catafalque with them, which, we imagined, must signify that the Christ was at rest in the tomb.

Next morning, Saturday, things were very quiet, and the town much as usual, except for the crowds of people everywhere, all crawling up and down the streets in very clean clothes, with innumerable tiny children.

Easter Sunday was very gay, beginning with deafening bells well in the dark hours of the morning, when even the cocks had hardly begun to tune up for the day. The great excitement was a children's carnival (at the end of Lent!), got up by the Spanish Club; which event resolved itself into the inevitable procession through the streets, for these people are as inveterate procession-walkers as the Swiss; and whatever comes off, they turn out and walk about the streets, quite conceited and perfectly happy, taking the whole mummery with invulnerable seriousness.

These children were really a very pretty sight, though, and the little things seemed to be enjoying themselves immensely. At about four o'clock they began to assemble, forming up and marching round the Plaza, and then up the Calle Real to the Gobierno (the Government buildings), round the grass plot in front of that building, back and down the street parallel to this, and finally along here, when we saw them from our balcony.

One of the prettiest cars was got up as the Sea, with clouds of pale green and blue tulle, the back of the car a great fan-shaped shell, in which sat a very pretty little *Mestiza* girl dressed as a mermaid, with a long pasteboard tail, and driving two swans. Another was "the world"—a huge globe with the four continents sitting one at each corner; another was a monster basket full of a miscellaneous collection of ballet-fairies, toreadors, Faust and Mephistopheles, gipsies, and so forth, all very solemn and perfectly happy. One tiny person of two years old was dressed as a cupid in pink muslin and roses—such a darling—and one little girl was a funny wee clown, as broad as she was long.

After they had all gone past, we went to the Spanish Club to see the prize-giving, which was very amusing. "Iloilo at a glance" was squeezing and surging about in the big room upstairs, and I thought the floor must cave in; but Mr M——, who is a member of that club, told me it was all right, as they always put props under the floor for a *funcion*, a characteristically Spanish and haphazard idea.

There was a band playing somewhere, and in an alcove a big tea-table spread out, while the whole of one wall was lined with long tables displaying the prizes—really lovely toys.

We walked about, talking to the children, all very keen to show off and explain their costumes, and the mermaid immensely proud of the little wheel on which her tail moved along the floor. One miniature couple in evening dress, looking like grown-up people seen through the wrong end of a telescope, were well worth watching and following about, for neither of them would have sacrificed his or her dignity to a smile for anything in the world.

The prize-giving went by vote, but the poor mites who had not got prizes were consoled by toys doled out in a novel and pretty fashion at the end of the show. I fancy I have seen it somewhere in a cotillon, but can't be sure. From the ceiling hung two huge Japanese umbrellas, with coloured ribbons dangling from each spoke, and when they were lowered at the end, the children filed past underneath, each taking off a ribbon and tearing away to see what present it was good for. We saw the little man, of the couple in evening dress, going about showing off his prize—the first prize, I think it was—which was a beautiful doll. Then, to our astonishment, we found that the couple were a pair of little sisters, Filipinas, of course, for there were, none but Filipino, Spanish, and *Mestizo* children taking part in the *fête*, though all the American Colony, as they call themselves, were in the room. I think there are very few American children here, and those that there are look miserably white, and thinner even than the Spanish or *Mestizo* youngsters.

We left about seven, before the rush, as we had the trap waiting outside, and the last thing we saw was the mermaid showing somebody her tail and the poor clown crying sleepily on her mother's shoulder.

In the evening there was a *baile*, which we summoned up energy to turn out for, but it was hardly worth the effort, as the floor had been spoilt by boots in the afternoon, while the band, half asleep, poor creatures, played intolerably slow and mournful music, to which the dancers crawled languidly about, for it was a very hot night, without a breath of air anywhere.

LETTER XXV.

A DAY AT NAGABA

ILOILO, *April 30, 1905.*

We went last Sunday to spend the day at Nagaba, a native village opposite Iloilo, in the island of Guimaras. We took the trip at the invitation of some friends who had gone to spend Saturday to Monday in a native house which happened to be empty and available for hire. I have often wanted to visit some of the places about, but the great difficulty is how to put up, for there are no inns, and no lodgings to be had in the villages. One can't go anywhere and back in a day, unless just across to Guimaras, but even that entails going out in the heat of the day, which is never very pleasant or very safe.

We were lucky, however, in this trip to Nagaba, as the sky was cloudy and the breeze very fresh, and, though we left as late as ten in the morning, we did not suffer from the heat. I am constantly reminded of a certain book of adventure, which as children we used to love, called *The Coral Island.* It is by Ballantyne, I think—you remember it, I am sure? Do you remember the pictures of the three boys in the Tropic Island, standing in white sunshine, and wearing loose caps or no hats at all? and all the stories of their adventures, and how they set off at "about the middle of the day" in a canoe with sufficient meat and vegetables to last for a week, and how they went in this fashion to other small islands? This did not seem to me odd as a child, of course; and I daresay I saw nothing peculiar in the daily life of *The Swiss Family Robinson*, either; and probably should have raised no objections to any of these stories a few months ago, or minded a bit being told that English boys went about unscorched and alive with no protection from the tropic mid-day sun, or that meat was fit to eat after one day in a canoe, much less one week!

Well, we got over to Guimaras in a very short time, landing from the launch in a small boat, from which C—— and I and the friend who was with us were carried ashore by our servants, who had come with us—we had also, by request, brought our plates, knives, forks, and tumblers!

The house we were going to was situated on a small rocky steep leading up from the beach, a few hundred yards from a tiny village of brown *nipa* huts amongst the green bushes and palms in a bay at the mouth of a river. The house was a regular native dwelling, built on high poles of bamboo, with walls of *nipa*, and floors of pieces of split cane half an inch or so apart for coolness. The whole abode consisted of one very big room, part of which was partitioned off as a bedroom, while all along one side of the house towards the sea ran a broad balcony, built out over the rocks, and shaded by tall thickly-leaved trees, with a glorious view of the blue bay, the open green sea, and a bit of rose-purple Panay in the distance. I don't think I ever saw a more lovely spot, and I could not help reflecting how different life in the Philippines must be to those who can live in such places as Nagaba instead of a street in a town. Though, to be practical, I suppose the food would be even worse, and ice—but one could not get less ice than we do now in the town.

NATIVE HOUSES.

Some of us spent all the morning loafing about and talking on the balcony, enjoying the deep shade and the fresh breeze blowing straight in from the open sea. One of the men of the party had contrived to catch the *anting-anting* lizard of the house, such as I described to you as having a call like a cuckoo and being considered very lucky by the Filipinos. He had tethered the creature by a piece of cotton tied round its body, so as to keep it for me to see when I arrived, and it was much larger than I had expected—about a foot long—and not unlike the desert lizards one sees dried in the bazaars in Upper Egypt, only the skin of the "Philippine cuckoo" is all a pattern of green and red. The poor thing was tame enough, but very shy, and inclined to get behind furniture or skirts, so when I had had a good look at it, they let it go again, when it vanished into the thick fringe of *nipa* that protected the sides of the balcony. This *nipa*, when one sees it close at hand, is a sort of palm leaf folded in two, lengthways, and tied to frames of bamboo, but it makes very nice, cool houses, and is absolutely waterproof.

One of the trees that shadowed the house was an Ylang-Ylang, from which the scent of that name is extracted; a tall, naked, light brown, smooth stem, with thin branches spreading out at the top, and leaves like an acacia. The perfume is in the small green blossom, which is not at all unlike that of a lime, and with infinite difficulty one or two of these were pulled down by means of a fishing-rod, and given to me to dry and put in my linen-cupboard in the native fashion. They dried up in a very few hours, but kept their delicious scent, and when I came home, I put them amongst my handkerchiefs, which are sweetly perfumed with them already.

Some of the men spent a riotous morning in a fresh-water swimming bath in a grove near the house. There is a spring of perfect water, which is brought in pipes past the house and out in long bamboo pipes on stands in the shallow water, where ships come and take it in to supply steamers, or to sell over in Iloilo. The flow of water is very great, enough to supply a city, and the main pipe is so contrived that by pulling out a plug one fills the swimming bath, which is a wonderful luxury.

We heard the others splashing and shouting in the swimming bath all the morning, and when lunch time came, they appeared radiant and starving, and I have not seen men do such justice to their food since I came to the Philippines.

After lunch we all settled down in various chosen nooks for a *siesta*, and our servant Sotero, who is a native of Nagaba, came and asked permission to go away for the afternoon, which surprised our friends very much, for they said they had never heard of a Filipino servant taking anything but "French leave."

I have not yet been able to acquire the habit of sleeping in the middle of the day, which is perhaps one of the reasons why I never feel well out here. So I sat about, and looked at some picture papers, and felt very tired—I could cheerfully have gone round to the sleeping forms and done them some injury simply because they could sleep!

About four C—— awoke, so we went a little walk amongst the rocks close to the house, and thought we were exploring the whole island!

We wandered about amongst scrub and rocks above the shore, where we came suddenly to a tiny hut perched up amongst big grey boulders, with fishing nets spread out to dry and a native lounging in the window-space. It looked such a nice little hut, just one large palm-thatch room on high poles, with a rickety step-ladder up to the door, where a round comfortable cat was sitting watching the fowls pecking about below. A little farther on we came to the banana patch, with brilliant green plants growing on a nook of dark earth amongst the grey rocks. All the rocks were very sharp; volcanic, with rough edges, which cut our shoes, even when we followed a tiny winding track. After we got to a little height, we could look down on the village and the sea and bay, which all appeared most bright and beautiful in the long rays of the low sun, and all so peaceful and quiet.

We turned back again by a path which struck more inland, past some more little banana fields and another little hut with its back to a tiny precipice. It is strange how near the towns the primitive sets in, for the people in both lots of huts were quite shy of us, and the children ran away and hid; while in the village, through which we passed, by making a round across some rice-fields, the people were quite country-folk, not a bit like the cheeky, independent loungers in the towns; answering one quite civilly and even happily when one spoke to them.

The village was delightfully quaint, all built on high poles planted in the sand of the shore, with many cheerful brown folk hanging out of the open sides of the houses, while mangy dogs with pups and fat old sows with immense families sprawled about down below. There are always quantities of pigs in a Philippine village, for, as I think I told you, they are the scavengers, and though the natives are not more unkind to those benefactors than to any other animals, to call one of them a pig is a frightful insult. In spite of all this, the favourite and most esteemed Filipino delicacy is sucking-pig, roasted whole.

Beyond the village we went across a field of emerald grass, bordered by a deep green hedge of curious bushes with no flowers on them. Our friends told us that these plants come into bloom in the wet Monsoon. Now, with the hot weather a very beautiful tree is in flower everywhere, called the Fire tree, which was only naked brown branches for a long time, and then burst into huge bunches of brilliant scarlet blossoms, rather like orchids, and very handsome at a distance, but coarse and common close at hand. The effect of these masses of showy red against the vivid green palms is wonderful and almost too bright. There is one of these Fire trees in the garden of the house opposite to us, here in Iloilo, which is a gorgeous display, and a delight to me just to look at as I sit here writing.

But, to get back to Nagaba, though there is not much to tell you, except that some of our friends joined us, and we ended our walk by a stroll through a cocoanut grove, where we saw an old man in a loin-cloth going up a tree to get the sap from which they make the *tuba*.[7] He had a long vessel made of a section of bamboo tied across his back, and a little round bowl of half a cocoanut tied in front of his body, with a big sharp knife beside it. He ran up the tree by means of notches cut all the way up the trunk, and at the top he tied the vessel under a bunch of buds, putting in it some of the stuff out of the bowl, which was red bark to dye the drink pink. This beverage I think I have mentioned to you before. One sees it anywhere, and the long tumblers of pink liquid are a feature in every little native shop.

This vessel they leave there for twelve hours, during which the sap drips out of the palm, and in the morning the man goes up and takes down the bamboo, now full of *tuba*, which is very fresh and nice, and tastes of cocoanut and water, and is very wholesome, not to say medicinal. If it is left, however, the *tuba* rapidly ferments, and by the evening is a very strong intoxicant, which constitutes the peculiar devil of the Philippines, and is the cause of most of the deterioration, physical, moral, and mental, of the race.

When the American Army first came out to the Philippines, the temperance enthusiasts in the U.S.A. hearing that a good deal of drinking was going on out here, started an agitation, by means of which they got the Army Canteens in the Philippines abolished. The result of this drastic mothering was that the soldiers went off and got *tuba*, about which, of course, the good folk in America knew nothing. Frightful scandals happened, which unfortunately did harm to the American prestige, and even the restoration of the canteens has not swept away the folly and evil which were thus begun.

---

[7] A corruption of *tubig*, Visayan for water.

This cocoanut grove, by the way, is kept for *tuba*, as are most of the palms one sees near the houses, for when the sap is taken in this way no fruit appears. Growing cocoanuts is one of the most lucrative speculations in the Philippines, as a tree bears fruit when it is six or seven years old, about a hundred nuts a year, the income yielded by a tree being about 2 *pesos*. So a grove of ten thousand trees or so is a very paying concern, if only the planter does not make the mistake, which I, myself, have often noticed, of placing his trees too close to one another, so that they do not get enough room to spread out at the top and find light and air.

We turned back from the cocoanut grove by a different path, and went back to the house along the beach. As the tide was far out, we walked across the firm, damp sand, where there were myriads of tiny crabs of bright metallic blues and reds and greens, which all darted sideways into holes as soon as one got within a yard of them.

After tea we loafed on the balcony, watching a lovely gold and rose sunset, while sailors and others took boxes and things down to the boat; and the man carrying our gear slipped on the rocks, and our plates and tumblers fell out and smashed to a thousand pieces. When it was almost dark, we returned in the launch to Iloilo, quite enchanted with our day at Nagaba and with the house on the rocks. We are determined to go over there one Saturday to Monday by ourselves, for it is a delightful change.

LETTER XXVI.

THE MONSOON—AN ITALIAN OPERA COMPANY

ILOILO, *May 5, 1905.*

I had two sweet little love-birds sent me yesterday, sitting jammed up in a tiny dirty cage in which they had travelled from China. They looked so uncomfortable and draggled, poor scraps, that I set off after my *siesta,* and went "down town," as the Americans call it, to see if I could get a cage for them. More Philippine shopping! I explained and argued at all sorts of emporiums, but no one had anything the least like a bird cage. At last I thought the wonderful English store might produce one, and when I got there, they said they thought they had something of the kind, made of wood, of native manufacture. I said I thought that would do very well, so after a lot of rummaging in a *camarin,* some very nice cages were found—large and clean, and made of split bamboo, with a little red and green paint here and there.

THE TRACK OF A TYPHOON.

I was delighted—till I found there was no mistake about their having been made by a Filipino! No water-pipkin; no tray to slide out; a door so small that I could only squeeze my hand into the cage with difficulty; and *no perches!* It was all there was to be had in Iloilo, however, so I took it with me, and climbed in under the apron of the *calesa*—it was raining very hard—and took my cage home and told the servants to make perches. This they did with considerable skill, and the results looked very nice, but when I put the birds on them, the poor things instantly tumbled off into the soapdish full of water, which was meant for them to drink from. After a lot of anxious thought, it occurred to me that the perches were much thinner than those in the little cage the birds had arrived in, and perhaps they could not wrap their long toes round these; and this was evidently the trouble, for as soon as larger ones were made and fixed in, the couple got up and stuck on, whispering to each other how nice the new perches were.

Of course the cat wants to eat them, and glares with greedy eyes, while old Tuyay is fearfully puzzled, coming to look intently, and snuffing very long and hard, which the wee birds don't mind a bit. They are such sweet things, with their tiny chirpings and pretty ways.

There is a strong S.-W. Monsoon blowing now—warm and tiring—and one's skin feels sticky and uncomfortable. In a month or two, however, this will be the chronic condition of the atmosphere, and will go on till October, but I suppose one gets used to it after a time, as to everything else. Yesterday a Typhoon was signalled by the meteorological office, but it has not arrived yet, and I hope it won't come our way at all, for the circular winds that sweep over these islands are the most frightful storms, tearing up trees, whipping off corrugated roofs, and setting the *nipa* houses on fire.

There are a great many rats here, which eat up whatever the cockroaches don't finish—*i.e.*, whatever is not in glass jars or tins. They get through nearly as many potatoes—at the price of new potatoes at home in May—as we do, so I invested in a large wire trap, which was set in the *dispensa* ten days or more ago. The boys and the *sota* (groom) watched the trap with the keenest interest, but never a rat would get into it to oblige them. Now, however, while I was writing this, Domingo came in, beaming, with the trap in his hand, and a huge grey rat in it. "What are you going to do with it?" I asked. "Are you going to kill it?"

"*Si, señora*, by pouring petroleum on the rat and setting it alight." He was astonished and obviously disappointed when I peremptorily forbade this horrible rite, which the Filipinos have learnt from the Chinese, who think that the poor, agonised, blazing animal runs away with the ill-luck of the house.

Then he suggested boiling water, and was again disappointed and surprised when I didn't join in this spree either, and went off quite gloomily to carry out my orders—to find something large enough to stand the trap in so as to drown the poor beast as quickly as possible.

Nothing could be found, till the *sota* fetched a tub from the stables, and this I made them fill with all the bath water—fresh water being far too precious to waste, even on sentiments of humanity! They collected all the water they could, and finally the flood reached the top of the cage, and though the sight of the rat struggling made me feel deadly sick, I waited till he was stiff and cold, as I did not know what cruelty these "little brown brothers" might not indulge in if left to their own devices.

The cook had been at market, and Sotero had gone shopping, so there was not the crowd there might have been on the Azotea, and only half the advice. They don't get excited, these Filipinos, unless they are fighting or massacring—one does not see frenzied little groups shouting in each other's faces, and throwing their fingers about like Italians, or low-class Arabs, or people like that—they are very slow, and their voices always soft and gentle. I mean the Filipinos, for the *Mestizos* differ from them in this, as well as in having curiously harsh, discordant voices, by which one readily detects their breed.

We went a night or two ago to a performance given by a wandering Italian Opera Company, who were really very good indeed, acting remarkably well, and possessing good voices. Three of them sang in various selections, and the fourth conducted an orchestra of bare-footed, flat-faced natives in ragged *camisas*, whose battered old straw hats hung about the footlight-board and on the piano.

The conductor played the piano splendidly, with incredible energy in such heat, and the result that he knocked out of his orchestra was astonishing. The theatre was very full, and we had shared a box with some friends, all sitting with our knees jammed together in a pattern like the ornamentation on a runic cross.

We enjoyed the show immensely, but, oh, it was hot! And if we, looking on, felt faint with the heat, what must it have been for the performers and for the *Chef d'orchestre*! Talking of heat, the thermometer now averages 90° to 93° all day in the dark, airy house, and a little while ago, when we got some ice by luck and manœuvring, I put the thermometer in the ice chest, and it only went down to 80°!

We have taken the house at Nagaba for next Saturday to Monday, and are busy making preparations for going over, with an anxious eye on the sky above and the weather-cock in the garden opposite. One has to take a good deal to the house at Nagaba, as all they provide is the four walls, a table, some chairs, a big native bed, and one or two hard cane couches. For this, however, one pays the same price a day as at a big London hotel for bed and breakfast for two people!

LETTER XXVII.

A WEEK-END AT NAGABA

ILOILO, *May 8, 1905.*

We were just going to Nagaba when I finished my last letter, I think, and now we have just returned, after having had a most delightful time over there.

We went over in the launch on Saturday, leaving here at half-past four, and to look at the start from here you would have thought we were going for good to China or Japan!

Before we set out, we sent a boy for a *carabao*-cart, inside which the gear was stowed:—two rolls of bedding; some large wooden cases with household effects; C——'s suit-case with what clothes we had to take; and Sotero sitting behind, carrying a mysterious bundle, with the cook beside him, got up in a clean pink and green muslin *camisa* and blue cotton trousers, carrying C——'s panama in one hand, and a long sack full of his beloved pots and pans in the other. C—— and I and Tuyay followed in the *calesa*, leaving Domingo in charge of the house, under oath to *mucho quedado* (take great care), but rather gloomy at not being in the outing.

At the Muelle Loney we embarked, with friends waving to us from the office windows as if we were going away for ever. The day was perfect and the crossing lovely, but a slight swell made it rather difficult for us to tranship into the small boat we had towed over. When we got to the other side, C—— did the complete and efficient sailorman in stowing the gear in the boat, handing me down (something after the fashion of the Arabs at Jaffa) into the cook's embrace, and giving orders generally; but he spoilt the whole effect by falling into the boat right on top of me, and bonneting me in my own topee, at which *debâcle* the cook showed all his dark red betel-stained teeth from ear to ear, and even Tuyay laughed.

The tide was very far out, showing long stretches of wet sand and reefs, all shining in the sunlight, with strips of very blue water in between. C—— quite redeemed his reputation for sailorising as he steered the boat ashore by the colour of the water over the sand banks; and we managed to get not very far from the front of the house, which we could just manage to make out amongst the trees and rocks, but the water-pipes on the bamboo frames going out into the sea, showed us where to look. The crew and the servants waded ashore, carrying gear, and Tuyay was chucked out and splashed along with them, while two skinny brown ragamuffins made a "chair" of their arms, and carried me—with puffings and groanings, so rude!—to land, and set me down on the beach with a sigh of relief. After landing me and the *ménage*, C—— rowed back to the launch to put the sailors on board, and she steamed away to Iloilo again. Coming back in the boat alone, he tied her up to a fish *corral*—a sort of wattle fence in the shallow water—and then waded ashore and came gingerly up the sharp rocks.

By the time he arrived I had unpacked, and it was about half-past five, so we put on bathing suits and filled the swimming bath, and the fun began at once. It was delicious, after the long, hot day, to splash about in the cool, fresh water, and we stayed there till it was quite dark, and we could see stars shining in the patches of dark sky between the branches. By-the-bye, I often think how strange it seems to see the same old Orion's Belt and Cassiopeia looking down on us here. We see the Southern Cross, too, low on the horizon—a disappointing exhibition, and no one would think it was meant for a cross unless they were told so.

We dined early, and were hungry, which was delightful. The cook and Sotero managed wonderfully, so that we were just as comfortable as in our own delightful house. There was a firefly flitting all about the big room, looking so pretty; appearing and disappearing like a tiny fairy light.

Next morning, when I woke up, I heard only a few cocks crowing—nothing to speak of—and some twitterings of birds as well, and I think the latter pleased me as much as the whole trip! In the Philippines "the birds have no song and the flowers have no scent," they say, which is a sweeping generalisation, but true for the most part.

We put on our bathing suits, had a cup of tea, and were out on the beach by six o'clock. The tide was far out again, with long stretches of shining wet, ribbed sand; the sea all fresh and blue, and glittering in the sunlight. But where we went was still in shade, for the sun had not yet come up behind the Guimaras hills, and the morning air was exquisite. We "ran races in our mirth" along the wet sands, till we got opposite the fish *corral*, where the water was deeper and the boat was tied up to a bamboo pole.

As we went along the beach, we saw people from the little huts we passed when we were here before, washing at a spring of water which flowed out from the rocks and down to the beach. They were some way off, though, and we were in the shade and they were in the still deeper shade under the cliffs, so we could not make them out very clearly, but we could see their coppered-coloured skins shining with water, and hear them laughing and talking.

We swam about the boat for a long time, and found the water quite warm in the shallows, even before the sun was up. I had brought C——'s panama, which I hung to the fish *corral* while I swam about in the shade, but when we went back to the house, I had to wear it, as the sun which was then on us is oppressively hot here as soon as it rises.

The fish *corral*, by-the-bye, is an ingenious trap, rather after the fashion of a maze, into which the fish enter but never have the sense to get out again.

When we got back to the house, we filled the swimming bath, which felt very cold after the sea, and it certainly washed off the salt water, but it was nearly as hard and harsh as the sea itself.

A FILIPINO MARKET-PLACE.

In the early morning a fleet of *paraos* (native sailing boats) goes across to Iloilo to the market with fowls, mangoes, maize, pine-apples, etc., and our cook took passage in one of these vessels to go and do his marketing, for it is impossible to buy a single thing in Nagaba, where the people only just keep enough for their own scanty consumption. He returned about nine o'clock, and I went into the kitchen to inspect the result of his shopping. The kitchen was in the regular native fashion, just a prolongation of the living-room, with the same split-bamboo floor, through which could be seen the fowls and pigs wandering about under the house. There was no ceiling below the thatch and rafters, and everything seemed very nice and trim—the fireplace being a high table of concrete with holes in the top. In each hole they light little pieces of charcoal, so that each pot has its own fire, which seems a cumbersome method, but it saves fuel, and must be quite enough trouble for a Filipino, who has probably one pot of rice to boil and no more. From the roof hang all sorts of dried fruits or vegetables, and queer little bundles of herbs for flavourings and for medicines as well. I noticed that amongst the things the cook had brought he had not forgotten the day's supply of *buyo*. When first I used to go into the kitchen here to look at the day's supplies, I saw this little packet, not unlike a lily-leaf, tied up with a wisp of twine, and classed it amongst the mysterious little odds and ends intended for flavourings. But one day I had the curiosity to ask, and the cook, with much shyness and shrugging up of his shoulders, told me it was *buyo* (betel-nut). I could quite believe it when I looked at his crimson teeth, and was thankful the supply was only for himself and not the other servants, for I could not stand being waited on at table by a person with a mouth as if he had been drinking fresh blood. The betel-chewers expectorate a great deal, though they can't possibly do so more than their compatriots and the Spaniards and Americans, but the red expectoration is horrible, somehow, and I've often seen all the pavement outside a house or shop quite crimson with the great splashes of betel-juice ejected by the inmates.

We spent all the morning pottering about and reading, and regretting that we could not carry out our plan of bathing again when the tide was up and deep below the house, as we were expecting a party of English and American friends from Iloilo, who had announced that they would visit us on Sunday morning. But the party never landed after all, which was rather a disappointment, as we were done out of our bathe, besides having no use for a dozen or two of sodas which we had brought over with infinite trouble.

After the *siesta*, we thought we would make use of the boat for a little trip, so we sent into the village for two men who could row; and they fetched her to the beach and rowed us up the little estuary, past the village and up the river. Unfortunately, the tide had gone out again—very far out—and the river was too low to go as far as we had intended, which was to a convent and church, the corrugated roofs of which we had seen from a height. So we just went a little way up the narrow, muddy river, but we could not see much as we were below the level of the thick bushes that fringed the banks. At last we stuck and could get no further, so we turned back and went up a little back-water, and landed by a queer sort of lime-kiln in a palm-grove.

We scrambled ashore, and walked up a track through the woods of mangoes and palms, till we got up a good height, with a map view of the river winding far below and a glimpse of the roofs of the convent. Down in the valley the land was all cultivated, chiefly in maize-fields and bananas, which looked green enough though uninteresting, but the hills were pretty, and wooded with trees of all tones of green, and the distances exquisite in gradations of mauves and blues. From where we stood, the sea was quite hidden, for we had our backs to it, and the hill between us and it; and the view spread out below was like some tropical version of the valley of the Doons. We went on up through the wood, still big dark mango trees with leaves like laurels—dark and shiny—and feathery, graceful cocoanut-palms in between. The ground was all covered with straggling plants, wild mint, and dead palm-branches, while wild pine-apples grew in quantities, each fruit sitting in a flat bush of spiky yellowish leaves, and looking delicious!

By a very primitive hut in a clearing we came upon some natives, clad only in short white drawers, who were very nice and cheerful; very different from the people in the towns. They knew very little Spanish, but we made out that their chief occupations were gathering the fruit of the pine-apples for food and the leaves to make into the thread to weave the *piña* muslin. They made charcoal too, and all this information C—— elicited in Visayan and a few words of Spanish. I don't suppose they trouble themselves much about even those simple occupations, and I should think the less thought they gave to the blessings of civilisation the happier they would be. What good on earth can education, whisky, votes, appendicitis, electric light, a free press, frozen meat, clothes, and pianos do to such happy simple souls? It seems so odd to think that in one part of the world cultivated, thinking men are trying their level best to destroy for others an ideally happy, simple life, while at home their one profession is a wish to return to it themselves, and their only idea of a holiday is to go off and camp in the Rockies, where they can approach as nearly as possible to the conditions one sees here in the country places. Indeed, as I told you, far from encouraging a simple, agricultural life, the land and other taxes, and the education they go to maintain, are having the effect of choking agriculture and hurrying the half-taught countrymen into the towns.

But even with the elect, with the Filipinos, the sums of money raised should be spent on roads, on remitting the poll-tax, on reducing the export duties—and then, when a generation or two has been peaceful and well fed, it would be time enough to educate the masses—if such universal education is necessary or beneficial to such a people, or any people at all. In the white countries, with all their thousands of years of progress through Greece, Rome, and the Middle Ages, one can't be sure, judging from the tone of literature that appeals to the masses, whether education has been an unmitigated boon; but hastily to apply the same methods to this infinitely lower development of the human race, is an absurdity that would be laughable if it were not pitiful and dangerous. And it seems so strange to think of a country being governed against its inclinations, not by legislators trained in its problems, but by a body of electors on the other side of the world, not one of whom knows more of its conditions and needs than the first cabman one would hail in London or Paris. Strange, is it not, when you come to think of it?

Well, to get back to our trip up the river in Guimaras, we came down through the woods again, and got into our boat about sunset, rowing back to the beach opposite the house in a pale crimson sunset glow, with long dark shadows of trees and houses falling on the sand, and when we got out at the house, we walked up over the rocks and pools, and saw the little bright metallic-looking crabs running into their holes again. We tried very hard to catch one, but it was impossible, for they run sideways at a great pace, simply vanishing like so many harlequins of crab-land.

We dined early, and spent the evening in long chairs on the balcony. It was a lovely night, fresh and cool, probably not more than 85°, with great stars shining brightly, making quite a silver light upon the sea. Many people from the village were out in the bay, wading in the shallows, and catching fish with spears and torches, shining a light on the water, and then plunging down a spear and bringing up the poor deluded fish. A man ran out from under our house, carrying a bamboo staff about 12 feet long, dipped in something resinous, and flaming at one end, and we saw another man join him, and they waded far out, till the torch was only a little speck of yellow in the silvery night. That was all very nice and primitive, but on the rocks below sat another engaging barbarian, squatting on his heels getting crabs out of the pools, and whistling "Hiawatha" perfectly in tune.

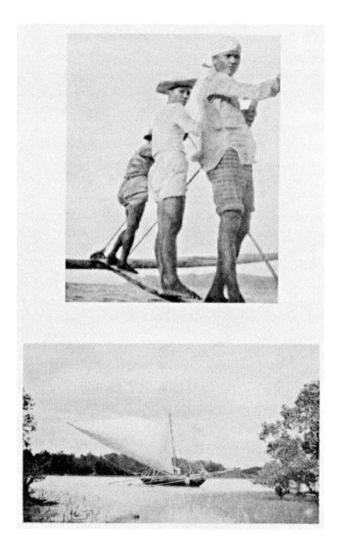

A THREE-MAN BREEZE OFF GUIMARAS.

A PARAO.

We had a very early start next morning, turning out at half-past five, and packing and breakfasting as soon as it was light, for we had to be back in Iloilo in time for C—— to be at his office at eight o'clock. We had not been able to get the launch to come and fetch us, so, when we were on our way back from the river the night before, we had stopped by the village and made arrangements to take one of the *paraos* lying at anchor there—long, thin frames of bamboo covered with *bejuco* matting, tarred inside and out, in shape sharp and narrow as a blade, with big canvas sails and great wide outriggers. The crews of these boats consist of several men, one of whom steers while the others control the sails or run out on the outriggers, for the art of sailing them consists in a very skilful balance, according to the direction of the wind; and breezes here are known as "one-man" or "three-man" winds and so on, by the number of men that would be required on the outriggers of a *parao*. They are said to be safe enough, but they look very risky, and skim over the water like swallows, also they draw very little water, and can anchor in very shallow places.

We got on board our *parao*, the *Soltero*, by about seven o'clock, and had a lovely, fresh three-man breeze, a glorious sunny morning, and I wished the crossing could have taken half a day instead of half an hour. C—— and I sat on the little narrow plank that served as deck; while the other half of the boat, where the "deck" stopped, was full of rolls of bedding and gear, and on top of all, sat the cook still clutching the panama and his sack of pots and pans. The boat towed behind, with one of the wooden cases in it, guarded by Sotero, holding in his arms a large and handsome rooster, to buy which he had asked for an advance upon his wages. I don't like cock-fighting, and was depressed by the sight of this poor animal; but it would be silly to make a fuss and perhaps lose so good a servant, and, after all, though you can train a Filipino to understand your ways, it is no more possible to alter his being a Filipino by your theories than to wash his skin white with somebody's soap.

I was so interested in watching the marvellously nimble way the sailors ran out upon the outriggers, first to one side, then we made a wide tack and the sail swung round, nearly knocking our heads off, and the crew rushed over to the other side, doing feats of balancing far more wonderful than anything I ever saw in a circus, for they had not got a nice safe net below them, with a lot of men in brass buttons holding on to the poles and looking up to see if they made a slip. On the contrary, there was nothing but their astounding balance and agility between them, and fathoms of choppy sea running with a swift current, and full of sharks.

They brought the boat to the beach at the end of the street which runs at right angles from our own, opposite the end of our house, and ran her broadside on in shallow water and then up on to the sand, where we could jump ashore from the bows.

The sailors and the cook and Sotero carried the gear up into the house, and when I went into the hall, I had the impression of having been some weeks in a strange country, whereas we had really only been within sight of our own town from Saturday to Monday. So many new things—and yet, though I have written till I am tired, I feel that I have not told you half what we saw and noticed.

LETTER XXVIII.

A LITTLE EARTHQUAKE, AND AN OPERA COMPANY UNDER DIFFICULTIES

ILOILO, *May 15, 1905.*

We had a slight earthquake here on Wednesday morning, the 11th. It was my first experience of that form of excitement, and I am sure I don't want another. The queer thing that everyone here tells me, and they have plenty of experience to go by, is that people do not usually think much of their first earthquake, but instead of becoming accustomed to them, they become more alarmed, and get to be horribly frightened at the mere suggestion of the earth's surface shifting about.

This one took place at about half-past four in the morning, and at first I thought it was a burglar or someone moving about the room, and was just going to call to C—— when he cried out: "Wake up! There is an earthquake!"

I woke up pretty quickly when I heard that! The shaking continued quite a long time, and I thought it a sickening sensation, and so horribly uncanny, with all the room trembling, and the furniture rattling and moving, while outside the air was deathly still. I think that what made the stillness was that no cocks crowed, and the eternal shrilling of the crickets ceased, which made a deadness in the ears such as one feels on coming out of a factory.

C—— invited me to go out on the balcony and "see the street moving," which I firmly refused to do. I am sorry now that I did not go on to the balcony, but at the time I felt too horribly frightened to move hand or foot.

I don't think I like earthquakes, but I expect I shall have to accustom myself to them, for they are so common in the Philippines as to excite no remark unless some building tumbles down; and the houses, as I think I told you, are built with a view to these hysterics of old mother Earth, with all the planks and beams tied with bands of *bejuco* to give them room to shift a little.

But besides the earthquake, we have been in more imminent danger since I last wrote, in the shape of the final and really conclusive and farewell performance of the Italian Quartette, which took place last Saturday night. The theatre was very full, and gaily decorated with loops of green leaves and paper roses of red and yellow, mixed up with perilous paper lanterns. The electric light, which has been weak for some time, chose, on this occasion, to go out altogether—in the midst of an impassioned duet.

There was instantly great excitement, for the paper lanterns were not lighted, and the theatre was plunged in blackness of the deepest dye. Reckless scratching of matches sounded all round, and the little lights were held up for a few seconds till they burnt out, and then dropped just anywhere. One did not need to look to gather that a Filipino did this thing! It made one's blood run cold to see them.

Of course, though the electric light was in such a precarious state, and expected to expire at any minute, there had been no provision made in case of accidents, and the remedy now was a wild rush outside to buy candles, which were soon produced and stuck in dabs of their own grease along the front of the stage and amongst the orchestra. One or two lamps came somehow from somewhere and were placed jauntily about the building, while the spare candles were secured by enterprising spirits in the audience and put about so that they shone in the eye, and no one could see anything, and little brown ladies in *camisas*, with huge gauze sleeves, leaned past the naked lights with admirable indifference. There was not a single accident, however, but how that was managed, and indeed how the whole matchbox theatre was not burnt to the ground and the audience roasted, is simply the eighth wonder of the world.

I can't say I took the affair very cheerfully myself; in fact, to be truthful, the sensation of impending doom, and the trouble of having to keep my eye on the wobbling candles, spoilt my enjoyment a good deal. The singing was very good, and in spite of the partial gloom, the opening scene of La Bohême was given very well indeed, and it was such a treat to hear that glorious music. Of course the darkness suited that very well, and made the scene in the garret most realistic, though I expect the Quartier Latin was rather *caviare* to the ladies in the muslin *camisas*. I loved to hear the Italian too, it sounded so full and round and pure after Spanish. I suppose one prefers whichever tongue one happens to learn first. After the opening piece the light suddenly went up, so we had a fairly good sight of the second part. They did a sort of shortening-up—I can think of no other name for it—of Cavalleria, acting really so remarkably well that the worn old story seemed as fresh and terrible as if it were just happening. I've never seen it done better in any part of the world—no, not even Caruso and Melba. One felt the full tragedy and pathos of the music, and the duet between Turiddú, and Santuzza, a handsome, graceful woman, was magnificently impassioned, leading up to an almost breathless moment when he cast the girl from him, and she fell upon the ground.

But, alas!—we were in the presence of a Filipino audience, who greeted the fall of Santuzza with hearty laughter, and continued to giggle while the girl sang her curse as she dragged herself to her knees.

I don't know how the Italians went on acting as they did. I am afraid I should have lost my temper and had the curtain lowered.

This great heat still continues, and is very exhausting, for the lightest clothes are always soaked, and the face and hands covered with little beads. No one thinks less of a "perfect lady" in this country if she mops her face with her handkerchief; in fact, it is the only thing for the poor creature to do. I simply long to feel fresh and energetic, and to be able to walk fast on a hard road on a cold day—what a dream of bliss! Even to enjoy food would be a pleasant change.

Those who can get away, but they are very few, go to Hong Kong, where the people are making a fuss about their hot weather. It is coolness after the Philippines.

The missionaries are the best off, with their nice little trips to Japan; and there has been a great exodus of these good people lately.

The lowest average of the thermometer is 93°, which means that is sometimes as low as 90° but generally up to 95°. Some people tell me this is the usual thing at this time of year, and others vow it is abnormal. Whatever it is, it has gone on now for three months, and I am getting rather tired of it, and don't think I shall be able to pull through another year out here. It is not only the climate that tells on one, but the scarcity and badness of the food. To think that you at home in an average of 60° think you would die off unless you had fresh cabbages, and peas, and beans, and gooseberries, currants, the first strawberries—how the very names make one's mouth water! Well, they say the Monsoon will change soon, and then the rainy season begins and the air gets cooler, and that is something to look forward to. The wind blows now some days from one side and some days from another, in an undecided fashion, with intervals of stifling calm, and then a sudden burst, which whips the sunblinds from their anchorage.

LETTER XXIX.

AN EVENING ON THE RIVER—RIVAL BISHOPS

ILOILO, *May 17, 1905.*

We went out on the river one evening last week at the invitation of two members of the boating club, which has its being in a *nipa* hut on the bank above the town, off the Molo road. It was a regular little native hut, with a rickety ladder up to the door, and boats slung underneath—a delightfully primitive place.

We went out in a boat and a canoe, making our way up-stream in the light of an exquisite sunset, all bright-red gold behind the mountains, and the river between its banks of low bushes like a path of pink crystal. The air was deliciously cool, or seemed so to us, and we rowed up a mile or more before landing at the bank on the farther shore from the town, where there were some fishing huts in a grove of palms.

We beached the boats on the mudbank, and then walked about through the trees till we came to some huts, looking wonderfully picturesque in the long stripes of pink light and mauve shadows amongst the tall trees. Here a number of half-naked Filipinos were loafing about, very civil, kindly people, and one was a very skinny old woman, who took a deep and unbounded interest in me, and asked all sorts of extraordinary questions about me.

The cocoanut trees in the grove bore many large green nuts in clusters at the top, like big green footballs, and as we were all rather thirsty, we asked if the hut folk would get one down for us to drink from.

With much politeness and amazing alacrity, one of the younger men ran up a tree, putting his toes in the notches in the bark, and not falling and breaking his neck by yet another Philippine miracle. He came down with a big green nut, such an enormous thing—the same in proportion to a cocoanut as we see them at home, as a green almond or walnut is to the nut in a shop. We asked him to open it for us, so he squatted down and chopped very deftly with a sort of sword which they call a *bolo*, and I fancy I may have mentioned it to you before. These *bolos* are a variety of the Malay *kris*, and are made in all sorts of cruel shapes, often inlaid very beautifully, but I believe the most frequent form is simply that of a short, thick, curved sword, which they use with deadly effect in fighting, and with great skill in almost every other event in life.[8]

The little brown people stood round and looked at us while we watched the man with the *bolo*. He chopped with marvellous dexterity, slicing off the outer covering of soft green flesh, and then making a hole in the top of the tender unripe nut inside. The nut had a thin lining of transparent meat, and was full of pale green liquid, like

---

[8] The fighting *bolo*, the more deadly and elaborate weapon is always kept concealed in the hut.

slightly soapy water in appearance. This "milk" we drank out of a small wooden bowl produced by the old woman, a neat little vessel made out of half a cocoanut, all in the most approved style of the story books! The drink was refreshing enough, but sweet and sickly. Then the man split the nut open and made a clever little scoop with his *bolo* out of a slice of bamboo which he picked up from the ground, and with this he shaved off some long strips of the white meat, of which we ate a good deal, but it was tough and tasteless.

A PALM GROVE.

So the opening of a green cocoanut was the means of dispelling almost the last of my illusions about a Tropic Island! I have so often read about the nectar and ambrosia of the green nut, and the wonderful yarns of travellers who say there is no drink on earth like the green milk—one book I remember went so far as to compare the stuff favourably with lemonade! Perhaps it is all right if you have been shipwrecked and your mouth is full of sea water, but then I imagine so few people who write the descriptions can ever have had that advantage.

From the huts we went on till we came out upon wide, open mud-flats, where there were a great many salt pits, which fill with water when the tide rises, for the sea water stretches right up to this place and farther. The pits were surrounded by pumps, after the fashion of the *shadoofs* on the Nile, and wells and all sorts of curious contrivances of bamboo, with long rows of pipes for drying the salt—it is marvellous what these people will do with bamboo. It was nearly dark by this time, and the mud-flats looked very weird and melancholy, the strange frames and poles appearing ghostly in the dusk.

We came out upon the river bank again and walked to the place where we had left the boats. On the way I picked some sprays of small pink blossoms which grow on big ragged bushes with thorns, and look like May, and smell like sweet currant. They look very pretty in a vase in the *sala*, and are the only flower I have yet brought home or had given to me, that has lasted for so long as twenty-four hours.

C—— has been having more trouble with the Customs, and this time over a boat he had to get from Hong Kong, as such a thing is not made and not to be had here. It is an ordinary boat for going out to the ships, and cost 40 *pesos*, but when C——, on being asked to value it, mentioned this sum to the Customs authorities, they exclaimed "Impossible!"

Unfortunately it happened that he could not produce a bill for the boat, as he had got it through an agent in Hong Kong, who charges it to his account with the Firm in Manila, and he had not even a bill of lading, as a friend had brought it from Hong Kong for him. The Customs flatly refused to take his word about the price, and sent for some local sages to value the boat. One of these worthies gave it as his opinion, off-hand, that it was absurd to say you could buy a boat like that for less than 60 *pesos*. Another said, "Probably ninety." A third, "Sixty at the lowest."

So the authorities, like Solomon, struck the happy medium, and charged C—— the duty (30 per cent.) on 80 *pesos*!!

And there is no redress, for the Firm's accounts will not be settled till the end of the month, or even later, by which time the dues on the boat will have been paid long ago, and when once a receipt is given by the Government, no power but a special Act of Congress can get one cent of it refunded. Oh, and we know this to our cost! For, during all these months, we have not ceased from appealing, reappealing, and worrying tooth and nail about the extra £40 we had to pay for our wedding presents. I wish to goodness we had a "pull." We should get it back in a week.

The tariffs here seem to be put on in an incomprehensible way. In a civilised old country it might help trade if there were an import tax against things the people could produce themselves, but the system here works out quite differently, for while a desire is being inculcated for things which the natives cannot and never will be able to produce, those articles are taxed at the same rate as they are in the most highly developed country full of manufactories. You will think I have become a regular bluestocking when you read these long discourses! But you need not have any fears on that score, for I am only trying to describe to you the conditions under which we struggle for existence in one of the most fertile countries in the world, and these questions are of such vital and burning interest that I hear them discussed by the most unlikely and domesticated ladies!

What the newspapers call "Religious Circles" have been in a great state of excitement lately, as the Pope has sent a Cardinal Delegate to the Philippines to rouse the Orthodox to a sense of their peril from the *Iglesia Independiente*, the Aglipayanos. When I was in Manila, this prelate was there, an Irishman of the name of Agius. I saw him and his suite at the Governor's reception, and people told me he was a very charming person. Now he is touring about the Philippines, and this week arrived here on a visit to the Bishop of Panay—an American, whose name I forget.

There were great ceremonies and processions, arches and welcomes on the arrival of the Cardinal. But the Aglipayanos did not let the occasion pass without comment, for they turned out in full force with counter-processions and, it must be confessed, with far larger crowds of followers.

The day before yesterday the Cardinal arrived in great state. He drove off to Jaro, and the road out to that town swarmed with priests, and little carriages dashing about full of mysterious, greasy-looking hangers-on in black coats and bowlers, the like of which no human eye has ever before seen this side of Suez.

The next day, yesterday, there was frantic excitement! The Filipino Archbishop arrived! With no official state, but greeted by an immense demonstration of crowds of *Independientes*, who went out to meet their pastor in decorated boats and launches, with bands playing, Chinese crackers popping about, and revolutionary marches with songs. He, also, went to Jaro, under more triumphal arches, with Welcomes, and one with his name, Monsignore Hijaldo, in huge red letters all across it.

We drove out to Jaro in the evening to see the fun, and were well rewarded, for the whole Plaza was as good as a play—far better than anything the Iloilo theatre could produce intentionally.

CATHEDRAL AND BELFRY AT JARO.

Jaro is a collection of rather fine old houses, of the prevailing two-storied pattern, but large and handsome, some of them with carved wooden ornamentations and balconies with pretty pillars. They stand round a very large green space, with a bandstand in the middle, which is the Plaza. At one side of the Plaza is the cathedral, a long, ugly building, like a stone tunnel, and alongside it is a smaller church, on much the same lines, which is the Aglipayano place of worship. Opposite the two, on the green Plaza, stands a handsome old grey stone belfry, thrown out of the perpendicular by earthquakes, and crumbling with decay. At each corner of the upper story is a huge white stone statue of a saint leaning forward with some giant emblem clasped in his or her arms—such a cumbersome, melancholy old edifice! We always stop by the belfry, when we drive into Jaro, to let the pony rest and crop the grass, which overflows liberally into the road, and five times out of six it happens that we are there when a small lamp is swung up over the cathedral door, and a couple of Filipino boys come across and go into the belfry to ring the Angelus, which they do by swinging themselves fearlessly about on the beams of the big bells.

When we drove out yesterday evening, we first met landaus containing the Delegate and the Bishop of Panay bowing and smiling to right and left, and lifting up hands of benediction; with many priests, secretaries, and retainers, most of them very fat men with very white faces.

Then, on the other side of the water, in the suburb of La Paz, which is a big town in itself, we met the Aglipayanos—Aglipay himself and his followers—all brown, flat-faced Filipinos, dressed something like the R.C. priests, only with fantastically bent up hats, and driving in the native *quilezes* or *calesas*.

In Jaro itself the fun was fast and furious, for both the churches had a great display of decorations outside—the *Independiente* considerably embellished by a long covered way built out, of latticed bamboo with palm-branches lashed to it, and paper lanterns, and quantities of little flags.

Across the Plaza were the two houses, both blazing with lights and flowers, the balconies full of men in white suits and women in their smartest dresses. In front of each house a band was playing, as if no other music were within a hundred miles, and the din was awful—the constabulary brass band, which was serenading the Papal Delegate, or his house, smashing and braying Sousa Marches; while the Aglipayano mandolines, guitars, and violins twiddled and thumped steadily at "Hiawatha" and other Filipino airs.

To anyone blessed with a glimmering of humour you may imagine that the whole show was a source of pure delight, and we lingered quite late, driving up and down in the hope that there might be a speech or a row or something. But apparently peace, if not goodwill, was the motto, as, when we at last had to return home, we left all hands as contented and jolly as if the other fellows did not exist at all, or lived in another continent.

You must imagine all this in heat such as you have never felt, all the priests, devotees, and bandsmen limp and dripping, and the faces of the Filipinos like wet mahogany. We are in a chronic state of discomfort, too, ourselves, which makes the sight of the black and purple robes, the berettas, and the outfit of the secretaries and hangers-on a very tangible addition to our own discomfort. I "guess" the "Dallergit" wishes the "call" had "come right along" in the cool season!

I told you about the little love-birds which had been presented to me, I think? "I had a dove, and the sweet dove died" ... but my first lovebird did not die of grieving, for I found him one morning with a gash in his throat which looked very like the work of a bad cat. When the wee bird was dead and buried, the other little scrap did not seem to mind much at first, but presently took to having fits, and soon expired too.

I miss them very much, for they were dear little creatures, and such companions to me, with their sweet little chirping noises. People tell me it is very difficult to keep birds at all out here, as the little ants that swarm everywhere get under their feathers and worry them to death in a few hours.

LETTER XXX.

PHILIPPINE SANITATION—DECORATION DAY

ILOILO, *May 29, 1905.*

I know you will be glad to hear that we are having a lull in the great heat, as the rain is beginning, or, at any rate, the Monsoon is blowing through rain, steadily from the S.-W., and the thermometer has gone down from 95° to 90°, which makes a vast difference to us, though it must still sound like great heat to you.

I have just had a letter from a Manila friend, who is spending the hot season at Benguet, whither the "Gubernatorial party" and the Commissioners have also fled; and where, according to the Manila papers, I see they are having gay times ... lots of Bridge. She says:—"We are very chilly people up here, fires every evening, and hot-water bottles at night! This is a lovely country, all pine-woods and tree-ferns—a curious mixture. We ride about here a very great deal, play cards, walk, and generally have a thoroughly quiet, lovely time. I am going to a euchre party this afternoon at a house near by; there are to be very nice prizes, I hear. This climate is like England. You and Mr Dauncey would like it when he can get leave. There is a sanatorium, hospital place here, where you can go for one dollar, gold, a day per head. There is also this house, but you could not live at that here, at least I think not. I think this climate would do most people as much good as going home. It is a beautiful place, and they shortly expect a railway to run within 15 miles of it, which will make it cheaper to get here, and quicker; at present it takes three days from Manila."

That all sounds very tantalising to us sweltering down here, but I *think* we shall wait till that mythical railway is ready, for we have several times discussed the pros and cons of a health trip to Benguet, but when C—— went into the matter, he found that the expenses from here and back would be more than to go to England! And then, if we did go to this paradise of pine-trees and hot-water bottles, we should only be that much to the good, for we should be still living on the awful Philippine food, and the question is, should we get rid of that cuirass of prickly heat? Also, would the water there still give *sarna*—which I think they call in India "dhobey-itch"? And these things being so, is it not better to go home? And being at home, would it not be the utmost folly ever to venture within a hundred miles of a Philippine island again as long as life lasts? I feel inclined to answer my own questions by saying—American fashion—"That's so!"

I missed my little love-birds so much that C—— got me some other pets, which we hope will flourish better—three baby mongeese. They are the dearest little things, so soft and gentle, and look like very fluffy weasels, with large dark beady eyes and long, busy, smelling-about noses. The people here call them *Gato del Monte*, which is, being translated, mountain-cat, though the animal we call by that name is a very different creature. They are found all over the islands, I believe, and there are many in

Guimaras, whence these were brought by a countryman who was going round the offices trying to sell them, with the little things nestled in his coat. So C—— bought them for me for a couple of *pesos*. They are very young and very tame, in fact more than tame, for they run after me all over the house, and as soon as I sit down, climb up and sit on my shoulders, or curl up on my lap, and I daresay the warmth of their woolly little bodies would be grateful and comforting amongst the pines and tree-ferns at Benguet! C—— has made them a beautiful large cage out of a packing-case and some wire-netting, where they spend their time asleep in a box full of cotton wool, or else clamouring to be let out, with a curious guggling, rippling cry, a sort of cross between a nightingale's "jug-jug" and a cab-whistle.

Half the ground-floor of this house was let a little time ago to a rabbit warren of low-class Filipinos, who keep all sorts of animals in the rooms, and throw all their refuse out into the narrow alley between this and the next house. Unfortunately, this is all on the side where our bedrooms are. After a time we got accustomed to the mysterious noises to a certain extent, though the bleating of goats remained tiresome, and the person with consumption who coughed all night still disturbed us. The natives here die like flies of consumption, and the dreadful cough, hollow cheeks, and glittering eyes are a very common feature in the landscape.

Well, we weathered through the noises, though we were often inclined to shift our quarters to the other side of the house, to the rooms which that persistent American wished to inhabit. Fancy breakfasting with them! I have not got over that yet! But on that side, unfortunately, the construction of the house is such that there is no through draught, without which one cannot sleep. Finally, however, the smell of the refuse gave C—— an attack of tonsilitis, with a touch of fever, and as I myself had also had some sore throats, we made the move across, and found it was not so bad after all, for the S.-W. Monsoon blowing straight in kept the air quite bearable.

The smells on the other side got worse and worse, and we put bowls of disinfectant about, and complained to the landlord of the house. He said he had no power, meaning that he was really afraid to offend and lose his tenants, but he "would speak to the people," advising us, at the same time, to go to the Sanitary Inspector of the town, who would set things right. Now, the municipality consists of natives, and the Sanitary Inspector is a Filipino with a Filipino's notions of sanitation, so he can't see what we have to complain about, and we went on sending in complaints and protests, which met with vague replies at first, and latterly with none at all. So at last C—— told the landlord that if he did not have the alley cleared, we would leave the house, whereupon *jornales* (labourers) were promptly hired, and unimaginable arrears of horrors dug out and removed—oh, the smell! And as to future transgressions of the laws of cleanliness and decency, C—— has adopted his own method for that, which consists in the simple plan of leaning out of the window when the people below do anything he does not like, and calling them "*Babuis*" (pigs), or "*sin verguenza*" (without shame) in a very loud voice, which they don't like at all; and this method has more effect than anything else, for he says: "You can always 'get at' a Filipino by making him ashamed of himself."

A SUBURB OF ILOILO.

We are lucky to be no worse off, however, for it is a marvel to me how this town is not swept clean of inhabitants by some awful plague, when one thinks that it is absolutely without drainage or sanitation of any sort, and when one sees and smells the awful and ghastly rubbish heaps which fester right amongst the houses in the town. The only saving of the place is the Monsoons, and it is no wonder everyone feels so ill and languid, even the natives, as soon as the wind drops. There is a costly School of Tropical Medicine in Manila, and many learned articles appear in the papers from time to time about germs and bacilli, and so on, assuring us that, when the Filipinos know more mathematics and Latin, they will know how to live more healthily; but sound common-sense would seem to lie in the direction of a strong and efficient sanitary control of white experts and a few schoolma'ams replaced by some paved and drained streets.

Oh, the streets! They are a disgrace to civilisation, for I have never, no, not in Morocco, not in little towns in the Canaries, known such neglect, such dirt, such squalor, and such smells!

Grass grows at the sides of the streets, and in wet weather many stagnant pools appear on pieces of waste ground and between the houses, looking very pretty indeed amongst the brilliant greenery when the sun comes out again, with beautiful reflections mirrored in their shallow depths, and making little gems of scenes like bits out of a fairy pantomime. All the same, one could quite willingly sacrifice their beauty in the cause of health, and for the sake of matter-of-fact drainage!

Mosquitoes breed in the swampy places in which the native houses generally stand, and at night the inhabitants frequently light fires under their flimsy dwellings to dry the ground and destroy the insects. At first sight these fires look very strange and alarming; we often pass them as we drive in the evenings, and it is yet another of the local miracles to see the dry thatch huts not taking fire from a pile of leaves and grass burning underneath.

In connection with the swamps too, or I suppose so, the Filipinos have another curious custom, which is, as soon as anyone is taken ill, to shut the house up tightly, with the screens let down and fastened over the openings that serve as doors and windows, and whenever you pass a house all dark and hermetically sealed with tiny slits of light here and there, you know some unfortunate soul is ill inside, and in all probability dying, for the Filipinos have no physique, and if they get seriously ill, they snuff out like a taper. When a poor person is dying—really at the point of death—he or she is taken out of bed and carried to the priest to be assoiled, which generally has the effect of killing the invalid outright. Only two evenings ago we met one of these melancholy little groups going along the Jaro road, two of the men carrying a long bamboo pole on their shoulders, with a canvas hammock slung to it, and I think the poor woman, whose head was lolling out, was dead already.

An American hospital, to which we have all contributed by request, is being provided for the town, and when we drive out, we often pass down the road where this remarkable building is rising slowly from a pile of beams and planks, all stacked ready, and cut to certain lengths. I say it is remarkable because the hospital has apparently been designed in America by someone who has never heard of the Philippines, for the main supports (the *arigis*), instead of being made of great trees of hardwoods, are quite slender posts of Oregon pine; and the cross-beams and, in fact, all the timber work, are of the same wood, which is about as much good as so many pieces of cardboard against insects, typhoons, earthquakes, and so forth. I daresay these plagues do not prevail in the country where this fantastic building was evolved.

AWAITING SHIPMENT.

Coffins containing Bones of American Soldiers
stacked in Malate Cemetery, Manila.

But if the substructure of the hospital was the laughing stock of the town, and the subject of many rather acid jests on the part of those who had contributed to such a monument of folly, you can imagine what was thought and said when the wards were seen in the making, and observed to consist of screens of *nipa* and *bejuco* matting! All so hasty, so shoddy, such a piece of blatant jobbery—but to hear its advocates talk you would think the finest hospital in Eu-*rope* was being rendered silly and out of date!

To-morrow is Decoration Day, the anniversary of the close of the war of the North and South, when the graves of the soldiers who fell in that struggle are decorated in the United States.

Out here the day has also been established as a public holiday; observed with bands and processions; and they have so ordered the ceremony that the graves of those who fell out here in the war with Spain and the Insurrection are supposed to be decorated, Americans and Filipinos alike. But the two events become hopelessly confused in the native mind; and it is no wonder that the Filipinos have some dim idea that they are rejoicing over the fall of those of the Americans whom they managed to kill in the Insurrection. There are not many American soldiers' graves out here to decorate, however, as the dead American warriors are being dug up everywhere and sent back to their homes—such a queer idea! Fancy if we dug up all the men who fell in our innumerable wars and sent them to their relations at home! There is nothing left but bones, of course, but each man is identified by a bottle containing his name, etc., which was buried with him. At least, they are identified to a certain extent; but a man who had the job of bringing a lot of these defunct warriors down the Pasig for shipment told C—— that the only thing to be done as a rule was to put a name on a coffin and then lay inside as many bones as you could find to make a complete skeleton. It sounds rather horrible, but I must say one can't have much sympathy with such unheroic and superstitious sentimentality, which seems to me no better than the customs of the Chinese.

LETTER XXXI.

MR TAFT—TROPICAL SUNSETS—UNPLEASANT NEIGHBOURS—FILIPINO LAW

ILOILO, *June 5, 1905.*

I don't think I have yet mentioned to you the great excitement in Manila, and in the Philippines generally, which are convulsed by the wind of the coming of Mr Taft, the Secretary of War in the U.S.A., who, as I told you before, used to be Governor out here. He is returning now to the Philippines on a sort of tour of instruction for the benefit of a party of Senators who, so say the papers, have been opposed to Philippine interests at Washington, owing to these interests clashing with their own sugar plantations, mines, and tobacco industries. Everyone seems to think this expedition a very good idea, and it is going to be gay and social as well, for a good many ladies—wives and other relations of the Senators—are to be included, and they say that the President's daughter, Miss Alice Roosevelt, may come too. Some say that she will come for the trip, as a pleasure party, and others declare that she is only to be sent as a pawn and symbol of the President's goodwill towards Mr Taft and his schemes.

In the meantime the papers are full of personal descriptions and puffs preliminary of the members of this party, but by far the most popular figure seems to be that of the President's daughter, about whom we get columns of description and narrative. She must be a very fascinating and charming and lovely girl, for though she is only twenty, she has refused numberless offers of marriage from all sorts and conditions of men, including the "effete hand" of Gustavus Adolphus of Sweden, he to whom our Princess Margaret of Connaught is now engaged. About this latter affair there is a very long account copied from another American paper—I mean a U.S.A. one, not a Manila paper—where it is said that Miss Roosevelt had declined to be a princess because she will not marry a man she does not love. I think that is highly creditable to her, don't you? And such a fine example to some of her countrywomen.

This last week has been sunny every morning, and then clouded over in the afternoon, and generally there is rain towards evening, so we cannot make up our minds about our second trip to Nagaba, which has been on the *tapis* for some time. We were going last week, but put it off for various reasons till to-morrow. Now, however, the weather looks so threatening that I doubt if we shall go at all. We are not without compensations, though, as the cool-looking grey skies are delicious, and the nights almost cold, so that a sheet is necessary, and sometimes even a blanket. In spite of the lowness of the temperature, however, I do not feel refreshed, as I had hoped to do, for the S.-W. wind is very enervating and relaxing, and everyone really feels more languid than in the heat. This wind has unshipped our green sunblinds, as it comes in great gusts, roaring and tossing in the thick belt of high palms that fringes the beach in the distance. The sound of the surf and the wind in the palms is delightful to me, for it reminds me of the pine-woods at home.

A few evenings ago we got into some real country by leaving the trap on the Molo road and walking along a path that led away through some tall brakes of bamboo. These clumps of bamboo are very graceful and beautiful, and the outline of their tapering stems and little flat leaves against the sunset skies always reminds me of that embroidered Japanese screen we have at home—by which you are perhaps sitting as you read this! We passed the bamboos and bushes by the roadside, and came at once to big grass fields and palm-groves, with ramshackle huts dotted about and half-clad native—how well I can sympathise with their prompt abandonment of the unnecessary extras of the civilised wardrobe, and only wish it were our fate out here to be able to wear one garment in a palm-grove! We wandered about there for a long time, up and down paths and tracks, and enjoying wonderful glimpses of glades and green vistas that were like impossible fairylands. There was the pink and orange bloom of a fine sunset, too, to add to the unearthly beauty of the palm-groves, where we lingered a long time, just admiring everything in sight, and smelling the delicious freshness of the wet earth.

We are very anxious to go there some day and try to get a few snap-shots, as a reminder of the scenes, though nothing could reproduce the colour. It is difficult to get enough light, as C—— is very busy just now, and does not get home before six. Eight to twelve and two to six—good long hours for office-work in the tropics! Still, we manage sometimes to get out before the daylight has quite gone, as the days are getting longer, but then it is, of course, too late to take the camera. That, by-the-bye, is another illusion dispelled, for I am sure I have always read and heard that the sun in these latitudes sinks suddenly at the same moment all the year round. I have already told you that I have watched in vain for this phenomenon. I don't know what happens in other places, but since the sun has come North here, the sunset has gradually changed to quite half an hour later than it was in December. In fact, it may be even later than that, for I can read on the balcony for a long time after tea before the light fades. Of course the twilight is brief compared to the length of time it lingers on at home, and I suppose it is sudden if it is compared to a long summer evening in England, but then you can think of our longest twilight as a flash if you compare it with Greenland!

About a month ago the basement of the empty house next door was taken by a typical Eurasian family—such a crew! beginning with an old father who goes about in a vest, slack, dirty trousers, and blue socks; an old mother, vastly fat, in petticoat, chemise, and slippers; some sons and daughters of all ages, and their husbands and wives and children, and two native servants. The basement they occupy consists of three large rooms. From our side windows we look right down into their windows, and get many astounding glimpses of their *vie intime*, including fearful revelations of *déshabillé*, which are the delight of C——'s life.

This family, who are quite well known in Iloilo Filipino and *Mestizo* society, and turn out great swells at the band, sleep about on *petates* (mats) on the floor, in native fashion, and some of their notions of sanitation are indescribable. The old father has a fearful voice, a loud, not-human bellow of insanity, which echoes in our rooms sometimes and quite frightens me, and C—— says I should be still more alarmed if I could understand the awful expressions he is using. They are always having horrid rows amongst themselves, all in slatternly rags in their filthy rooms—in the streets they are well-dressed and well-behaved, in true Eurasian fashion, all the world over. The sons are in various employments, which would keep the whole family in comfort, if not in decency, but one need hardly say that it all goes in *Monte* and buying diamond rings.

About a week ago, just as we had finished breakfast, there was a terrible hullabaloo coming from the dovecote next door, and we said to each other that they must be having a worse row than usual; when we heard yells and loud voices, and the old man bellowing out even worse words than the awful things he shouts out when he wants salt, or a cigarette, or a sock. We rushed to the side of the house looking on their windows, but a hand was pulling the shutters together, and the screams and yells and oaths were terrible. So we ran out on to the balcony in time to see one of the sons-in-law shoot out of the house, as from a cannon, yelling "*Policia! Policia!*" and go running up the street to the police station at the corner. A crowd began to collect at once in the street, while heads appeared at every window, and the pandemonium in the house became deafening.

Then, suddenly, a young woman in two garments ran out sobbing, with her hair down; followed a minute later by the fat old woman in her chemise and petticoat, wringing her hands and moaning, and running up and down, till someone caught hold of her and led her away to a house up the street. Then Juanita, the little native servant, with her hair streaming, rushed out with the baby in her arms; and the little girl of six came running in to the people below us, terrified and white and blubbering. Then another daughter—with a white, handsome face like a Bouguereau Madonna—hurried out, and after her a woman carrying clothes, whereupon a polite native clerk stepped across from an office and conducted her to the shelter of a friendly house.

All this time the bellowing and voices in the house went on undiminished, till the son-in-law arrived with a trim blue linen-clad native policeman. They went into the house together and shut the shutters and closed the door, and the noise died down, and the crowd outside melted away!

Nothing more happened all that day, and no human eye saw the policeman come out again. But next day we noticed that the old man was living with the natives under us; and C—— made some enquiries, whereupon they said, "The old man is mad," adding quite casually that he stuck a knife into someone, so his family chucked him out.

Well, so he lived there for a few days, with the windows of the house next door all shuttered so that he should not be able to see in, and every now and then he roared out "Ramon y Ju—a—ni—ta—aa!" or "Juanita y Raaaaa—mooooon!" always the names of both servants, when the two natives would go trembling to him, with the children for him to play with!

This went on till yesterday, when there was an afternoon of shouting and cursing and futile advice, and the street blocked with *carabao*-carts, and natives swarming in and out of the house carrying furniture upside down, and trying to force it into the carts broadside on. We hear the reason and result of all this is that the old man has moved, some say to Manila, others, to the next street. I think the poor trembling old fat wife must have gone too, as I have not seen her about again since then. The house next door has its windows open on this side again, and there seem to be more people than ever lying about there—they never *do* anything—and Juanita-a-a-a still takes the babies out in a large wicker washing-basket mounted on squeaking wheels; and the young men and women look great swells at the bandstand on Sundays and Thursdays.

I mentioned the way these people slept on the floor. That is a curious Filipino habit, but I daresay it is very nice and cool, and the floor can't be any harder than the Filipino bed. The servants sleep about on mats, generally in the hall of the house, but ours refuse to sleep in this house, as they say it is haunted by the spirit of a young Spaniard who died here when it was occupied by the Spanish Consulate. So they spread their mats on the Azotea, and if I wake up thirsty and go out into the hall for a glass of water, I see them through the open door, lying asleep on their mats in the moonlight, looking like pictures of the corpse on the battlefield, out of the *Graphic*, and rather weird and uncanny, with their clothes very white in the moonlight, and their dark hands and faces and dark bare feet; but on damp or cold (or what we call cold!) nights they look still more uncanny, rolled in blankets, and looking like mummies.

A friend who was here the other day told me an amusing instance of Filipino methods which happened a few days ago. A policeman came for his cook one morning, with a summons on the part of the cook's wife for assaulting her. So off the cook went to the court, not the High Courts where American dignity administers the highest justice with his boots off and his feet, with holes in his socks, on a table before him, but the police court where a Filipino tries to deal with small offences.

In the evening our friend noticed that his own cook and not a substitute was in the house, so he asked the man what had happened in the morning.

"Oh," said the cook, "they fined me five dollars and my wife five dollars too, and sent us away."

"But," said Mr —— "you beat her."

"No one said I did not beat her. But they fined us both, you see, so I was allowed to go away again, free, in time to cook the *señor's* dinner."

And you may think that sounds like a sentence out of the *Hunting of the Snark*, but it is perfectly clear logic to the Filipino mind, and all parties seemed to think the most lucid and satisfying law had been administered.

LETTER XXXII.

OUR MONGEESE—A FIRE—THE NATIVE EDUCATION QUESTION

June 15, 1905.

You must forgive the writing of this letter being rather bad, as I am ill in bed again, and likely to remain there for some time, for I have developed a tiresome complaint, which takes, so people tell me, a long time to heal. It sounds very simple, for what has happened is that the mosquito bites, with which my feet are covered, have become poisoned with something in the water, or the touch of a fly, and I hobbled about for a long time in great pain, being doctored and told to lie up, but I would not consent to, as it is so dull, and the warmth of lying even on a mat makes one's prickly heat unendurable. Now, however, I am forced to give in, for I can't walk across a room. An American friend tells me she has had this malady, and it extended all the way up her limbs, and she suffered great pain, and was ill for months. I am afraid this does not console me much, for I am a bad patient, as I have never had anything the matter with me before I came out here. The climate is certainly trying, but some people seem to be able to weather through it pretty well, though I have never met anyone who is really what one would call robust. Some become wrecks, as I apparently should do if I stayed much longer. I can't tell you how thankful I am to think that there is a chance of going home!

Our dear little mongeese are flourishing. We let them out of the cage nearly all day now, and they go running and smelling about the house; squeaking when they think they are lost, and then I have to go and find them, when they crawl up me as up a large tree, and go to sleep on the branches, quite safe and happy. I think you would love them. They have the sweetest little innocent faces I ever saw, and such pluck and individuality, each with its own little fads and manners. In India, I believe, people keep mongeese to kill snakes; but here they seem to be ready to pursue any and everything, and the house evidently affords good hunting, especially the space under the roof. I saw one of the mongeese under my wardrobe the other day, struggling with what looked like some dreadful grey insides of a little animal, and I hauled her out, thinking she had got hold of something that might poison her. It was the mangled body of a house-lizard—horrible sight! Then another of the little creatures caught an immense spider yesterday, and sat under the *sala* table tearing off the long hairy legs, and then choking the body down in great gulps—ugh!

One night last week I was awakened by a police-whistle in the street, sounding an alarm, which is one long note and two short ones. We found this alarm note out in a rather curious fashion, as one evening we whistled for one of the servants like that— we were sitting on the balcony at the time—and a few moments later a policeman knocked at the door and wanted to know what murder or other trouble we were in! And when C—— enquired about it at the police station, they asked him not to blow a whistle in that way in the street again unless we were in danger. It was a comfort to know that the signal would work so well.

So when we heard the long note and two short ones in the night, we turned out on to the balcony, whence we saw the glow of a big fire at the end of the street towards the point, and Filipino policemen were running along below with clanking buckets.

The building that was on fire was the Military *Corral* (stables), which made a fine blaze, and there was a stirring scene when the poor frightened horses came tearing down the quiet, dark street in a maddened rout. They were the American horses, which look so big and powerful and quite alarming to eyes accustomed to the little Filipino ponies. They clattered down the street in batches, tossing their heads and trying to pass one another, with the glow of the fire in the sky behind them, and we heard the sound of their hoofs dying away and away through the empty town. After a while the light in the sky faded out, the policemen with their buckets returned slowly, and we went back to bed; but no one else in the street had so much as looked out of a window!

We learned afterwards that many of the horses were found wandering far out in the country, but I believe some of them have not been caught even yet. The *Corral* was burnt to the ground, as they had to wait till the police arrived to put it out, because there were only two soldiers sleeping there, all the rest living in houses in the town and suburbs with their *queridas* (native mistresses). This seems a very strange state of affairs, but it is a well-known fact, and on this particular occasion was referred to quite casually by the soldier on duty (of whom C—— was asking information), and who apparently thought it was the most natural arrangement for troops in a disaffected country.

I have been reading a great deal since I have taken to bed, and besides all the home papers you send me, I have the Manila papers and *El Tiempo* (Iloilo), which I find I can read quite easily now. *The Manila Times* of June 10 had a long article about the eternal education question, headed "Arbitrary Race Distinctions," in which, as you may gather from the title, some American works out his nation's theory that there is no real difference between East and West. The writer very amiably wishes to point out that Filipino children are just as intelligent at school as are American children, and I think this is about the hundredth article I have read to that effect; but I have still to read or hear any observation to the effect that precocity is the natural heritage of every Oriental child. Americans always appear to judge the Philippines by no standard, precedent, or parallel; which I suppose is very natural for anyone coming straight from such an absolutely different country as the U.S.A. In this article, of which I am speaking at present, there are many long and fine words recklessly thrown about, such as "introspection," "collective individuality," and so forth, which I think are meant to prove that if a Filipino child is precocious, he will grow up a clever, cultured, and enlightened man or woman; whereas every unprejudiced person knows that the Filipino people learn with intelligence (an intelligence which is, after all, only remarkable when compared to a very ordinary white child) till they reach manhood or womanhood, and then it is as though a veil were drawn over the brightness of their minds, and they not only progress no further, but even go *backwards*!

This optimist also pictures a future "in three generations," when "the iron horse will spin merrily up and down the passes," by which I take it he implies that means of communication will at last (instead of at first) be established; and after a lot of hyperbolical descriptions of machinery, he winds up with this, "a sleek, well-nourished Filipino will garner the grain and check the tree boles"—which is very fine talk, but, to begin with, no one ever saw a Filipino who was not sleek and well-nourished, and what one wants to know is, what labourers will toil at the "iron horse" and the machinery with sufficient thrift and honesty to make those concerns worth the attention of the American or even Filipino capitalist? It is easy to imagine that some day the natives of the Philippines may be allowed to administer their own government and deal out laws of life and death to each other, but where is capital to come from? For the notion of Wall Street putting money into a business run by a Filipino, would be beyond the wildest dreams of the most uninstructed voter in the remotest State.

Now, what I can't make out is this, are all these essays and writings and leaders about the absolute equality of the Filipino mind with the best white intellect really genuinely what the Americans think of these people, or are they just so much dust in the eyes of the native as well as the foreign critic to excuse and justify the position the U.S.A. has chosen to assume towards these Islands?

LETTER XXXIII.

A PAPER-CHASE—LACK OF SPORTS—PREPARATIONS FOR MR TAFT

ILOILO, *June 26, 1905.*

C—— and another man got up a paper-chase last Sunday, and, by way of being cordial, advertised the event in *El Tiempo* a day or two before, C—— and his friend arranging to be the hares, and let all Iloilo chase them, if it cared to. They were very keen and excited about their venture, which was something quite new in the way of local enterprise. The "meet" was in Plaza Libertad at six in the morning, and when they got there and found a large company of Spaniards, *Mestizos*, Swiss, and one or two other Englishmen, they were delighted, and set off in great feather. Our pony is a very good "goer," and can fly along ahead of almost any other pony here, so C—— and his friend started and tore along the Jaro road in the cool morning, with the "field" after them.

Beyond Jaro, where they were out in the open country, they noticed that the hunt was far out of sight and hearing, so they ambushed in some bamboo brake, and hung about, peeping round bushes for about a quarter of an hour, and then went cautiously back a few yards and hung about again, and so on till by degrees they got back into Jaro. Imagine their disgust when they at last tracked the other sportsmen to a bar where they were sitting at little tables drinking cold beer! Their fury about the incident is comical, but one cannot help sympathising with them after all the trouble they took to infuse a little sport into the place.

One of the chief things Cebú crows about is possessing a race-course and a Jockey Club, and I think they are quite right so to crow, as something of the sort would be a boon here. One need hardly say that when anything like that is done in Manila or anywhere else, the Americans have no part in the initiative, as they are not a very sporting people, and all they do to keep themselves alive is base-ball. It seems so odd to be in a garrison town, and not see officers with sports or a club, or polo or gymkhanas or anything. The Filipinos have no games, and the great idea is to teach them base-ball, which, by-the-bye, the Americans call ball-game. When I say the Filipinos have no games, I forget a sort of ball they throw about, in the streets or anywhere, made of strips of bamboo bent into a hollow, spherical frame; but the throwing about is not conducted on any principle or according to any rules.

When I am feeling well again, I should like to ride in the mornings, but I wish I had brought my saddle, as there is not such a thing as a side-saddle to be bought in Iloilo, or, the shopkeepers tell us, in the whole Islands. This is because the *Mestizas* never ride at all, and the American women ride astride in large loose trousers that look like two skirts.[9] There are very few here who ride, but I saw several going about in Manila, and am confirmed once and for ever to my allegiance to the side-saddle, for a more hideous and ungainly effect than women astride I never saw, to say nothing of its vulgarity. The attitude also brings out all the disproportions of the female figure, making it look top-heavy and ill-balanced. It is all very well for the Amazons to look well on a Greek sarcophagus, but no modern woman of over sixteen is shaped like that—and I very much doubt if the ordinary ancients were either, quite apart from corsets, boots, and collars. Besides all that, from the point of view of sense, a woman's knees can't be strong enough to grip the saddle. So as I have not brought my own saddle I shall not be able to ride, and now we are thinking of going home, it is not worth while to send for it.

I read in my Manila papers that there is a fearful row going on in Manila now, because the committee who are arranging the banquets and receptions for Mr Taft and his party have invited heads of every religious sect except the Iglesia Filipina, and the latter are making a terrible fuss, and insisting on Father Aglipay being included amongst the official guests. Of course, if he is asked, the R.C. won't come, and the Pope will be furious, and the Insurrectionist Party will score one important point in the public eye. On the other hand, if the authorities fall out with Aglipay, they fall foul of his powerful following, who give quite enough trouble as it is, so they are in a very uncomfortable cleft stick, besides the fact of partizanship for any one religion being entirely unconstitutional. And the trouble is aggravated, you see, by Mr Taft being such an ardent pro-Filipino, and all the natives believing that his advent is to be a sort of second coming to announce the millennium of freedom.

What he *is* coming for, besides the personal conducting of the anti-Filipino Senators, is a staple subject of conversation, many thinking he will be allowed to announce a great reduction in taxation as a sort of halo to his visit. Whatever it is, I am so anxious not to miss his visit, and I do hope our return journey will not have to begin before he and his party arrive.

Besides the Taft excitement, Manila has been convulsed for months by efforts to get fireworks from America for "the 4th." Already in the month of April there were huge "scare-heads," as they call them, in the papers, with letters big enough for a poster, beginning

FIREWORKS NOT GONE OFF YET,

and then another headline to the effect that

---

[9] This breach of Oriental decorum is one of the most fatal and irreparable mistakes the Americans have made in the Philippines. It is a subject on which the Filipino or *Mestizo* is not slow to speak his mind. Alas for misunderstandings!

THEY WILL NOT REACH MANILA TILL JUNE.

Sometimes these headlines are very comical, whether intentionally or not I don't know—for instance, when the transport *Sherman* left, there was a headline in enormous letters,

Sherman's LIVING FREIGHT,

which I at first took to mean cows or horses, but found to my surprise it was only a list of officers' names.

I am sure you will be sorry to hear that one of our dear little mongeese is dead, the little man of the party. He was very sick for a day or two, lying on the floor on his stomach as if in pain, and when the others came running into my room in the morning, he could only crawl very slowly after them. At last, at about ten in the morning, he died, poor, gentle little beast, and I made Domingo take him out and bury him in the garden. We don't know what he died of, but we think it was tough cockroach, as his poor little throat was full of hard brown wings, which we hauled out, but it did him no good to get rid of them. What I fear is he may have picked up a cockroach which had died of rat-poison. I gave him weak sherry and water to revive him, but he brought it all up again with pitiful little groans and squeaks, and soon afterwards he died.

The little widows did not seem to mind much, they hopped about as usual; but now one of them has injured an eye in some way, and has gone blind in it, and is very sick and sorry, and I am afraid she won't live long either. I bathed the poor eye with cold tea, which gave the little creature some relief, for she lifted the lid slowly, and then I saw that the eye had a cut right across, as if some animal had scratched it. She can only move very slowly, with her head on one side—a very sad sight—just able to crawl as far as wherever I am, and then sit in a heap waiting to be lifted up, when she goes to sleep on my lap, and lies still for hours.

LETTER XXXIV.

TRYING HEAT—AN AMERICAN PROSPECTOR—NEW LODGERS—BARGAINING FOR *PIÑA*

ILOILO, *June 29, 1905.*

The weather is becoming more stormy, and typhoons are signalled, but so far they seem to go wide of us, which is a very good thing. The thermometer the last few days has been very low, 78° to 80°, but the damp makes it more trying and relaxing than when we had over 90° to contend against. With the rain, all sorts of trees have come into bloom—things with coarse, strong foliage and huge bright flowers. The fields are all covered with very vivid green grass and corn coming up, and sometimes when there is a purple thunder-cloud across half the sky and all these colours in the sun, wet with rain, shining against it, the effect is simply like a scene cut out of glittering metals.

As I explained to you when we first arrived, life here is adapted to dry heat, and the fears I had then about the wet season are being justified every day, for steel and silver rust while you look at them; clothes come out in feverish patches of blue mould; silk and satin "go" so that they tear like tissue paper; and all sorts of mysterious "beasts" are stowed away in our garments, while shoes have to be shaken before putting on more carefully than ever.

C—— amused me the other day with an account of an American millionaire who came down by the last boat from Manila to "prospect" in this island and Negros for sugar. It seems that the fancy of this plutocrat, who is quite a common, roughly-dressed old man, is to buy up half the island, with which object he went to the office, as C——'s firm are the largest, if not the only exporters of sugar in these islands. C—— said the old chap's notions filled everyone with amusement, for he wants to get control of some plantations, and put up sugar mills that will crush 10,000 tons of cane daily! The price and scarcity of labour were represented to him as a factor in his schemes, as well as the Export Tax, lack of roads, and other trifles. But he was not much depressed, and I daresay he will tackle the enterprise in the American sink or swim style, which seems rather a pity, as what the Philippines want is small and prosperous farms—not huge trust-like businesses to produce vast sums to be spent in New York or Paris.

You remember my telling you about the *fracas* next door? That family all moved away, eventually, but not to Manila, only to the next street parallel to this. The next-door basement is now occupied by a dressmaker, a jolly fat old Tagalo woman with a deep voice like a man, and her hair scraped up into a knob with a comb (an ordinary white bone one for *combing*) stuck across it. Besides the comb, she wears nothing but a chemise, petticoat, and slippers. The work-girls are all natives, and they sit about the big front room on mats on the floor, sewing and cutting out and talking all day long. They are there at five in the morning, and often work till after dark. Two have sewing machines on tables, and they look so queer in their tight native *sarong* and muslin *camisa*, sitting on a Viennese cane chair at a treadle-machine.

The husband of the Tagalo is a fat, greasy Spaniard, with side-whiskers, and an eternal cigar, who lounges all day in a cane chair in vest and trousers, reading the *Heraldo*, and balancing his slippers on the tips of his bare toes. They appear to hit it off very well, he and his old native wife, for he is quite content to blowze and loaf all day, and roll off to his club now and then, while she is a typical, thrifty, hard-working Tagalo,[10] always amongst her work-girls, and generally sewing herself. She sits in a chair, though, and every now and then picks up an old cigar-box that is for ever within her reach, and rolls herself a cigarette, scooping up very carefully every crumb of tobacco that falls into her capacious lap.

This Filipina keeps the house much cleaner than the *Mestizas* did, and has more regard for privacy, in the shape of curtains of bright cretonne nailed across the side windows. The old lady has a very pet dog, which is exactly like herself—a huge, fat, sleek, brown creature, perfectly good-natured, with a deep, full voice. They have a spaniel too, and other dogs that run in and out, and I can't make out how many belong to the house, or how many are only friends; but I got to be quite certain of one, which nearly always lies on the window-ledge, and to know it by sight. After a time, however, it gradually dawned on me that this particular spaniel never moved— and then I discovered that he was *stuffed*! Till I knew that, he was, to me, a quiet, contemplative dog; but since I found he was stuffed, he has become a horrible, uncanny demon.

Yesterday morning a little old native woman appeared wandering round the balcony with a bundle under her arm. When she caught sight of me she darted away, and in a few minutes Sotero came into the *sala* saying that a *mujer* (a woman) wanted to sell some *piña* to the *señora*.

I said I did not want *piña* particularly, but that the woman could come and show it to me if she liked; so in she came and squatted on her heels in the doorway while she undid the bundle, first a piece of cotton, and then an old newspaper, then more cotton, and at last a lot of rolls of muslin. They were very pretty pieces of stuff, dyed in pale greens, pinks, blues, and mauves, but she wanted sixteen or eighteen *pesos* apiece (thirty-two to thirty-eight shillings) for them—dress lengths of fifteen narrow yards. I said: "I will give you nine *pesos*."

"*Santa Maria!*" she threw up her hands. "I could not live. My mistress would beat me!"

I said that was nonsense, because she knew no Filipino lady would dream of giving her more than seven.

---

[10] The Tagalos are a much more industrious race than the Visayans, and are always in demand as clerks, workmen, or servants, in preference to the Southerners.

"Fourteen at the very lowest, *señora*, and the American ladies gave me eighteen without any questions."

"That is very silly of them," I said. But I knew it to be true, for I had been present at a great buying of *piña* by American tourists, and the prices they gave were simply idiotic.

"I am not *Americana*," I said.

"I know that" (I daresay she did, for on that point a native rarely, if ever, makes a mistake), "so I would not think of asking the *señora* more than thirteen, which I hope she will not mention to anyone."

"Why should I pay thirteen for stuff that I know is to be had in the Filipino houses for nine?"

"If I say twelve, may the *señora* say a prayer that I may not be dismissed by my mistress."

"I am *Protestante*. I think each person must say their own prayers."

"The *señora* is wise and good. She will give me eleven and a half."

And so on, and so on. Before we had done, I was the kindest, wisest, most humane, and beautiful and polite woman the sun ever shone on; I was blessed by all the Saints in turn—but I paid nine *pesos* for a roll of blue *piña*, and the old woman said she would come any day and sell me any amount more at the same price.

LETTER XXXV.

DECLARATION DAY—THE CULT OF THE FLAG—A PROCESSION, FESTIVITIES, AND A BALL

ILOILO, *July 4.*

This is a tremendous day here, and a universal public holiday—Declaration Day, you know; the anniversary of the day when the States declared themselves independent of the Mother Country. All the town is gay with palm-branches and myriads of Stars and Stripes, while the fun began at sunrise this morning by a great letting-off of Chinese crackers, and Americans coming out on their balconies in pyjamas and firing pistols into the air.

I think the Americans must be a very patriotic people, for out here they keep up these anniversaries with even more fervour, I am told, than they do at home, where they are a tradition of the soil. The cult of the national flag, too, is a perfect passion with them, and I have yet to see an American house out here where the Stars and Stripes do not appear in some part or other. In very many houses the flag is used as window-curtains, as ceiling-draperies, as *portières*, as tablecloths, besides little extra sort of Christmas-cake flags being stuck about wherever an ornament is wanted. One does not see this sort of thing in colonies of other countries, but the American flag devotion is really so sincere that one cannot cavil at its excess. Nevertheless we should consider it odd if the houses of high officials, and of everyone, in fact, in one of our colonies were decorated with Union Jacks in this fashion! Of course the Spaniards laugh at it very much; but then they are, very naturally, rather critical of all things American. One of them was holding forth bitterly to me on this flag question a day or two ago, and when I said that I thought it very nice to see so much patriotic feeling, he waved his hands and replied, very hotly: "It is not patriotism! It is farce! We, who have been born and bred for hundreds of generations on our native soil and love our country as a mother—we hold our flag sacred! We do not use it as furniture!"

I was much amused at his vehemence, but did not dare to smile for fear of hurting his feelings. Instead, I tried to soothe him down by saying that I thought the flag cult was perhaps a benefit as a direct appeal to the elementary natures of the Filipinos. This move of mine was a failure, however, for he burst out with renewed fury: "The Filipinos! What they think of it! Ha! You should hear them!" So I gave him up as a bad job!

To get back to the Declaration Day. The popping of pistols and throwing of crackers into the streets went on intermittently till about eight o'clock, when a procession began marching about the town, and luckily the day is extremely fine, though it is very hot indeed, as, though the thermometer is as low as 84°, there is not a breath of wind stirring, and all nature is very still and bright and shining.

The procession began to pass our house at about nine, so we had no more trouble to see it than just to lean over the balcony with some friends who had come round to profit by our position. C—— tried to get some snap-shots, but I am afraid they may not come out very well, as the camera is damp, like everything else in the house, and has a good coating of the prevailing blue mould.

The first spectacle that came along was a number of American officers on horseback, in khaki, with sashes of any colour they seemed to fancy—pale blue, pink, scarlet—slung round one shoulder and tied in a large bow on the hip. They rode the big army horses, which are no larger than ordinary horses at home; but, as I told you before, they look like pantomime animals after one's eye is used to the Filipino ponies.

There was some hitch, out of sight, as the procession reached us, and all the officers pulled up their horses and turned round to look back. I don't know what it was, but they halted a long time, trying all the time to get into the shade of the houses, for the heat was already very great. The men's khaki suits were dark with perspiration, quite a different colour! Their horses dripped puddles of sweat when they halted, and one white horse was gradually turning *purple*!

The Americans rode in the style which I notice they all adopt. It does not look well according to our ideas, for they slouch in the saddle and flap their elbows, sitting with their legs sticking out straight as if the horse had tar or something on its ribs which the rider wanted to keep clear of. They seem to hold their reins in any sort of way, in each hand and up to their chins being the favourite method, which looks awkward, to say the least of it. After them came one or two Filipinos, who all ride very well by instinct, sitting their horses firmly and gracefully, with flat thighs, and moving as if they were part of their mount, so that it is a pleasure to look at them. The little ponies and horses of the Filipinos pranced and curvetted about in a most engaging manner, which desirable result is brought about by means of an ingenious contrivance, borrowed from the Spaniards, of a sharp iron spike which runs into the roof of the horse's mouth when the rein is pulled, causing the animal to fret and foam and sidle to the admiration of beholders, who wonder how the rider can be so brave and cool with such a spirited steed.

After this little cavalcade had got past, the procession proper came along, headed by a military band from Guimaras, playing extremely well, and a long column of American soldiers, all in khaki and wearing khaki felt sombreros, such as our troops adopted in the Boer War, turned up at one side and with a narrow blue cord knotted in front, the ends finished off with two small blue acorns. They marched very well, all looking as exactly alike as so many toy soldiers on an expanding frame—you know the things? All very tall men, with long, handsome faces, narrow shoulders, and long, thin legs, not at all a robust type, no wiriness and no depth about them.

After the soldiers came a dozen or so of ordinary civilians in white linen suits and *sombreros*, with stars and medals on their breasts. They were followed by a similar group of men on foot, and these two little bands represented the Veteran Army of the Philippines, which includes anyone who volunteered in any capacity during the War.

We told C—— he ought to be in that company, or at least to have a medal, as he was once made a temporary "lootenant," and fought for the Americans in Samar. I think, however, that the V.A.P., as they call it, confines itself to American volunteers. With the American craze for societies and so forth, the V.A.P. are a sort of brotherhood, and have lodges and badges and meetings, and all that sort of thing. They gave a dance when we first came here, to which we went, and were awfully disgusted when we arrived to find that we had come too late for a solemn Lodge Meeting at which some ceremony had been performed.

After the V.A.P. came a lot of Philippine Scouts, quite the opposite build to the American soldiers, as they were very small, square men, with brown, square faces, high shoulders, long bodies, and short legs. Sturdy-looking little people, and looking very trim and smart in their neat khaki uniforms. Their band followed them, and behind that came the Constabulary, more little square "brown brothers" in white gala suits, with *their* band.

A string of carriages came next, decorated, wheels and all, with Stars-and-Stripes flags and filled with all sorts of Americans, Filipinos, *Mestizos*, and Spaniards, men and women, a very gay crowd. Following them was the Fire Brigade, consisting of natives marching on each side of an old hand-pump, like a thing on a sailing ship, and carrying a most amusing banner, painted with a picture of a house on fire, where a man in the middle distance worked a hose with a Niagara pouring out of it, while in the foreground a huge woman holding a giant baby sat on a packing case amongst a lot of very small furniture.

Next came a Filipino Base-ball Team, in khaki knickerbockers and black shirts, with ATLETICA in large white letters across their chests, after the fashion of that base-ball team we once saw play in the gardens of the Borghese.

The great feature of the procession was a large car decorated with a quantity of American flags and portraits of Washington, surmounted by a big pasteboard column, striped red and white, on the top of which lay a scroll of paper, held down by a gigantic gilt ink-pot with a mammoth quill stuck in it, and on the scroll was written CONSTITUTION in big letters.

All the men in the Port Works went past, some carrying hammers, and some bearing, between five or six of them, immense long boring-rods for blasting. They were Filipinos, of course; in fact, with the exception of the American soldiers and a dozen or so of the occupants of the carriages, the whole procession was Filipino—all quite pleased and childlike to march about with banners to Sousa's stirring tunes. I don't suppose one in twenty of the "little brown brothers" had the vaguest idea what their big white brothers were so rejoicing about; or if they had ever heard of Townshend and the Stamp Duties they would think the commemoration of the removal of a yoke of foreign bad government and taxation was something to do with their own everlasting struggle for independence. Besides this comical side to the rejoicings, there was the absurd anomaly that a great part of the funds for this celebration had been contributed by the British commercial houses!

Well, it was an interminable string of people. The Normal Schools of Jaro, La Paz, Molo, etc., each under their own banner, a long file of boys and then girls in all sorts of outfits and colours, but the girls all wearing the Filipino *camisa*, and many of them carrying the branches of artificial and gilt flowers, which they use in religious processions. It was particularly noticeable that there was no priest of any sort in the procession, nor were the priestly colleges or the Convent Schools represented in any way.

We got quite tired of watching them at last, especially as the whole thing kept on getting muddled up and having to stop for long, weary halts. We came to the conclusion at last that as there was no crowd in the street or at the end of it; there must be a tiger round the corner. But a very literal Scotch friend said: "There are no tigers in the Philippines."

A dance was given by the Spanish Club last night, and there is to be another to-night, at the invitation of the Presidente of the town, at his official residence, the Gobierno. I am not well enough to go to both, for I have not been out of the house for weeks, and even now it is rash to stand at all till my feet are healed, but I felt I must go to one of these functions, so I have chosen to-night, which is, according to Iloilo notions of etiquette, far the less exclusive of the two, so it will be much the more amusing.

I have been writing this, lying in my long chair in the *sala*, while C—— went out to the Plaza to see if he could hear any speeches or anything funny. He has just come back, and tells me there was a platform erected in the Plaza, where speeches had been rolled off, but he had been too late to hear any of them. A great pity, as I daresay they may have been amusing, because one of the speakers was a rabid pro-Filipino and the other (both Americans) a keen pro-American. I will finish this letter to-morrow, so as to be able to tell you all about the ball.

July 5.

We went for a drive yesterday, late in the afternoon, and when we got as far as the Plaza, we found a terrific *Fiesta* in progress—all the lamp-posts decorated with Stars and Stripes and Japanese lanterns; and a huge stage, covered with palms and more Stars and Stripes, put up opposite the bandstand, and full of Americans, while vast crowds of Filipinos surged below—the men in white and the women in colours like those in a cheap church window—and it all looked very gay and pretty. I was very much surprised to see all this, as I had had no idea anything of the sort was in contemplation, and I was sorry that neither I nor the other Englishwoman had been invited to the stand, but I suppose they thought we would not care to take part in rejoicings over the Declaration of Independence although our countrymen had contributed, by request, a great part of the funds for the celebration.

We pulled up and looked on for a little while, much interested in a tug of war which was unlike anything we had ever seen. The two sides, Filipinos, stood on a long wooden frame like a gigantic ladder lying on the ground, and on this they lay at opposite ends, with their purchase on the rungs, and pulled at the rope with no effect whatever to the amateur eye; but apparently some man in command thought otherwise, for a voice suddenly sang out that one side had won, whereupon the competitors all let go the rope and fell quite limp, and then got up and walked away.

They had races, too, and a greasy pole—no, two greasy poles—of bamboo, with a packet of money at the top, and, of course, a flag of Stars and Stripes. Up these the enterprising native youth of Iloilo swarmed, to the intense joy of the onlookers, who howled and roared with appreciation. All sorts of dodges were allowed, which were ingenious if not particularly sporting. One small boy tried to get to the top by covering his hands and feet with sand, with which his pockets were laden and bulging, while the man who eventually got to the money hoisted himself by a device of bars of wood and rope, which betrayed him at once to C—— as a sailor. We very nearly gave up waiting for this enterprising mariner, who took an immense time to get up to the thin part at the top of the pole, where he could abandon his contrivance and get his hands round the bamboo—but he secured the prize, and the people below bellowed with delight.

There were very few Americans amongst the crowd, all the officers and officials being in the stand, with many ladies in light frocks and big hats, while the rank and file could be seen in the bars round the Plaza, not caring a rap about tugs of war or greasy poles, or their "little brown brothers." In the gaol the prisoners were crowded at the barred windows, getting what fun they could out of the general atmosphere of liberty; and as we drove round the Plaza, I saw a most ragged and miserable young countrywoman carrying a sad, puny baby at her breast, talking to her man through the bars of the prison, where the female relations come and hand food in to the dark ragged fellows inside. She slunk away round the Plaza, and her face was too pitiful for words, she was so gaunt and haggard. We had no money with us, but I doubt if she would have taken it if we offered it to her, as the country people are very proud, and very sensitive about "*verguenza*," which is Spanish for shame. Very few of the white people seem to understand this *verguenza*, by an appeal to which, as I told you before, wonders can be done with a Filipino.

This little incident put me out of humour with the Declaration celebrations, so we drove out on to the Molo road a little way and then returned, and I had a good long rest before dinner to prepare me for the evening's festivities.

The day wound up with the ball at the Gobierno, which is a kind of Government House comprising public offices, and the Law Courts, and so forth. It is a big building across the end of the Calle Real, with a large over-hanging balcony or verandah, under which the carriages pulled up on a stone-flag pavement, all muddled up anyhow, anywhere, each one turning and going out in any direction the horse chose, with the usual shouting and confusion and swearing on all sides.

The big stone basement was decorated with palms tied against the columns, and Stars and Stripes, and all up the staircase more Stars and Stripes and more palms.

The ball went on chiefly in the Court Room, a long narrow apartment, where the scheme of decoration was half a dozen huge American flags draped over the walls;

and, stowed away over one doorway, a few folds of the red and yellow of Spain. On one side of the Court Room, through wide arches, was another long room, and on the street side was the long balcony, open to the night, and cool when compared to the rooms.

When we arrived, the ball was in full blast with the Official Rigodon, which C—— and Mr M—— who went with us, did not care to dance, and I could not, so we sat in a row and looked on, and I talked to an American friend we had met as we came in. He asked me to dance, but I said that was not possible for me, as my feet were still unhealed, and all bandaged up for this dance.

"Oh," he said cheerfully, "I guess you are right to be careful, because if you neglect those things they turn into tropical ulcers, which are *in*-curable."

"Do they?" I said.

"Why, yes, I had a friend who got mosquito bites poisoned just so, and he died of them."

In spite of this, however, I spent a very cheerful evening, and was quite rewarded for the trouble of going out by the spectacle itself. For some time our American friend remained by us, as he said it was the last chance he would have of seeing us to say good-bye, because he was going back to the United States. We asked him if he were going on leave, but he said no, he was giving up his appointment; which rather surprised us, as he is one of the chief officials here, and has a very good position. But he said he simply could not stand the Philippines any longer, and would rather work for half the pay in any other country.

"Besides," he said, "I am entirely out of sympathy with the whole thing, and can't see what we are doing here anyway."

I said, "But you have the country to develop."

"Oh, I'm sick of hearing that," he said. "What I want to do is to go right back to the States and see some development done there."

"Where do you mean?" we asked.

"Why, in my own State alone there are hundreds of miles of virgin soil which I reckon I want to see developed before these silly old islands."

"Ah," I said, "then you don't like the Philippines?"

"Have you ever met anyone who does?"

"No," I said, "at any rate not one American who does not loathe the place, except one woman, the wife of a missionary, who says she likes it, but then she spends all the disagreeable season in Japan."

"That's so," he said. "And I guess if I come back it's going to be on the religious stunt, with no work and lots of *va*-cation."

The guests at the ball were all sorts and conditions of men, rather what C—— calls a "heterogeneous mass," but most of the Americans were there too, and several new people whom I learned were officers and their wives from Camp Josman, over in Guimaras. One little woman particularly took my fancy, with her pale, pretty face and masses of fair hair, and a really lovely pink silk ball-dress. She looked so fresh and charming, but I felt quite anxious about her nice dress, as my own black skirt was a source of trouble on such dirty boards, where, I am sorry to say, some of the guests did not hesitate to expectorate when they felt inclined for this national pastime.

The floor, as I say, was simply rough, unpolished, dusty, dark-wood planks, and all the American men, except our friend and two others, wore day suits and boots, while many of the women had on walking shoes, which did not improve things.

The natives were all got up in blinding colours—little, dark, square-faced women in the harsh aniline dyes of thirty years ago—and some of them had on very handsome diamonds. C—— and I and Mr M—— were the only English people present. I believe the others, as well as many of the Americans, all thought the official ball not sufficiently select, which seemed to me a very amusing point of view in a place like Iloilo—or anywhere else for the matter of that.

After watching the ball-room for a little while, we thought we would like some fresh air, so we moved out on to the balcony, where the air was fairly cool, and where the band was stationed on a platform of two steps in height. This was the Constabulary, native brass, which sounds very well out of doors in a procession, but is rather deafening in a room. On the platform were two or three music-stands at which a few men lounged, but the rest of the twenty-five sat and blew (all brass and two flutes) wherever they pleased, most of them festooned gracefully about the steps of the stand; some lying almost full length on one elbow; and some huddled up with their chins on their knees, looking exactly like performing monkeys. One man with strips of black sticking-plaster on his flat, brown face, lay on the steps of the stand, gazing at the ceiling, and playing his cornet in one hand.

There were benches all round the balcony, and on one of these we sat, in company with a lot of other guests, while some energetic and perspiring dancers came out and extended the ball to the balcony, dancing solemnly up and down in front of the band. When some people moved away from the bench nearest the platform, half a dozen bandsmen instantly took possession of their vacant places and sat there, leaning back and blowing away at greater ease. They seemed to be playing instinctively while thinking of other things. One small boy on the bench by us was fast asleep, with his fingers still moving up and down on the stops, which so interested Mr M—— that he got up and put his ear down to the fellow's trumpet, but declared he could hear no sound coming out of it at all. The other bandsmen watched him do this with impassive, expressionless faces, if they looked at him at all. This was during the second Rigodon, which we could see going on in the long Court Room, and when the last figure was reached, a bandsman suddenly sprang up from a recumbent position on the steps and tootled the first few bars of "Hiawatha," which they all struck into with a swing, and some of the sleepers opened one dull eye, while the man with the black sticking-plaster on his face was suddenly galvanised into walking up and down to the tune—a sort of dancing walk—in front of the bandstand.

While we sat by the band, we were joined by another American friend, also a "prominent citizen," with whom I had a long and interesting shout about the Philippines in general, and Mr Taft in particular, which was most entertaining, for this friend was as ardent a pro-Filipino as the other had been anti-Taft and anti-everything. This man was very enthusiastic about Mr Taft's scheme, as he called it, and when I said, "What scheme?" he replied:

"Why, the way we run these Islands."

Whereupon we entered upon a hot discussion, for I was all in favour of roads and irrigation, and he was all for school-desks and more teachers. I quoted a paragraph I had seen in the Manila papers, where the public were informed that some new and wonderfully fertile valley had been opened up in the Island of Luzon, and that the Government's first care had been to send ten thousand school-desks to this favoured spot. Whereupon he said:

"Well, what is the matter with that, anyway?"

I begged him to consider what Ceylon would be now if Sir Samuel Baker had opened it up with school-desks instead of roads and reservoirs.

"Oh," he said, "I never thought of it in that way. But perhaps our idea of raising these races is right. It is an experiment which time will prove."

And that we argued too, with a running comment of amusement on the *baile*, in spite of the loud blasts of the band.

Before we left, we had excellent supper in a side-room, where two long tables stood covered with food, and all the ceiling was draped with loops of greenery and paper lanterns. There were plates set out, each with a helping of excellent cold turkey in the middle surrounded by little piles of stuffing and vegetables and things, which we followed by very nice meringues, and accompanied with delicious iced drinks—ice from the Government factory—such a treat! While we were at supper, standing at one of the long tables, a paper lamp flared up and fell in a flaming mass just behind me. C—— and some Spaniards promptly stamped it out. But some of the women were frightened, so the Spaniards sang out:

"Terminado! Terminado!"

And everyone went on eating again.

A little group of natives and *Mestizos* came into the room immediately afterwards, but they had not seen the lamp fall, and one of the women in a light trailing gown passed over some smouldering fragments. C—— sprang forward and said in Spanish:

"Your dress! There has been a lamp burnt there!" And pointed to the sparks.

But the woman merely glared over her shoulder, as if he had offered her some insult. I could gladly have stuck my fork into her impudent, bold, brown face, and can't, as yet, see why in the Eternal Fitness of Things she did not catch fire and flare up.

After supper we watched a waltz and a two-step, and then went away about twelve.

On our way out I passed one of the alcove openings into the inner room, where I saw a sad, white Bouguereau Madonna face looking up at a man bending down, and recognised one of the heroines of the late *funcion* (a delightful Spanish slang word) next door. So I perceived that the Marble Misery was a chronic pose, and nothing at all to do with her relations stabbing each other. Only, I must say she looked more "in the picture," running down the street with her hair streaming, than in a bright ball-room.

We had gone to the *baile* in a hired *quilez*, as we did not want to take our own frisky pony out on such a night of Chinese crackers underfoot and rockets overhead, and we had told the *quilez* man to come back for us. To our astonishment, he did so. Not that it was much of a treasure in the way of a carriage, for it was so badly balanced that our weight at the back would have lifted the pony clean off the ground if the driver had not kept the balance by squatting on the shafts over the pony's tail. The little animal tore along, and it was a wonder and a mystery to see how the driver stuck on at all. It was probably chiefly done with his toes, for Filipino toes stand apart, supple like fingers, and are used in the most marvellous and uncanny ways. In the streets the Filipinos wear, or ought to wear, only slippers of gaudy velvet, called *chinelas*, but many of them now affect stockings and pointed shoes, which I think must be one of the most doubtful blessings of civilisation. In the procession I noticed many of the little school girls and boys with stockings on and awful shoes, and one or two of the little girls even wore hats, but, if I described them to you, you would not believe me!

Well, have you ever had such a long letter in your life? And yet there is any amount more to tell you if I only had the energy to write it.

LETTER XXXVI.

COCK-FIGHTING—PULAJANES

ILOILO, *July 14, 1905.*

I know you will be sorry to hear that the last of our dear little mongeese is dead—killed by the dogs next door a week ago. We heard squeaking and barking and scuffling in the alley-way one evening, and rushed to the windows, but it was all dark below, and we could see nothing. So C—— and Sotero went down with a lamp, but there was nothing to be seen, and when we sent in to ask the old Tagalo dressmaker about it, they all swore they had heard nothing. So we hoped it was only a rat; but we waited in vain for our poor little pet to come back, and she never appeared again.

I could not bear the sight of the empty cage, and made the boys take it away after a day or two, and now I find it stands on the Azotea, with Sotero's rooster sitting solemnly on a perch that has been fixed across the middle. This is the same cock, by-the-bye, that travelled back with us from Nagaba, and when C—— asks the boy about it, he always says it is "going to fight for fifteen *pesos*" on some Sunday—which never comes. The cock is as tame with Sotero as a dog, and allows itself to be combed and stroked the way one sees all the Filipinos do to their fighting-cocks.

A VILLAGE COCK-FIGHT.

In the native huts the fighting-cock is a very precious and sacred person, enthroned on a special perch at one end of the living-room. The night before he fights, this warrior is watched with the greatest care to see which point of the compass he faces, as on that omen hang many events, for if the creature faces the east he is bound to win, but if he is turned towards the west you may as well not take him to the battle at all. A little hope is left, however, for when the cocks all crow before the dawn, he who makes the first scrawk is bound to win, and you can put your last *peseta* on him.

The poor beasts are taken to the ring, where spurs of curved steel are fastened to the back of their heels, which makes the fight pretty short and decisive, and may be indirectly merciful if it helps towards a swift death. The making of the blades is a fine art, and they are carefully carried about in a small box with a little stone on which to sharpen them. When one sees a Filipino on the way to a cock-fight, with his bird sitting on his arm, there is generally another native walking beside him, carrying this little black box containing the spurs and the little whet-stone.

There is as much roguery and "doping" amongst these cock-fighters as there is about horse-racing amongst "civilised" men, and some of the dodges are really very ingenious, such, for instance, as taking tiny pills of opium or other poison under the finger nail and dropping them in front of your opponent's bird when it is pecking about before the contest begins.

Before the fight the interested parties are allowed to test the roosters, like looking at a horse in the paddock, only they enjoy advantages which I believe are not to be indulged in a paddock at a race-meeting, for they may form their opinion of a bird by picking the animal up and feeling its muscles, looking at its thighs and examining its feet, of all of which points the Filipino is a wonderful judge, being able to graduate his large bets on the feeling of a muscle with great certainty. All the same, this is the occasion, if he is so minded and the other man is not quick enough, to injure the animal by means of a sharp pin point hidden in the palm of the hand or between the fingers.

I notice that the fighting-cocks here don't have their breasts pulled bare of feathers like those poor birds we saw in that old man's house below the walls of the Alhambra. Do you remember how bald and horrible they looked? And how the old villain who kept them told us he pulled the feathers out and rubbed in spirits to keep the skin hard? They don't seem to do that here, for I have never seen a bare-breasted cock, and never met anyone who has heard of such a custom.

The General has gone off to Samar, the long island parallel to this, and on the other side of Cebú—though I can only use those terms vaguely, and by way of a general indication to you where to look on a map. The island is now under martial law, owing to the patriotism and enterprise of certain jolly fellows, called Pulajanes, going about with big curved *bolos*, and old Spanish flint-locks, and in fact anything they can catch hold of. These persons are really patriots of a most irreconcilable type, but it suits the programme of the Government to label them *ladrones* (robbers), and to refer to their own hard fights with them as "cleaning up the province." On the strength of this nickname, the Americans cut down these patriots freely (when the Pulajanes do not do the cutting down first), and if they catch them alive the poor devils are hanged like common criminals.[11] The papers continue to publish long eulogiums on the peace and prosperity of the Philippines, and all the time the richest commercial centre of the Archipelago is under martial law, with all its business houses shut down; and soldiers and officers continue to arrive at the hospital here every now and then, with more or less severe wounds. Also waggons occasionally go past from the barracks, piled up with baggage, and followed by troops in service kit, and one hears that they have "gone to the front."

For some time past the staff of C——'s firm has been increased here, in this Iloilo branch, by the absorption into it of one of their men from Catbologan, the chief town of Samar, as their business there, along with all the others in that island, has had to be shut down.

There is desultory fighting even here, in Panay, but we never hear of it except as an occasional paragraph in a Manila paper.

So much for peace. As to prosperity, there is general scarcity, many districts suffer actual famine. In Cebú the lower classes are chiefly dependent on an allowance of so many sacks of rice a day, the gift of the Chinamen! In that town, indeed, matters are so bad that siege-like conditions prevail, and amongst other horrible things that happened, a starving native woman lately killed and ate her own baby. This is not hearsay, but sober reports in the *Manila Times*.

I am paying the penalty of my recklessness in having gone to the Declaration Day ball, for the little walking I did that night made my feet very painful again, and I am laid up in bed once more, reading papers and trying to forget my American friend's optimistic remarks about tropical ulcers. The doctor tells me I want feeding up to get the poison out of my system, and this I can quite believe, but fail to see how it is to be brought about. I have tried drinking a little wine, but that makes my prickly heat unendurable. The Spaniards here drink *tinto*—the red Spanish wine one gets at *tables d'hôte* in Spain—but it has to be spirited up for export, so out here it is rather heady and sour; but I am sure it must be more wholesome than the whisky and soda of the English people, or the eternal tea of the American women. You will be tired of hearing about my mosquito bites, but I must just tell you one new thing that I have heard about this unpleasant ailment, which is that many people think the poison is introduced by flies—one fly would be quite enough! There were no flies, or very few, when we came here at first, in the dry season, but with the rain they have appeared in black swarms, and we live surrounded by large sheets of sticky paper with Tangle Foot written on them—a delightful American expression! Here again I am reminded of the amount of indifference shown to an animal in proportion to its size—comparative with that of a human being. For can you imagine anyone being tolerated, who caught cats or horses in deep, thick glue and let them slowly struggle to death? Yet what are

---

[11] I have before me a cutting from *The Manila Times*, containing an account of the arrival in Manila, by the Transport *Dix* from San Francisco, of "eleven strong-limbed, square-jawed bloodhounds" ... "for the work of trailing the *Ladrones* of Cavite and the *Pulajanes* of Samar."

you to do with flies? You can't catch each one—first catch your fly, in fact—and then kill it in the quickest and most scientific manner. No. It must be Tangle Foot papers. But even though I find I am simply compelled to have them about the house, when I see a fly trying to haul one foot after the other out of the dreadful Tangle Foot, I can't help appreciating the poor insect's point of view.

The old millionaire I told you about is still here, and everyone is trying to be civil to him, but I hear he is very difficult to entertain, for he insists on being the only man to talk, which he does very slowly and in an almost unintelligible accent. He gives considerable annoyance, too, by his bad clothes, dirty hands, and unshaven face, and one can't help sympathising with the men who are irritated by such slovenliness, or agreeing with them, that it is not much good being a millionaire if you can't get hold of a decent tailor and a razor and some soap!

I think I told you that our friend Mr —— sent his wife and family off to Hong Kong when the heat began? They have come back, and are giving me so much annoyance by rhapsodies over the climate, the cheapness of everything, and the good food in Hong Kong that at last I had to *beg* them to say no more! Mrs —— is still comparing prices here with prices there, and she brought back pretty things for her house, which make me wild with envy—or would if we were not soon to pass to happier climes! Her husband went to fetch his little tribe, and he is raving, not so much about the comparison of prices and the joys of fresh milk, fruit, and vegetables as the horrible imposition of being compelled to pay the Philippine Cedula Tax all over again. Five *pesos* a head—10 shillings each for his wife, the three children, and the nurse! And what annoyed him most of all, I think, was his having been away about three weeks himself and having to pay it again too. However, it has been worth the money to them, I should think, for they all look quite brown and jolly compared to the people here, and quite different beings to the washed-out folk they were when they went away. At this time of year, as I think I told you, all the Hong Kong people who can afford it go home or to Shanghai or Japan, as they consider Hong Kong at this season not fit to live in!

LETTER XXXVII.

A PEARL OF GREAT PRICE

ILOILO, *July 14, 1905.*

We are having much cooler weather now, the thermometer sometimes as low as 77°, and hardly ever above 80°, and at night it has even been down to 64°. We have had some spells of hot sunshine, which have brought the flowers out in the few gardens and the cemeteries. We get a trayful now and then of all sorts of queer-looking blossoms, mostly bright reds and yellows, with no smell, and very gaudy and handsome. Many of them I have seen in hothouses at home, especially one big bright yellow funnel-shaped flower; but I don't know any of their names, except the native words told me by the charming white-haired old Filipino gardener who brings them. Amongst the last lot was a thing exactly like a large periwinkle, which made me think at once of the garden at home, and some stuff like May-blossom, which made me feel more homesick than ever! They are beautiful, all these flowers, when they come in fresh, but there is no scent about them, and they seldom live twenty-four hours. One I do recognise, and that is the Canna lily, which I have seen in hothouses at home, and some irises of different sorts. I am feeling much better, so we went for a drive yesterday between the showers, but got caught in two tremendous squalls—one in the town and one on the Molo road. The *calesa* has a hood, which is raised on crooks, and one can shut oneself in altogether in heavy rain, with an arrangement of waterproof curtains, the reins passing through a hole in the high apron. It looks so funny, in wet weather, to see the bottled-up *calesas* going about, being driven as by magic, with the miserable *sota* (groom) trying to make the best of his narrow perch behind.

The roads were a maze of huge pools of water, through which we just splashed anyhow, and all the palm-groves were brilliantly green, and full of new little fairy lakes, which looked so lovely that they were well worth the discomforts of the drive. Near the huge Priests' College, a little way out of Iloilo, we saw some *carabaos* having a glorious time in various new pools. They looked very picturesque, with their great dark curved horns, standing out against the shining water and the green grass. The greenness is wonderful—too wonderful. There is no beauty of purples and soft blues about a wet day here; it is all grey and green, and even the little lakes in the palm-groves are very garish, and all exactly alike. One longs for a change of colouring, and these crude tints get on one's nerves like an oleograph in a hotel.

Talking of nerves, the perpetual sounds were added to, as soon as the rainy season set in, by the bell-like voices of countless frogs, singing in every ditch and pool. They sing in the day, but at night they are loudest, or else most noticeable, and their melodious notes might be pretty if one heard less of them and a long way off.

WATERING CARABAOS.

A day or two ago Sotero came to me saying that a woman was at the door wanting to sell me a ring. I said I would look at it; so he went off and brought me a dirty little piece of newspaper, out of which emerged a huge pearl set in a very common, florid, claw setting. I looked at the pearl and saw that though it was white enough, it was very rough, with no iridescent lustre, what connoisseurs call "skin," I believe. I also noticed that as the stone tapered away, and was discoloured under the setting, it could not be worth more than £10 at the most. But Sotero said the woman wanted two hundred *pesos* (£20), so the incident came to a rapid close. When C—— came back in the middle of the day, and I told him about the ring, he said he knew it quite well, for it had been hawked all over Iloilo; and everyone thought the price asked a preposterous sum. In spite of which the woman refused all reasonable offers.

The pearl came from the pearl-fisheries of the Philippines, which are chiefly in the Sulu Islands, far away South, where the Philippines almost touch British North Borneo. They say the pearls are not very good ones at the best, but none of the best specimens find their way about the Islands, for they are sent straight away to Singapore by the Chinamen who own the fisheries. Here there are oysters with beautiful, transparent, white pearl shells, of which the small panes of the rain-shutters are made; but these shells have no pearls in them, and are of very little value. Besides these oysters, we get all manner of shell-fish—crabs, cray-fish, clams, shrimps, as well as soles, sprats, whiting, and quantities of other fish. Indeed the supply of fish is wonderfully varied and always exquisitely fresh, except on Fridays, when the servants of all good Catholics clear the markets, or even secure the fish before they get into the markets at all. In stormy weather, too, we don't get much fish, but, as a rule, the supply is a great boon, and one of our chief sources of sustenance. I was astonished to find in Manila that fish was very scarce and dear, and people there envied us the fish here, while those who only knew Manila refused even to believe that we could have such a supply at all!

A FILIPINO FISH-MARKET.

LETTER XXXVIII.

AGRICULTURAL POSSIBILITIES

ILOILO, *July 31.*

I think I told you we had been very lucky in the selling of the greater part of our furniture, and now we have got the *calesa* and pony off our hands as well, which is a great loss in the evenings, but we had to take what chance we could. Some of the young Englishmen got up a Gymkhana on the beach yesterday, and C—— rode the pony for the last time, when he was lucky enough to win two races out of three, and only missed the third by a misunderstanding about the start.

It was a dull, showery afternoon, unfortunately, but when the rain went off, I strolled down to the beach to see if anything was to be seen. I found crowds of Filipinos standing about the upper part of the beach, and a few hurdles down on the sands, which the receding tide had left quite firm. The competitors, who included some of the young Spaniards and *Mestizos*, were riding up and down, and just as I arrived on the scene, a race came flying along in great style, to the intense joy of the native onlookers.

The occasion was enlivened by the *banda de musica popular*, the members of which had been on their way to play in the Plaza, but had strolled down to the beach, where they stood amongst the crowd, and every now and then blew and tootled a tune while they goggled about.

I signalled to our *sota* and made him go up to the house and fetch me a chair, on which I sat and watched the race. As I sat there a Filipino youth came up and very civilly asked me if the *señora* wanted a *muchacho*, but I said I did not, as I was quite content with the servants I had at present.

We have had one or two very fine days again lately, and have been for one or two drives, but some very blood-thirsty road-mending has been going on, to prepare the town for the critical eyes of the Taft party, who are to arrive here from Manila on the 14th or 15th of next month. This road-mending is done by hauling the volcanic gravel out of the river beds, and dumping it in huge piles along the middle of the roads, and as the thoroughfares are not lighted, the result is a wild steeplechase with one wheel in the air. Sometimes fellows come along and spread the gravel out, but more generally it just spreads itself. It makes very soft roads, which the heavy *carabao*-carts plough up at once.

One of the last drives we took was to visit the foreign cemetery, which is on the outskirts of the town, on a road running parallel to the beach. We got out of the trap at a tall wooden gate, which an old man opened to us, and walked up a short avenue of flowering bushes and palms. The graves stood on a grassy plot, with bushes growing about it, laden with large red or yellow blossoms, and crossed at right angles by sandy paths bordered with tiles. They were not ordinary graves, like those one sees at home, for each one was a sort of small brick tunnel some feet from the ground, and closed by a cemented tablet. There were names of some English people on one or two of them, and one had just been opened to send the bones of the occupant back to his native land. The man had been dead twenty-five years, and it seemed to me hardly worth while to disturb him.

A little behind the main row of tombs we came on a Jewish grave—a big marble sarcophagus—with an iron rail round it and inscriptions in Hebrew on the flat top. The marble was native to this country, I have no doubt, as there is plenty of it in the Philippines; in fact some of the small islands are known to be of solid marble, but it does not pay to work them—did I not tell you this before, though?

Mr B—— came to call this afternoon, and was very indignant about local justice, as it appears that one of his Filipino clerks was impudent to a white man in his firm, whereupon the white man naturally struck the Filipino as any ordinary man of grit strikes a man who is rude to him. However, the cur Filipino went off to the police and lodged a complaint. The white man was had up, and has been heavily fined for "assaulting" the Filipino, and Mr B—— says:

"What on earth are you to do with impertinent natives if you don't hit them? They don't care a straw if you dismiss them, and take not the least notice of reproof."

But I think there is right on both sides, for the way some of the white men hit their servants about is brutal and foolish. I said something to this effect, whereupon Mr B—— said, very much surprised:

"Why, doesn't your husband have to kick your fellows about?"

And he was quite incredulous when I assured him that C—— had never dreamed of such a thing except once, when our first cook had muttered impertinences, and been kicked out on to the Azotea for his rudeness.

"But they are such stupid fools," argued Mr B——.

We replied that we did not think blows would make them any brighter, on which he laughed and said perhaps we were right, as we certainly had remarkably good servants.

Another guest, Mr M——, was talking about Philippine food, and observed that tomatoes grew so well here. I said I thought they were miserable failures, as they are about the size of walnuts, and quite green. But he maintained that that was because the Filipino just sticks his tomato plants in the ground and goes off to sit in the shade or to a cock-fight, and when he sees any sign of fruit on the plants, he picks it and takes it to market. Any notion of tilling the soil—weeding or manuring—is absolutely unknown to these people, or if known, carefully avoided. Mr M—— said he had seen tomatoes, grown by Chinamen, as good as the very best out of a hothouse at home. There are several Chinese *potagères* in the town where rows of trim little beds may be seen thick with extraordinarily luxuriant crops of vegetables of every sort, but out here no one will eat anything grown by the Chinamen, as those enterprising people employ some dreadful and unmentionable methods of agriculture. Besides this, there are many germs in the teeming, prolific air which invest vegetables such as cabbages, lettuce, etc., and make them very unsafe experiments, even if one can procure any. When I was in Manila, there was a good deal of talk at dinner tables, and much writing in the papers about some American scientist who professed to have found out a way to "treat" the Philippine green lettuces before eating them, so as to destroy some dreadful germ which causes horrible complaints. But it seemed to me less trouble and a great deal safer to give up lettuce as a bad job!

The great and terrible fear in the Philippines is the germ of a disease called "sprue"—a sort of wasting away—which is very difficult to remedy, and almost ineradicable.

Melons would grow well here, for in the wet season anything in the nature of a gourd springs up like a weed—a habit which suits the Filipino agriculturist to perfection. Some of the more energetic spirits fasten a piece of *bejuco* from the marrow plant up to a window, and gourd vines may often be seen obligingly toiling up a string to hand fruit in to the weary dwellers in a *nipa* hut. Nevertheless, melons are only to be got from Hong Kong, and even then they are a costly delicacy. Some friends sent us half a watermelon a few days ago, as a present, but we did not like to accept anything so valuable, and insisted on paying for it. What a treat it was!

With the rainy season we also have a tiny hard native fruit that looks like a damson outside, but has white flesh with a stone like a date-stone, and is entirely devoid of any flavour of any sort. I tried having this fruit stewed, but it was even nastier than when raw. When we were at Nagaba for the day, in the spring, we got some fruit like knobs of rose-coloured wax, pink all through, with black pips, and rather tart, but also tasteless. I suppose all these insipid, nasty little native fruits could be cultivated into something nice, in the way that cherries have been developed, and apples and everything else, from the tasteless wild fruit. At present, however, they are tolerable only to the native palate. The best of them is a tiny brown fruit called *lazones*, which has a fluffy thin brown skin, and grey brown flesh in divisions like an orange, each division containing a large green seed. The flavour of the *lazones* is sharp, rather nice, and very refreshing, but this fruit only comes from Luzon, and is very expensive, besides being half-rotten by the time it gets here. Bananas, pine-apples, and mangoes—that is all. Bananas one gets unutterably sick of, and pine-apples too—and mangoes, even if one likes them (which we do not), give one prickly heat. In fact tinned strawberries and raspberries are about the best Philippine fruits.

We have received an invitation to the banquet in honour of Mr Taft and his party on the 15th—on the payment of 12 *pesos* each. But we may have to sail before that date if our Hong Kong steamer comes in. I shall be very sorry if we miss that event, for I think the Taft utterances would be well worth 25 shillings a head, though that does seem a pretty stiff sum for an Iloilo banquet!

LETTER XXXIX.

A LAST DAY AT NAGABA—THE "SECWAR"

ILOILO, *August 11, 1905.*

We went a last trip to Nagaba on Sunday, but only for the day, and were lucky in having very fine weather and delightfully cool, only 80°, with a lovely breeze blowing, and the sky a little overcast.

We roused ourselves up after lunch, and two friends came to the house to join the party, and we sent the "boy" for two *quilezes*. When we went down, I stepped into the first one; there was Tuyay lying in it already! How she knows when we are going out is simply marvellous.

We drove to the Muelle Loney, at the farther end of which *paraos* are moored for hire, and chose a nice big boat, the *Valentino*, with an upper deck of split bamboo, a rabbit-hutch cabin of *nipa* matting, and a crew of eight men, and set sail for Nagaba.

The sun came out soon after we started, so we lay half in and half out of the cabin and the shade it cast. It was a "three-man breeze," so some of the crew ran out on the outriggers and others hauled ropes, while three ruffians sat on the deck, which was 3 feet wide, by-the-bye, and spread out a piece of blue paper, which they held down with their bare brown toes. We could not think what they were going to do, when, to our astonishment, one of them produced a pack of greasy cards and pieces of money and began the three-card trick! They did their best to get us interested in the game, the chief little old brown swindler losing to his confederates all in the best Derby style. We looked on with deep interest, but showed no signs of wishing to take part in the gamble, except for C—— to ask casually if they knew he was in the Secret Police, which made them look quite serious for a few minutes. This remark about Secret Police was no empty jest, for it is an Institution of the Free and Enlightened U.S.A., worthy of Russia or the Dark Ages. Well, after this disquieting joke about the Secret Police, the three-card trick seemed to lose its flavour, and the gamblers shifted billet again, to our intense amusement, crawling along the outriggers, and past the "cabin," and on to the tiny space of after-deck, where the steersman sat huddled up with his legs round the tiller. Here they spread the blue paper out again, one of the confederates lying airily across the stern entrance, betting excitedly, with an occasional squint into the cabin to see if anyone was inclined to slip aft on the sly. But we never even looked round, so they soon abandoned that tactic and climbed on to the "cabin" roof, where they crouched like monkeys, chattering, and now and then a great flat brown face hung over the edge and looked down in on us; but we got rather tired of them, so C—— leaned out and hit one of them, and they gave that up too.

All this time we were skimming through the water, going at a tremendous pace, the boat leaning over first to one side and then to the other, with the white foam spurting up from the brilliant green sea, the half-naked brown sailors running out on the long poles of the outriggers, and the big sails filled out tight. It was most exhilarating.

We went straight across, a little wide of Nagaba, and then made a wide tack, which enabled the boat to go quite close to the beach, as the tide was high, and we came up right opposite the village. One of the boatmen carried me ashore, and the moment Tuyay saw me leave the ship, she flung herself into the water and swam after me in a sort of tragic despair that made us all laugh very much.

Then other brawny little natives took C—— and our two friends astride on their shoulders and set us all down on the dry sand, and we walked up through the little village of huts, all amongst the babies and dogs and pigs. There were several new swamps to be seen, and everything was even greener than when we were last there, which was before the S.-W. Monsoon had really set in. I noticed, too, that the bushes had flowered, as our friends had predicted, and one of them was a beautiful, scentless yellow blossom, a little like a snapdragon.

We had meant to go for a real walk, but the sun was too hot, as it was not more than four o'clock, so we wandered along to "our" house, through the fields and village. It was delightful to feel the fresh country air, and to smell the earth and plants after the streets of Iloilo, and we actually felt hungry, and began to ask each other what was to be done about food. Nothing was to be had at any house in the village, as we all knew by experience, but by luck we came upon a sort of open *nipa* shed, where a little Filipino woman was standing behind a wooden tray containing ears of maize, little heaps of rice, and betel-nut, which was by way of being a shop. From her, and a youth who cropped up from nowhere and conducted the bargaining, we bought what the Americans call corn-pone, which is whole ears of young maize roasted. We munched the corn, which was very sweet and tender, and uncommonly filling—after about half a "pone" one could hardly breathe.

A little further on we regretted our haste in satiating ourselves with maize, as we saw a big open shed, with two steps up to it, and all sorts of glasses and dishes glittering on a table spread with a white cloth, evidently a sort of *Fiesta* restaurant. We cheered up at this, and hurried along with talk of fizzing drinks, but when we came nearer, and out of the full glare of the sunlight, we got a horrible shock on finding it to be the Aglipay church!

So we trailed on, rather despondent, and very thirsty, between the huts and boats, through the deep soft sand, which was unpleasant to walk on. We saw a big *parao* lying drawn up, hewn out of one vast tree-trunk, which is the original model of these long, narrow boats, and it looked like a huge *baroto* (canoe).

When we got to the house, Tuyay was greeted most enthusiastically by a little spaniel friend, and the caretakers were civil enough to us, but incredibly stupid about a request for coffee. At last C—— made them understand by talking to them in Visayan, but it is really very strange how very few of the people in the country know any Spanish, and the town's-people can only say a few words or phrases at the best.

We took chairs out of the house, opened the sliding bamboo frames shutting off the balcony, and established ourselves out there in the cool shade. There we sat for an hour, munching maize, and watching three fowls and three brown babies picking up mysterious food on the rocks and in the shallow pools. One of the babies was an elderly person of five or six, who was "minding" the other two, and one could see that he was older and more important, as he had on a very short and entirely foolish white muslin shirt, but the other two were in nothing but fat brown skin. The tiniest was a very serious and bullet-headed little chap, with thin arms and legs, and a huge rice-tummy. All three mites were squatting about, very busy and solemn, finding some little shell-fish, which they cracked between stones and ate with the gestures of monkeys.

They were to us a source of absolute delight, and it was not till the elderly pastor in the muslin shirt led his flock off to fresh pools out of sight that we went into the house and drank the coffee which the woman had prepared for us. It was excellent black coffee, made in the native fashion by holding the grounds in a little bag at the end of a piece of bamboo in a coffee pot—simple, but effective. With it went large flat cakes of yellowish sugar, called *caramelo*, and she had also produced from somewhere four ship's biscuits. The latter were rather a relief after the maize, and indeed we thought the meal a delicious feast, though I have no doubt we would not have looked at it over the other side of the Guimaras Channel.

After this, as it was about six o'clock, and the sun was going down, we walked down to the river mouth and got on board the good ship *Valentino* by crawling along another *parao*, which was beached in the shallower water further inshore, and thence by perilous ventures along those outriggers on which the sailors run about in a gale as if they were on firm land!

The sail back in the sunset was exquisite, all the mountains of Panay dark blue against an orange sky, a young moon overhead, and the air exquisitely fresh.

Altogether it was a most delightful trip, and I only wish we had had more such days, but with only one day a week to choose from it is often too hot, and sometimes too wet to go on the water. Most of the time, too, I have not been well enough for expeditions under the most favourable circumstances, and then, over and above all these reasons is the fact that one seldom has the inclination here to do anything or go anywhere. I think it must be owing to this latter phenomenon that there is no sort of "week-end resort" at Nagaba, for one can hardly understand how such an enterprising people as the Americans have neglected this golden opportunity for a business that, I believe, they understand so admirably—I mean sort of Simple Life Hotels. I remember an American whom I met at home once, in England, telling me a long story about some place in the Adirondaks, where people from New York (or was it Chicago?—no matter) go and live in tents; and millionaires catch food, and their priceless wives and daughters cook and sweep. The story came up *à propos* the daughter of a millionaire who had just married an English duke, as this personage had been roughing it in the next tent to my friend. I think I may have told you the story at the time. But I have read so much and heard so much about the American love of country life that I am astounded to see how they all sit grilling in Iloilo when they might have a hotel at Nagaba. The truth is, of course, that such an enterprise might be a doubtful undertaking, as every American I have ever yet met or seen, from the highest to the humblest, is simply saving money to get away from the Philippines and back to "God's Country."

We are still undecided about our departure, as the *Sung-Kiang* (the sister-ship of the *Kai-Fong* and the same Line) has come in before what the Americans call her "scheduled" time. That is a very queer word of theirs, by-the-bye, and they work the poor thing to death, making it do all sorts of unnatural gymnastics in place of good, ready, useful English. Probably we shall wait for the *Kai-Fong*, but whichever we decide for, we shall not miss the Taft party after all, which I am very pleased about, and we have put our names down for the banquet.

They are in Manila now, the first intimation of their arrival having been a telegram in the Iloilo *El Tiempo*, headed "Impresiones de Miss Alice Roosevelt"—who had not been an hour in the Philippines, if she had landed at all, when the impression was what newspaper language calls "voiced."

Now we have *The Manila Times* of that and the following two days, which are "all Taft," of course, set forth in the quaintest concoction of cheap picture-writing, bad grammar, and awkward, slapdash slang. Much about "Miss Alice,"—a whole column of an interesting description of that lady's every gesture at a race-meeting—in fact she looms so large in the Philippine eye that it looks as if she were here for a very good reason; perhaps to take the fierce, white light off Mr Taft a little. They allude to the latter, by-the-bye, as "the *Secwar*," which, when I first came across it, I took to be the name of some Indian chief, but it at last dawned upon me that the word was a contraction of Secretary of War, and I have since been told that it is his telegraphic address used as an affectionate nickname.

The American reporter seems to be as virulent in Manila as anywhere else, for before the party had landed one of these human mosquitoes asked a Senator what he thought of "these islands," but the visitor cleverly replied that he had come to gather impressions, not to furnish them.

The papers are still full of guesses about the true reasons for this visitation, for so many of them persist in the theory that Mr Taft is not entirely actuated by altruistic wishes for the welfare of his "little brown brothers," but has a wary eye upon the elector at home, and will pose as the Saint of the Philippines just as far as his own interests are safe. I think it is a great shame to say this, however, for it is obvious that he has done the best he can for the Philippines according to his views; and whether one agrees with his theories or not, his good intentions are not to be denied. I had a long talk with a man who has been here in a good business for thirty-three years, and is supposed to know more about the Philippines than any other white man alive; and he told me that, as far as enlightening the Senators went, he thought the Taft visit was a costly farce, for they are to be allowed to see and hear nothing that does not "suit the Taft book." A week in Manila of meetings, balls, parties, and banquets, followed by flying visits to the principal towns in the provinces and more banquets, all feasting and flags and anthems; but not a glimpse of the miserable, wasted agricultural districts, the abandoned rice-fields, and the real truth of the labour problem. Moreover, their opinion of the self-government problem is to be formed by the conversation of a few well-educated and carefully selected *Mestizos* in the towns.

The natives, themselves, however, are tremendously jubilant about the approaching visit of their Patron Saint, and expect all blessings to spring up miraculously in his footsteps.

Talking of natives, I am glad to say that our three excellent servants have found good billets, with a rise in importance and wages, and they are all so pleased, poor souls, that we took the trouble to recommend them to our friends. They did not want much touting, for the spotless tidiness of their appearance is an advertisement that speaks for itself and their honesty is patent, for we trust them in a way that no one else dreams of doing with their Filipino servants. I don't know how the two house boys will get on with impatient Englishmen, for they are both very shy, faithful, simple countrymen—real unspoilt Filipinos. But if they were spoken to sharply, or muddled in their work, they would become confused and stupid at once. Not that there is anything peculiar to the Filipino race in these traits, because they are perfectly familiar to me in many kindly, simple, limited souls in other latitudes. You have to take them as you find them, only hoping, as with the same type at home, that their secret cunning may be ranged on your own side, and that if you can't make a silk purse out of a sow's ear, you may perhaps manage to contrive a useful little leather bag if you are patient enough.

> *Note.*—I have before me *The Manila Times* of 17th January 1906, from which I give the following extract:—"While the municipal and ecclesiastical dignitaries, etc., were awaiting the arrival of Secretary Taft, a Government vessel slowly made her way up the Pasig river filled with the dead and wounded from the island of Samar. During the stay of the party in Manila, four native men were brought in from the adjoining province of Cavite frightfully mutilated because of their pro-American sympathies."

LETTER XL.

PREPARATIONS

ILOILO, *August 14, 1905.*

We have now decided to go to Hong Kong by the *Kai-Fong*, which sails next Saturday or Monday, the 20th or 22nd. The *Sung-Kiang* loaded up as much as she could and shoved off on Saturday, as she did not want to be paying port dues here the whole of to-day (Sunday) and to-morrow, which is a public holiday, being the anniversary of the taking of Manila by Admiral Dewey.

The transport conveying the Taft party is *scheduled* to arrive here to-day, and this evening they are to be present at a performance of the Filipino Amateur Dramatic Club, to which we have been invited by means of a huge printed invitation, couched in elaborate Spanish, and adorned by many ornaments and flourishes.

We heard the sound of a band going past very early this morning, and when we went out on to the balcony, we saw it was the Infantry band from Guimaras, with the regiment behind them marching down the street. They marched splendidly, and the band was playing a most sad and beautiful tune, which made one think of war, and troops marching away, and women crying in the morning. The soldiers had just arrived, I expect, for everyone from Camp Josman is pouring into Iloilo for the *fêtes* for the Taft party.

Arches are being put up in the streets, and, as everybody has been requested to decorate their houses, we have hoisted a Union Jack on a long pole, and all this morning the servants were very happy, in the pouring rain, sticking up palm-branches which they had stolen from some plantation. They are much excited about the arrival of this hero of theirs, and one of them—who gets confused when we accuse him of being an *Independiente*, because he has his watch hung on a nail in the kitchen, with a portrait of Rizal over it, a sort of little shrine—is simply beaming with delight, and can't haul up enough palms.

In the office opposite, the native clerks are surpassing themselves with archway and window decorations of greenery and flowers; while the old Tagalo dressmaker next door has been busy for a week past making paper flowers of all the hues under the sun. In that house, by-the-bye, the stock of domestic pets has lately been increased by the addition of a sheep, which is quite tame, for we can hear its little hoofs tap-tapping over the bare boards, and see it sitting amongst the work-girls in the big front room. They have a nice little black pig, too, also running about the house and equally tame, and in the evenings the old man goes out for a walk to the beach with the fat old brown dog, the pig, and the sheep all running after him and playing about. I have often seen them go along the street—such a curious company! And people who live near the beach tell me he takes them all down to the sea, washes them, and then walks about to give them an airing. They are all sharing in the popular rejoicings, too, for the brown dog and the pig have got on necklaces of paper flowers, while the sheep is crowned in the most arcadian fashion.

Mr Taft has made a lot of speeches in Manila, but, so far, they have only contained very nebulous references to the Independence question; though he has cast a sop to the malcontents by promises of abolition or reduction of certain export duties, by which the excited Filipinos argue and predict a millennium of agricultural improvement and general plenty.

But none of the business men are very clear as to how this miracle is to be wrought, for the Government will not lower the standard of wages; Chinese labour will not be allowed in; and the Filipino will not suddenly, if ever, become a thrifty, hard-working tiller of the soil, even if he passes all the standards of the American schools.

One paragraph stowed away in a corner of *The Manila Times* made us laugh very much, for it was an account of how Poblete de los Reyes (a Filipino *Independiente* agitator) and Father Aglipay were "haunting the corridors of the Ayuntamento" (the *Gobierno* of Manila), "but up to noon to-day they had failed to get the ear of Secretary Taft."

This gave me a delightful vision of those two anxious flat brown faces peering out of all sorts of shadowy places, and Mr Taft for ever making a break for another room, and rushing through suites and up and down little staircases to escape the gen-u-*ine* patriots. This is only a fancy picture, of course, but still it may contain a grain of truth, and at any rate it afforded us much amusement.

Many people think Mr Taft is reserving some great pronouncement for Iloilo, as he favoured this town above all Philippine communities in that he made here his great pro-Filipino speech, two years ago, when he was Governor-General of the Philippines. In this famous oration he used these words: "These Philippine Islands are going to be governed *for* the Filipinos, and no one *but* the Filipinos, and any stranger or American who does not like it can get out."

This did much to ensure his popularity with the natives everywhere in the Islands, and in Iloilo in particular. However, even the easy-going Americans seem to have grasped that these words went a little too far, for they tried to hush up that part of the speech, but the Filipinos, already fully alive to the blessings of a free press, seized on this utterance, and it was published in *The Nuevo Heraldo*, which is the Iloilo *Independiente* organ. The phrase got about everywhere, and did much to shake public confidence in justice towards the white man, with incidental harm to trade and enterprise, but it pleased the "little brown brother," and added another step to the pedestal on which he has placed the Patron Saint.

To the mere observer, however, this cry of Altruism is not very convincing in face of the fact that the Philippines lie so conveniently on the west of the future Panama Canal. It was not brotherly love which prompted astute American politicians to wash off the Spaniards with rivers of blood and treasure, and I think the Filipino will find that he gets just as much of "Philippines for the Filipinos" as is contained in the other famous phrase of "little brown brother"—and no more. Gradually, too, he will find that to be a "little brown brother" out here will be the same sort of distinction as being a big black brother in the U.S.A.

In one of the last magazines we received from home is a description by some woman of a cruise in a tramp steamer in the Pacific. Lotus Islands, and all that sort of thing, and who-wants-to-return-to-fretful-Europe rhapsodies, which it struck me I should better have appreciated this time last year. But now all I think of is the utter, mental sterility of such a life, which appears to me, in the light of experience, still more like the impression made by a beautiful and stupid woman. She winds up with a fine peroration about the "spell of the Ancient World," which "binds one to the Island home and the Island life for ever."

I can't think what there is of the "Ancient World" about a Pacific island; but the spell, if there is one, must be that of indolence; or the attraction, as in the case of Stevenson, simply a matter of health; for it seems to me that no other inducements could make one willingly lose touch of all that civilisation has to offer to distinguish one from a south sea islander. Of course, in the temperate climes there are the inconveniences of dress, frost, and drainage, but those are small when compared with art, books, good music, and intelligent fellow-creatures. Oh, you can't imagine the deadliness of the lives the white people lead here—the indifference, the stagnation, the animal round of food and sleep! I think if it had been my fate to stay on in the "Island home and the Island life" for ever, if I had not become physically ill, I must have become mentally an invalid for the rest of my life.

LETTER XLI.

THE FESTIVITIES

ILOILO, *August 17, 1905.*

I must tell you all about this *Comitiva Taft* dissipation, of which we had the first taste on Monday, the 15th, when a printed notice was left at our house, saying that the "Congressional party" had arrived that evening instead of next morning, and another large, flowery, and handsome invitation, bidding us to a reception to be held at the house of the De la Ramos, very rich Filipinos, who have a fine house in a broad, shady street, where the Bank and some other big houses stand within gardens.

The reception was to be followed by the performance at the Filipino theatre, to which as I told you we had also been invited, but we thought that the reception, which was "scheduled" to come off at eight, would be quite enough for us for one evening.

We dined early, and sent Domingo out for a *quilez* "with a good horse." He came back after a long while and said all the carriages in the town were already hired, but he had got what he could, and the *caballo* was *poco bueno* (little good). He was right. It was a horse to make one's heart ache to look at; and when we stepped into the dirty old broken-down *quilez*, to which he was attached with odds and ends of old rope, the poor beast started going backwards all down the street. The driver roared profanities, and clicked his lips, and chucked the reins, but all to no effect; till at last he called one of our servants out of the house, and they each seized a wheel by the spokes and forced it round, so that the pony was shoved along, when it started off at a great pace; the driver sprang on the box, and we tore like the wind to the house of De la Ramos.

There had been a great deal of rain, and the roads were very deep in mud, but the sky had cleared, and a bright moon was shining.

In spite of this natural illumination, there was a reckless profusion of arc-lights in the streets, which, as I told you, had been in black gloom for months. We had seen the lamps being repaired for some days when we went out in the evenings, and the general furbishing-up and improvement extended to a sudden serving out of ice from the Government factory, so that everyone was wishing there could be one of these Visitations to Iloilo every week. Well, when we got to the De la Ramos house, we found all the front really extremely pretty, with *huge* stars-and-stripes flags—stripes the size of palm-trunks and stars like soup-plates—draped right across the front, with green palm-branches stuck about, all in the light of brilliant illuminations. Great doors stood open to a vast lighted and decorated hall, with a very big cut-glass chandelier in the middle.

The *poco bueno* horse was pulled up on his haunches abruptly in front of all this magnificence, and some white men leaning against the doorway picking their teeth, looked at us, but offered no remark. So C——, in evening dress, got out and asked one of them if this was the house where the reception was to take place. One man, keeping his toothpick in his mouth, said:

"Waal I guess there is *naht* going to be any great shakes of a reception *to*-night."

"Oh," said C——, "we got an invitation from the Reception Committee, and heard the *Manchuria* had come in."

"That's so, sirree," said the man, "but Secretary Taft and Miss Alice is not coming ashore; leastways, they're on board now eating their dinners."

"Will they go to the theatre, then?" we asked.

"No," said the man vaguely, "I guess naht. Leastways, I don't rightly know. But Secretary Taft says he don't want to come ashore before his skeddled time to-morrow morning. I reckon he's gettin' a bit sick of goin' around."

The man was quite civil, but he and his fellow-loungers were so vague and depressing that we drove away again, feeling rather sorry we had taken the trouble to put on evening dress.

We made our driver go down the end of the street to the quay by the Customs landing, where there was a very pretty arch, all lighted up, with portraits painted on it of Mr Roosevelt, and "Miss Alice," and Mr Taft. This had been erected by the Filipinos, and the decorations, which were the work of a native artist, were really not at all discreditable. Across Calle Real was another arch, put up by the Chinese, at the entrance to where their shops begin, with more electric lights and pictures of angels, and more medallions of Mr Roosevelt, with an entirely different face from the Customs one, and "Miss Alice" looking about thirty, with fat, red cheeks and masses of black hair.

After admiring these marvels, and noticing what could be seen of the decorations on the houses, we drove home and consoled our hearts very successfully with cold mutton—a treat from the Cold Storage in Manila—which would have made up to us for anything. You see, you can't have cold meat in this climate without ice to cool it on, and we have been without ice for so many wretched months. Faddy people should be sent to Iloilo to learn to say a fervid and completely heart-whole grace before cold mutton, and I often think out here of the delicious cold meat which our servants at home may be, at that very moment, refusing to eat!

Next day we were awakened by a brass band walking up and down the streets, and blowing Sousa and "Hiawatha" for all it was worth. It was not yet dawn when this festivity began, so after we had sworn at them, we went to sleep again, for the music did not mean that anything was happening, beyond that its playing was a sort of general rouse-out and reminder. We had been informed that the reception was to be held at the *Gobierno* soon after the party landed, so, as we determined to bring this function to bay somehow, we sallied forth after breakfast to see what was to be seen.

A *quilez* was not to be had for love or money, nor, indeed, a "rig" of any sort, so we walked to the Plaza, and in the Calle Real picked up a *carromata*—one of the fearful little vehicles into which you climb over a muddy wheel and sit jammed up behind the driver.

After sending back Sotero, who had followed to look for a *quilez* for us, and making him carry away Tuyay, who insisted on not leaving us, we got into the *carromata* and drove down the crowded streets to the *Gobierno*.

All the houses were very gay with stars and stripes and greenery—the decorations very little spoilt by the rain—and the streets full of people in clean clothes; all the principal thoroughfares crowded, but the others very empty.

The day, which had begun with rain, had cleared up, and was very fresh and jolly, as it had not yet had time to get steamy, and a cool breeze was blowing, the flags fluttered in the sun, bands were playing everywhere, and it was all very gay and sparkling. In one of the streets we began to pass a long procession, waiting behind the scenes, as it were, with flags unfurled and bands ready to strike up.

There were crowds and crowds of people making for the palace, and we were told that the *Comitiva Taft* had already landed and driven there, so we followed as best we could. There was a great deal of shouting of *Tabé*—and we were as near as anything over some of the revellers who were mooning about as if the streets were deserted.

By-the-bye, I don't know whether this expression *Comitiva Taft* is bad Spanish or good Filipino, but it is the one employed by the Philippine newspapers, and I prefer it to the American "Taft Circus."

When we arrived at the *Gobierno*, we found large crowds of little, brown-faced Filipinos in white American suits, all looking up at the broad balcony—the one where the band had played on the night of the 4th-of-July ball. The whole expanse of balcony was full of people, with many ladies standing in front in light frocks and big flat hats.

We struggled through the crowd of sight-seers and into the big basement, which was decorated very profusely, and where a lot of people were standing about. A man told us he guessed the reception was going on upstairs; and we thought perhaps he had guessed correctly, so we mounted the broad stairs, between sheaves of palms and American flags, and found ourselves in a huge crowd in the outer room of the suite I described to you the night of the ball. The court room had been arranged with rows of chairs and benches facing the daïs, and the balcony beyond, with the bright blue sky and white glare of sunlight for a background, was a seething mass of white-clad humanity. I noticed the Americans were all at one end and the Filipinos at the other—an arrangement of choice, I imagine, rather than accident.

Amongst the visitors I met again Mrs Luke E. Wright, and several other people whose acquaintance I had made in Manila, as the party had been nearly doubled by the numbers absorbed into it after arriving in the Philippines. My friends said they had heard I was ill, and that I was going home, and envied me, calling heaven to witness that they wished they were going "back home" too. The Governor's secretary told me that the party now amounted to 170 people, and they had a very jolly time on board, and were expecting to have a very pleasant trip round the Islands.

There was no regular presenting being done, and no one offered to introduce us to Mr Taft or "Miss Alice," and we did not like to ask them to do so, which I am sorry about now, as I should have liked to have met them. However, Miss Alice was standing next to the Governor's wife while I was talking to the latter, so I was able to get an impression of her appearance, which I thought quite pleasing; a young girl with a fluff of fair hair tied behind with a big bow of black ribbon, a very pale complexion, and heavily-lidded blue eyes. She had on a coat and skirt of stiff white pique, which did not do justice to her pretty figure, and a plain straw hat with blue ribbons on it tilted over her forehead.

All the American ladies amongst the visitors were very plainly dressed in shirts and skirts, as for the country in the morning, with large, flat hats and floating gauze veils—just like the American tourists you see in London out of the season. The residents, however, had on pretty muslins and hats, and the Filipino ladies sported their most beautiful *camisas* and finest jewels. I heard afterwards that the very plain costumes of the visitors were considered as rather a poor compliment, not to say a mistake in tact, for of course the Manila papers had given glowing accounts of the lovely dresses they wore at the entertainments in Manila, and Orientals think such a lot of that sort of thing—and so do Occidentals, too, for the matter of that!

Mr Taft and the Senators were all in white linen suits; the officers in white linen, too, plus the badges of their rank. Mr Taft, who is a very tall, fair man of enormous build, towered over the heads of everyone about him. I don't think I ever saw anyone so vast, and could quite believe that he weighed 250 pounds—though I must say that to hear a weight expressed in pounds does not convey much impression to my mind. He has a large, clever face, which creases up into an amiable smile for which he is famous, and which has helped him enormously in life. In curious contrast are his eyes, which are small, and placed rather close together, and very shrewd in expression. When he is serious, it is a stern, rather hard face, and not very pre-possessing, but when he smiles the "Taft smile," it is altered in the most extraordinary manner, and he really looks charming.

After we had been on the balcony a little time, the procession began to come into sight, headed by a brass band. At this the people on the balcony sorted themselves out, Mr Taft and "Miss Alice" standing in the front of the balcony with the chief personages behind them, and less important Americans in the doorways and on the outskirts, all in the most approved "democratic" style, while the brown faces all clustered at the other end of the balcony. I thought it a great pity that it did not occur to Mr Taft, or Miss Roosevelt, or the Governor, or anyone like that to go and stand amongst the Filipinos and give a real and tangible demonstration of the theories they were there to express. I did not see anyone talking to the visitors but Americans, either, and I thought that a pity too.

You see, a little thing like that would convey more truth about Equality than miles of bombastic print or hours of windy rhetoric.

The Governor's secretary found me a place in front of the balcony, but I was foolish enough to move away for a moment to speak to someone, and so lost my place. Then we saw that people were beginning to stand on the benches, so C—— got me a place on one by asking some men to move, which they were rather huffy about.

On one side of me was a tall, thin young Senator with a large hand-camera, who showed his resentment in tiresome little incivilities; but the man on the other side was a nice, good-natured soul, who tried to make room for me, and spoke very agreeably. He seemed to be feeling the heat very much, and complained that it was so fearfully hot, but I laughed and said: "This is the coolest day we have had for a long time."

"My!" he exclaimed, "I guess I'm not fair crazy to come and live in these old Phaluppeens."

"Oh," I said, "then you have not joined the party at Manila?"

He said he had come from America all the way, and told us he was a newspaper man with a mission, come to write up the trip. This made us understand better his asking from time to time such extraordinarily elementary questions. He wanted to know what a *carabao* was, and was surprised to hear that sugar cane only flourished in Panay and Negros. I had to explain to him that we were in Panay, and pointed out Negros and Guimaras!

I did not grudge the trouble of teaching him the A B C of the Philippines, but I could not help thinking it rather odd that he had no more preparation for his mission when his opinions would probably be "voiced" and quoted as oracles on his return to "God's Country."

Of course he was choke full of long words about the American Ideal, and told me a lot about the absurdity of such narrow prejudice as race-distinctions; but I let that go without remark, and without even taking the trouble to draw his attention to the demonstrations before his eyes; for I have found out by this time that you might as well talk to the wind as to a race-equality American who won't sit "on a car" with a negro in the States.

C——, who was standing behind me, joined in the conversation, whereupon the American journalist instantly whipped out his visiting card and handed it to him, but of course C—— was quite unprepared, and had to spell his name and explain himself generally. It is very amusing, and at first rather embarrassing, the way Americans hand you a card as soon as you speak, but it has its advantages in getting names right.

The procession was remarkably like the one we had seen on Declaration Day, only with different "floats." I don't suppose you know what "floats" are, and no more did I, for when I had read descriptions of the processions in Manila, and how the "floats" were "gotten up," I concluded the function had been a water-pageant on the Pasig. I heard some people about me using the same word, however, and mentioned it to my journalistic friend, who informed me that the word was one which was employed in the U.S.A. to signify cars in a procession, and that its origin was in New Orleans, where they had processions on the river with decorated "floats" or rafts.

This was a very long procession, and some of the agricultural cars were prettily done up with banana plants, and one had sugar canes growing in it; and there were ploughs, and rows of men carrying spades and hoes and things. Mr Taft stood and watched it all, talking to Miss Roosevelt; but he got what the children call a good deal of powder in his spoonful of jam, in the shape of huge white banners with large inscriptions on them about the financial situation and the tariffs. Some of these reminders were of a very ingenious pattern, like huge three-sided lanterns, with the inscription in English, Spanish, and Visayan, so that no one should make any mistake about what was meant. "A square deal" was written on one, and some of them were, to me, quite pathetic, for they said: "We are at your mercy," and others were frank, not to say abrupt, requests for liberty, "to govern ourselves our own way."

At all these and at the strings of labourers from the Harbour Works, the Fire Brigade, etc., Mr Taft stared very solemnly and steadily, standing upright in front of the balcony, with Miss Roosevelt beside him, his arms folded across his chest. I was much struck by his expression, and could not help looking at him as much as at the procession and wondering what he really thought of it all. When the workmen came past, our journalist friend suddenly betrayed his knowledge of Philippine affairs by saying knowingly: "Ah, these are the Chinese labourers, I guess."

"No," said C——. "Those are Filipinos. There are no Chinese labourers in the Philippines except in some mills in Luzon."

This information apparently took the man's breath away; if he believed it, which he probably did not. He was quite silent for a long time. Perhaps some of his most elaborate perorations had been damaged, and C—— and I thought afterwards that it was rather a pity we had disillusioned the poor creature as we did. Another of his cherished illusions was what I may call the St Louis "Exposition" idea of the Philippines, and we had the greatest difficulty in trying to persuade him that all he saw was not the direct result of the American occupation!

At last the interminable lines of school children came past—all the Government schools, of course—as on Declaration Day; no priests or convents. Mr Taft had looked on unmoved and unsmiling at the Agricultural and Industrial displays, but when he saw these scholars, he broke into the "Taft smile," and clapped his hands above his head. All the Americans followed his lead by bursting into applause, which they kept up, as he did, all the time the schools were passing. I turned my head to the right, where the little brown parents of these children were crowded together, and saw that not one single Filipino made one gesture of applause!

The schools took a long, long time to crawl past, and the continuous applause became rather tiring. But even a Filipino procession must come to an end if only you can wait long enough, and the last of them went past, and we got down off our bench.

Then followed a great surging and shifting of all the people on the balcony, everyone trying to secure a seat in the Court Room, and we were lucky enough to get near a door and not very far from the front.

On the daïs were placed two or three rows of Vienna cane chairs, those for the important people in front, with arms to them. In these sat the Governor, Mrs Luke E. Wright, and "Miss Alice." Next to the latter Mr Taft took the chair assigned to him, into which he wedged himself with infinite trouble; but the chair at once broke to pieces. Everyone laughed very much, Mr Taft most heartily of all, saying in a good-natured, jolly way: "Here! Someone give me a chair I can sit down on. I'm tired of standing."

So they brought him another chair, and he took his place, and the speechifying began.

The *Presidente* of Iloilo—a very courtly old Filipino of the name of Meliza—made a speech of welcome—a very long affair—which included the subjects of Taxation, Duties, and Independence, to which Mr Taft replied elusively, repeating nothing tangible but his old phrase of "Philippines for the Filipinos."

Then some more people made speeches—natives—and at last they drove Mr Taft into a corner about the Independence, and he said, "I am not come to give you your Independence, but to study your welfare. You will have your Independence when you are ready for it, which will not be in this generation—no, nor in the next, nor perhaps for a hundred years or more."

Even though I have told you how up to then no one had any idea of why he and his party had come to the Islands—most people thinking he was going to say something definite about the Americans retiring from the Islands—the natives all firmly convinced that he was coming to ratify the undated promise of Independence he made them two years ago—even though I have told you this, you can have no idea of the effect these words had upon the audience. We were simply staggered, and the darker complexioned amongst us sat quite still and immovable.

The speeches lost some of their force by being translated as they went along by an interpreter, who spoke English and Spanish with equal perfection, and, indeed, he was quite marvellous; but all the same the utterances lost point, and it was not easy to follow the thread with long halts between. What was more serious was that the translations of Mr Taft's opinions were softened by the courteous Spanish phrases, and the fiery patriotism of the Filipinos was marvellously toned down in the English rendering.

During a question of taxation, Mr Taft said:

"I want to know if you think it would be any good to reduce the Land Tax, or if, by suspending it for three years, the trade and agriculture of the country would benefit?"—or words to that effect. Whereupon he and old Señor Meliza had quite a long argument about this weighty point.

The whole ceremony was indescribably free and easy, and even commonplace. Most of the Senators took very little interest in the proceedings, while the ladies with them did not even pretend to care about what was going on. As to "Miss Alice," she was honest enough to make no pretence at all of listening to anything, but sat staring before her, drumming with her pretty, slender, white fingers on her lips, only waking up to signal and laugh to some friends in a doorway near the platform. She was very girlish and natural in this and in all her other gestures, and if she lacked the pose necessary to the occasion, one could not be too critical nor take objection to her lack of grand manner when people were presented to her, for, after all, such situations are only to be carried off with ease by those born and bred to State ceremonies. Besides, it would have been unreasonable to have looked for scrupulously aristocratic bearing amongst such a party of professed democrats.

In spite of all that, however, the Filipinos, who, with their traditions of *custumbres*, are themselves a very polite people, were much shocked by the free and easy ways of their rulers, benefactors, or whatever they are. I afterwards heard many little comments upon the American lack of dignity, which made me feel sad, for these two peoples will never understand each other—even the good sentiments of the heart being conveyed by differences of manner, which are meat to one and poison to the other.

In talking of taxation, the word "sugar" suddenly arose, on which Mr Taft, who was getting obviously bored, and mopping his face freely, rose and said:

"See here. We've come to this place to talk about sugar. Now, look here, have you got any room where the gentlemen who are with me can meet your representatives? They would like to see a sugar plantation growing, too, if you can show them one."

The Filipinos said they thought that could be arranged, and, as a matter of fact, the hall for this confabulation was already prepared, and the growing cane ready as well.

"That's all right," said Mr Taft. "All I care about is to get out of this room and get some of that nice cool wind on me!" He looked simply *melting*. So everyone rose up, and Mr Taft gave out that Mrs Carter, the wife of the General, invited the ladies of the party to luncheon with her at her house "on" the Calle Real at one o'clock. Then everyone filed away, and we went home to rest before the evening. It was then half-past eleven—very late for this country—and the sun very hot.

I was afterwards told about the ladies' luncheon party. It only consisted of the visitors, most of whom were already personal friends of Mrs Carter, so, of course, it was not an important function. Here, again, I thought, was a golden opportunity wasted, for a few invitations extended to leading Filipino and *Mestiza* ladies would have done more good to the American cause than all the utterances of the cleverest orators.

In the evening we went, in the usual pantomime *quilez*, to the Santa Cecilia Club, where the Filipino banquet to Mr Taft and his *Comitiva* was to be held. Or at least, that was the official description of the entertainment for which, as I told you, we each paid a preposterous sum.

The whole building was ablaze with lights and bunting, while the familiar perilous medley of vehicles surged about in the mud outside, with hairbreadth escapes going on every minute, any one of which would have made the fortune of a clever paragraphist.

The top of the stairs, the big landing, and outer place, were crowded with people, but the main room was still comparatively empty, so when we went in we had a good chance of seeing the decorations and tables. The latter were most ingeniously arranged to form the letters ILOILO, with a long table for the first I, then two long ones each with an elbow to make a sort of flat O, and then another long one with a long elbow for L, "and repeat," as they say in knitting patterns. The only attempt at decoration was a mass of greenery all down the middle of each table, lying flat on the cloth, with oranges and *lanzone* fruits lying on it, and salted pistachio nuts all thrown about anyhow. By each plate lay a small spray of flowers (gardenias, little roses etc.), a list of the guests, with a plan of the tables and the *menu*, which was a small blue paper book with a *nouveau art* picture of a woman on the cover. On the back of this *menu* was printed in large, clear type these words: "La situacion di Filipinas es como La de un enfermo que necesita una radical y eficaz medicacion. La supresion de la Tarifa Dingley es la mejor medicacion para Filipinas." The interpretation of which is: "The situation of the Philippines is like that of a sick person for whom a radical and efficacious remedy is necessary. The suppression of the Dingley Tariff is the best medicine for the Philippines."

This *menu* amused me a good deal, with the idea that poor long-suffering Mr Taft was to have politics written on everything he saw or touched, and certainly the Filipinos did not appear to be going to let slip any of this golden opportunity of "voicing" their grievances. The room was lighted by electric lights on the ceiling, arranged in the form of letters, spelling Taft on one side of the room and Visayas on the other, and flags, palm-branches, and paper roses were employed in the usual profusion.

The people dropped in gradually, and when the Taft party arrived, Mr Taft took his place at the middle of the first L, under the picture of Washington. The rest of the party were scattered up and down the tables anyhow, with no scheme of precedence, which was very sensible, and the first tangible display of democratic principles I have seen since we came to the Philippines.

About 258 guests were "scheduled," and less than three-quarters of the places filled. When I looked round the hall, I saw that the English and Germans were fairly well represented; but there were very few Spaniards, only about half a dozen Filipinos, some *Chino-Mestizos*, and one or two Eurasian ladies in lovely *camisas*, and wearing magnificent diamonds. All the rest were Americans.

Everyone seemed disappointed that Miss Roosevelt did not put in an appearance at the banquet. The rumour went about that she was too tired with the morning's fatigues to be able to go out again. Afterwards I heard this discussed, when some said that "Miss Alice" was not at all strong, and that the round of gaieties in Manila had worn her out; while others declared that she always shirked the serious side of the trip if she could possibly do so; but I don't expect the latter theory was true, and I thought it rather a shame of her country folk to say it.

The feast began with tinned *julienne*, the Constabulary band playing at the side, in the outer room, with a vigour which quite relieved one of any necessity for conversation. I examined my list of guests and plan of the tables to find out who the people were, and saw that all the blank places were those of Filipinos! Fancy! Their welcome to their Patron Saint! But he had so disappointed them by his avowed sentiments at the reception at the *Gobierno* in the morning that very few of them could be induced to come to the banquet.

As far as eating went, the banquet was a haphazard affair, for it was almost impossible to persuade the dazed Filipino waiters to attend to one. At least, they did attend, but in a very Filipino way, for I got four bottles of white wine brought me; C—— had never a taste of soup; and we both had three plates of fish put down before us, which the people on each side took away, as they could not get any at all. Everyone was very good-natured, so it was all very amusing.

There was considerable liberty of conscience displayed in the costumes of the guests, some of the American men being in soiled white day suits, conducting female relations in high cotton blouses; while others were got up in full evening dress. One handsome woman, who I heard was the wife of an officer in Camp Josman, was so much in evening dress, possibly to make up for the others in the blouses, that she was instantly nick-named The Mermaid. Her finely shaped head was dressed very low, and set off by classic bands of gold, with huge bunches of flowers and ribbons over each ear, and I heard a man near me suggest to another that someone should go and ask her to take some of the ornaments out of her *coiffure* and put them round her bodice. But no one had the courage to do this thing, so the little *Mestiza* ladies stared and giggled, and as for the few Orientals present, they looked at the Mermaid as if they thought Equality was going to be great fun.

When we were just about to fall on some beef *à la mode* which had at last, after incredible pertinacity on the part of C——, been placed before us, a man at one of the tables behind us suddenly got up and began to make a speech. Everyone slewed their heads round to see him, and forgot the beef, which the waiters instantly fell upon and swept away beyond recall.

The speechmaker proposed a health, which we drank in very good red or white wine provided for us, and then he made a speech, and someone—one of the visiting party, I think—got up and replied.

After him, another got up. But many people listened to him and still held on to their helping of turkey, which they tried to eat as noiselessly as possible; a most amusing sight.

Then another; and another; popping up in all sorts of places, with the interpreter appearing suddenly beside them like a harlequin. Some of the speeches, in spite of the halting of the translation, were very good, and very interesting; for the speakers did not mince matters much—the natives saying things very plainly, and the Americans replying with equal frankness.

Next me at table sat a Filipino swell in European evening dress, with splendid diamonds on his hands and in his embroidered shirt front, who turned his chair round when the speeches began, and sat astride, leaning on the back. He cleared his throat, and spat on the floor in such a dreadful manner that I felt sick, and at last I turned quite faint, and had to get up and move to an empty place further on. There I was not so well off, as far as hearing went, for the head of the next table was occupied by a cheery party of "prominent citizens," Senators, and officers, who were drinking champagne and making a horrible noise.

I moved again, this time to a doorway at the upper end of the hall, where a polite young *Mestizo* offered me his chair; so I ended in being very well off as to a place, and heard and saw very well.

An old Senator with a venerable beard was making a long speech on the subject of freedom and the folly of race-distinction. In defence of the latter theory, he rather rashly quoted Tennyson, repeating the lines about "Saxon and Norman and Dane are we," which could not be applied in the remotest way to either Americans or Filipinos and came out pure gibberish in the translation.

To him replied the editor of one of the Iloilo papers, a small, full-blooded Filipino, with sharp, clever features. He made a most fiery and eloquent speech, in which, with angry brown face, and clenched fists thumping the back of the chair on which he leant, he declared that the Philippine Islands had been discovered as long as America, and that the Filipinos had the same spirit as that which had caused the Americans to revolt from England.

He got fearfully excited, and called God to witness that his people were only asking for their rights in wishing to have this foreign burden removed; he and they demanded, insisted on, their Independence! When he sat down, the waiters and the band, and the Filipino spectators who had strolled in, all applauded frantically.

The applause, by-the-bye, was most instructive, for the American speeches were applauded to the echo with shouts by the Americans; but the Filipinos and *Mestizos* received the Spanish translations in *utter* silence. On the other hand, the brown folk roared with applause over their own speakers, and the Americans did not take the least notice of the English translations. It was a most odd and unique scene.

Last of all came Mr Taft, who spoke better, more clearly, and more simply than any of the others, and my only regret was that such a splendid delivery should have been impeded by the interpretations.

He repeated all the things he had said in the morning at the *Gobierno*, walking even more boldly up to the Independence question, and saying that the people would be given their Independence when they were worthy of it, which was the sacred duty of the American people, who had received these Islands as a Trust from God.

This was received with rapturous ovations by his countrymen, but the translation was taken in absolute and embarrassing silence—all but two or three hisses!

He went on to expound the theory of educating the Filipino people up to Western ideals, and laid great stress upon the dignity and power of labour—"and you must work with your hands—your hands!"—thunders of applause from the white men. Absolute silence after the translation. For my part, I can't say I felt much carried away by these phrases when I recollected the speaker's attitude towards manual labour and book-learning a few hours before.

When they were on a level with the free races, "in a hundred years, perhaps three hundred, four hundred, they would be worthy to stand and face the nations"—or something like that. He also said that he had certainly promised the Filipinos Independence, and he was not going back upon his words, no—he was come to uphold—to ratify them. "Dear Wards from God," he called them, spreading his arms out and smiling the Taft smile, and saying "that the Philippines were a solemn trust, and the Americans would not fail in this great duty towards humanity."

So these fine words were all they got out of Mr Taft, and we all rose and trooped out to find our "rigs."

At the top of the staircase I met a very Prominent Citizen, who remarked that this had been a great occasion for Iloilo; and I said: "Yes, Mr Taft is a clever man and a brilliant orator."

"That's so," agreed my friend, "he made a *vurry fine* speech."

I said: "He spoke a great many truths; what he said was very straightforward."

"Yes," said the P. C., "but he should have said all that two years ago."

And that, I find, is the unanimous verdict of every class and nationality about Mr Taft's subtle and rather tardy interpretation of the promises he made when he was Governor of the Philippines.

Next evening, when the party had gone, and there was nothing left but to discuss what had taken place, we were leaning over the balcony when a Prominent Citizen of our acquaintance came walking past, and stopped, in the friendly, half-Spanish fashion of the country, to say good evening and make a few remarks.

"It was a fine show," we said.

"Why yes," he agreed, "I guess the Filipinos did their best for the *Secwar.*"

"I think he disappointed them, though," said C——.

"Well, I should smile! I guess Secretary Taft's the best hated man in these islands now."

And that, I believe, is the unfortunate truth.

LETTER XLII.

WEIGHING ANCHOR

HOTEL ——, ILOILO, *August 22, 1905.*

We are up-rooted at last, you see, out of our own delightful house, and enduring the cooking and service of the best hotel this place has to afford, while we wait for the *Kai-Fong*, which is reported to be loading hard wood at Cebú.

This is not really such a bad place for Iloilo, which means that it compares unfavourably in comfort, cleanliness, and sanitation with a second-class Commercial in a small town in Spain. However, I have a very nice big cool room, opening on to a broad balcony, where little trees and plants stand in tubs, and that is very agreeable to the eye, as we are right in the town and not near any gardens. There are four doors in this room, and six windows, so that the room is capable of the necessary draught without which it is impossible to sleep. So far so good, but the Filipino bed has to be reckoned with—in this case, a vast four-poster, with a very handsome piece of carving at each end. That at the head is particularly beautiful, a very free and graceful design of leaves, and corn, and fruit, which I wish I could take home with me. We took the precaution of bringing our own *petates* and pillows when we left our house, as well as our own towels, and are continually thankful that we did so!

It is the chief hotel of Iloilo, as I said before, and therefore frequented by all the Prominent Citizens and their families, to say nothing of the military, as many of the officers board here. I think they must be such good-natured people not to make any fuss about the dirty linen and unwashed plates, or the cold and greasy food. I am afraid we are not so amiable, for we began at once to have it understood that, as we were paying the prices of a first-class hotel in London or Paris, we expected comfort and some cleanliness, and C—— said very definitely to our waiter that he would knock him down if he attempted again to hand things on the wrong side. This cleared the air a good deal, and when they found we insisted on having things nice, they did their best for us, and really they have made us so comfortable that we are quite patient about the *Kai-Fong*.

We cleared out of our own house on Friday (this is Monday), and spent all the following day making over the furniture to the various people who came, like Joseph's brethren, bearing money in their hands. We were so sorry to see the rooms dismantled, for we loved that house, and had lived in it in such comfort, and so well cared for by our good servants. When C—— paid the latter off, he gave to each an extra present of money, which pleased them enormously; and the cook, really quite sad, said over and over again that he wished we would take him with us to England, and asked to be allowed to shake hands with us, which great honour we permitted. Sotero we have brought here to wait on us, as we would not allow Filipino hotel servants into our rooms, of course; but Domingo has been paid off, though he refuses to consider himself dismissed, and I believe he is sleeping in the empty house and standing guard over our big cases, though no one is likely to run away with them, as they take about five coolies each to move. I begin to realise here what our openness to the Monsoons meant, for I have just had to clear out of my bedroom, where I was writing, and come into the public *sala* (which is really a furnished corridor), because the wind shifted a little, so that it no longer blew into the bedroom. By this I mean that when the wind was off me, I burst into perspiration, my face dripping on to the paper, my hands as if I had dipped them in water, my clothes soaking, and my head beginning to ache and throb. Oh, I can't find words to express how thankful I am to be going away from this horrible, everlasting heat! It gets on one's nerves not to be able to move a chair, to walk two yards without dripping at every pore, and one's clothes feel so irksome and heavy. If one takes exercise it is acute discomfort—if one does not, one is ill!

We are now having the echoes of the *Comitiva Taft* visitation, and it is really most amusing to see how the popular idol has fallen. Fallen for the Filipinos that is, for the Americans all think him very great and "cute" to manage as he has done, though they are all declaring openly that he should have said all this two years ago, as our friend shrewdly observed to us when we were leaving the banquet. Of course, there is something to be said for Mr Taft, for if he had made such unpopular utterances when he was Governor here, his life would not have been worth two cents a day. All the same, to the lay mind, such subtle change of front is not very palatable, and one cannot help wishing that politicians could afford to say straight out what they mean, and stick to it for good or evil.

The papers from Manila with the account of our festivities have arrived, and I never read such brazen lying in my life; in fact, the reports are so cooked that they leave off being annoying and begin to be funny. The wild scenes of popular enthusiasm, the crowded banquet, the frantic love of the people of Panay for their idol, and so on, and so on. And as to sheer reporting, Mr Taft's speech (which the Manila people are informed was greeted by the natives with thunderous applause) is given at great length, but the impassioned utterances of the patriot who clutched the chair-back are dismissed in a few mild words. No mention, too, of the ominous banners in the procession, of the note on the back of the *menu* at the banquet, and not the faintest hint of the one or two hisses which greeted the sentiments of the *Secwar* himself. So much for the local papers. And if that is the way they dally with truth out here, one can only faintly wonder what impression of this trip is being disseminated amongst the intelligent voters in the far-off U.S.A., by our well-informed journalistic friend and others of his kidney.

The Iloilo banquet, by-the-bye, wound up rather disastrously for American dignity, as the rowdy party at the table near us got up some quarrel with one of the Filipino waiters; there were blows and fighting, and the whole lot were chucked out into the street. This, as you may imagine, has made a horrible scandal, and produced a very bad impression.

About the banquet, too, it now appears that the Filipinos subscribed 70 *pesos* towards that and the general expenses, and the rest of the community, ourselves included, made the sum up to the 4000 required, plus a grant from the Treasury.

C—— went to see our poor old Spanish friend about something a day or two ago (the ex-courtier, whose visit I think I described to you), and when C—— said that he had not seen him at the banquet, the old fellow replied that he had sent the committee 12 *pesos* towards the expenses, with a letter of well-wishing, etc., as he thought it was his duty to do so, and to contribute what he could.

"Well," said C——, "but didn't they answer with an invitation to the banquet?"

"No," said the old man, "they did not even acknowledge the money."

He seemed rather down on his luck about the whole thing, and more anxious than ever to sell his piece of land and go home to Spain to die.

LETTER XLIII.

HOMEWARD BOUND

S.S. *Kai-Fong, August 25,* 10 A.M.

Iloilo is now far away below the horizon astern, and if I look over the side, I am afforded the delightful spectacle of one Philippine Island slipping past after the other into pale blue fluff, and I hope they will stay down under my horizon for ever.

We scraped out through a network of taxes, like fish trying to get out of a fish-*corral.* Our two large cases had to get a Customs permit before they could be put on board, for which they got from us a *peso* in the form of a stamp upon the Export Entry, and another *peso* and a half for what they call wharfage. This means that they did not examine the contents of the cases, but gave C—— a paper to sign and an export permit. Another item is an Internal Revenue tax of a *peso* on each passenger ticket. Fancy if we at home had to pay 10 shillings in taxes before we could go across the Channel!

It is so nice to be in such a clean and comfortable steamer, and to have fresh vegetables and fruit, brought on ice from Hong Kong; and one wonders how the Americans can tolerate the contrast between this and those dreadful Spanish cockroach-traps which they dignify by the name of the Mail.

All the crew are Chinese, of course, looking so straight and tall and intelligent after the stumpy, stupid, little Filipinos. With them too, as with the Filipino horses, the eye has been thrown out of focus, for the Chinese simply look colossal. I keep on thinking to myself what a very tall man that is, and he is only the usual height of ordinary men.

Most of the second-class passengers are Chinese, and they have queer meals on the lower deck, all squatting round a wooden tray on which are one or two big bowls of rice and bits of meat and vegetables. Round these are piled little bowls, into which the mixture is served out, and the Chinamen all set to work with chop-sticks, which is so like a conjuring-trick that one can watch them as long as they will go on with it! Amongst these people is a Chinaman with his Filipino wife, a little ugly woman, with her lips jutting out beyond the end of her nose, dressed in a gay *camisa,* and for ever smoking a huge, ragged cigar. Some children of theirs cling to them most of the time, and a very gaudily-dressed little chap of a more purely Filipino type, whom the Chinaman is exporting to a friend in Amoy who has bought the child for 10 dollars. You can buy children very cheaply in the Philippines; and away from the big towns, and very often in them, they are openly offered for sale; and most of the rich native and *Mestizo* families have servants which have been bought as children. I daresay, though I have never inquired about it, that the Americans strenuously deny this officially, but unofficially it is a perfectly well-known custom. This small slave was a very native little chap of three or four, got up in purple cotton coat and a crimson jockey cap, and radiantly happy in his new clothes, and we could not really feel very sorry for him. The Chinamen all take the greatest care of their hair, combing it out every day, and some of them have magnificent, glossy, black locks, right down to their knees; but others, whose hair is thin and scanty, eke out their pigtails with long cords of black silk gimp.

Talking of servants, when we came down to the Muelle Loney (to think I shall never see that place again!) this morning, we found Domingo waiting, in his smartest clothes, spotlessly white, and his skin shining with soap, to see us off. Poor fellow, he hung round, blubbering quietly, and carrying anything he could catch hold of, and when he said good-bye his face was quite pathetic. I think he felt he was losing the only people in the world who had ever treated him well, and he was one of the best specimens of a typical, unspoilt Filipino, stolid, obedient, humble, and faithful as a dog, and C—— said he would have given anything to have been able to take him with us, as the poor creature implored us to do. At the last, when the launch was pushing off, Domingo made a wild rush to spring on board, but was too late; and the last we saw of him was standing on the quay with his hat off and the tears streaming down his big, brown face.

We discussed this rush of Domingo's, but can arrive at no satisfactory solution of what he wanted to do, for I think he only wanted to come out to the *Kai-Fong*, but C—— says he is certain he meant to follow us to Hong Kong and compel us to take him with us. Well, we can't do that, but we have done our best for him in making him from a rough coolie into a clean, smart servant, who can get double the wages he received from us; and we found him a good place before we left, though, as I said before, I am not at all sure how either he or the other will do with the impatience and curses with which the average white man thinks he impresses his dignity upon the coloured person. It is not to be done in the Anglo-Indian method; no, nor in the American extreme of familiarity. Of that I was persuaded before I came here, and am still more convinced now that I have more experience.

The only way to impress anyone, black, brown, *or* white, with the idea of your dignity, is to be dignified yourself. But I suppose this is too much of an obvious truism for anyone to attempt to think over or act up to. Well, it served me in very good stead; and all I know is that, though every soul I spoke to had endless complaints about the impudence, laziness, or dishonesty of their servants, whether they were of the nation who kicked them, or those who allowed them to wear a vest in the house and not say *señor*, we never had any trouble once we got rid of our first Americanised cook—my house went as on oiled axles, and we never missed one single thing from start to finish. So what am I to say of the Filipinos? Those with whom I came in contact, as well as my own servants, were a narrow, cunning, good-humoured people, vain, superstitious, stupid, great gamblers, kind to their children, and bitterly cruel to animals—oh, the poor hens hung up by the heels in the sun! and the wretched pigs with their four feet lashed together that used to lie all day scorching in the Plaza at Molo! the awful open sores under the harness of the starving ponies! the brutal, sickening, cock-fighting! For those horrors alone, I should be thankful to leave this country, even were it the paradise which it is not. No, no terrestrial paradise, for one has the laziness, the heat, the apathy, and cruelty of the East, without the compensations of artistic beauty, cheapness, plenty, and luxury, which make up for those drawbacks in other hot countries. A shuffling, drab, discontented, thick-headed, costly East—with all the worst traditions of four hundred years of the off-scourings of the Spanish monkish orders, overlaid by a veneer of shallow cock-sureness hastily assimilated from a totally incongruous alien civilisation.

We carry a cargo of sugar, and from the ventilators come up gusts of that peculiar, heavy, nauseous odour, which carries one back instantly to the *camarins* of Iloilo. I can't believe that the Philippines are really a thing of the past for me—it is not that I was there so long; but there was so little variety, and we saw and did and heard the same things so often, that I am left with an impression of as many years as we have been there months.

THE END

THE PHILIPPINE ISLANDS

Lightning Source UK Ltd.
Milton Keynes UK
UKHW040617211119
353970UK00001B/233/P